Madame Bovary and the Critics

Madame Bovary
AND THE CRITICS
A Collection of Essays

Edited by B. F. BART

Department of Romance Languages
Syracuse University

NEW YORK UNIVERSITY PRESS 1966

COPYRIGHT © 1966 BY NEW YORK UNIVERSITY
LIBRARY OF CONGRESS CARD CATALOG NO. 66-12596
MANUFACTURED IN THE UNITED STATES OF AMERICA

The essays in this collection represent a sampling from the more than five thousand studies dealing with Flaubert which have appeared since the publication of *Madame Bovary* in 1857. Primarily I have sought to provide the reader with a number of differing ways of looking at the novel. More than that, however, each reader, by the act of reading it, joins the long family extending back for more than a century now of those who, like him, have read and lived with the novel. I have attempted in this collection to make the reader aware of this family which he has joined. It can be intriguing to follow the course of other readers' estimations of the novel from its original *succès de scandale* because of the trial which it occasioned on through denigration or praise for this aspect or that, as one set of criteria or another was applied to it. The reader of this collection will find that his own responses have a long history and that they tend to be variants on one or another type of reaction experienced before him and elucidated, with more or less success, by earlier readers. He may have been interested by the characters or the plot, or the descriptions, or the subject or moral of the story. Or his concerns may have been broader: the form of the novel as a genre, or the concept and theory of the novel in general as exemplified in *Madame Bovary*. Or he may have become interested in the personality of the author and his biography. Within one or another of the warring camps in one or another of these areas—for *Madame Bovary* has always been a battleground—he will wish to find his own position and take his own stance. These critical essays will help to guide him as he sees what has been said by those who read the novel before him.

I have, with apologies, included two of my own essays in order to represent certain types of criticism. Perhaps the reader will forgive this the more readily as he discovers from reading them that in each case he is provided with all the ammunition he needs to disagree with me and to come to his own, perhaps diametrically opposed, conclusions. In any case, with my own articles or with those of other critics, he has always the novel itself to turn to. And this is what really matters.

For those who may wish to pursue the matter further, the best biography in English is Philip Spencer, *Flaubert* (New York: Grove Press, 1952); and I shall be publishing a general study of Flaubert's life and works during 1966. An earlier study may also be of interest: *Flaubert and Madame Bovary,* by Francis Steegmuller (revised edition, New York: Farrar, Straus, 1950).[1]

B. F. B.

[1] Page references to Flaubert's works will be given in terms of the Conard edition (Paris, 1910 ff.).

CONTENTS

Margaret Tillett

1 · On Reading Madame Bovary

INTRODUCTION

Too frequently in studying a great work we only end where
in fact we should have begun: by examining directly our impressions as we read the work. For such a reading there is no
need for outside references, no searching of relevant data is required. All that is needed is a sensitive reader who knows and
enjoys the work and who can guide others to the scenes that
matter, the queries that must be raised, the reactions that must
be evaluated. One does not have to share all of Miss Margaret
Tillett's experiences in reading Madame Bovary to profit from
her report of them. Those who differ from her here or there—and
not infrequently these disagreements will appear in the following pages—will still return to Emma Bovary and her plight and
read it the better for Miss Tillett. Let her introduce the novel
and these essays.

The most famous of Flaubert's works, published in 1857, has
now weathered over a century of praise and blame. It is difficult
to imagine that more could be discovered about the origins and
composition of any work of fiction, than has been discovered
about *Madame Bovary*. But if it were possible to forget all the
mass of information that now exists about the book, to imagine
a state of not knowing of Flaubert's correspondence, or the story
of his life, or that he ever said *"Madame Bovary, c'est moi"*—to

imagine that one simply possessed the last edition corrected by him in his lifetime, without any notes or comments—in fact, that one was reading it as he meant it to be read, and as most people probably do read it for the first time—what impression would it give?

An impression of power, authority perhaps, of being the work of a writer free of any affectations or pettinesses. The famous "realism" has of course lost its edge by now; it seems improbable that the most memorable aspects of *Madame Bovary*, for a reader familiar with the novels and plays of the 1940's and 1950's, would be the description of the results of the bungled operation on the club-foot of Hippolyte the ostler, or the love-scenes between Emma and Léon, or even certain details of the death of Emma. Artists of great sincerity and integrity, in Flaubert's time, were never entirely free from the desire to *épater le bourgeois*; the same is certainly true for present-day artists, but the *bourgeois* has become infinitely more difficult to *épater* [startle]. To read the speeches for the accusation and the defence in the notorious trial of Flaubert for "outrage to public morals" is to enter another, perhaps wryly amusing, world. No; the story is certainly firmly anchored in the human "real" of a certain time and place—here, the province of Normandy towards the end of the July monarchy—and the subtitle, *Moeurs de Province*, suggests that this is important; but it is not all-important. The great thing in *Madame Bovary* is the impression it gives of the continual vibration of an acute sensitivity held in control, an instrument finely tuned, giving a true note. The main character lives as a series of recognizable moods conveyed with remarkable feeling and power; in these the universality of the work lies. Emma Bovary is a Romantic, and the Romantic outlook on life as it appears here, caricatured by Flaubert, is immediately recognizable to everyone, to those who suppose that it is a symptom of adolescence and must be outgrown, and to those who know, as Flaubert himself did, that at its best it is admirable, the only defence against insidious soul-destroying materialism. There is no real opposition between Romantic and Realist; the great adversary is the Materialist, the anti-poet.[1]

[1] Flaubert uses the expression "anti-poète" in a letter. *Correspondance*, III, 141.

Unfortunately Romanticism is all too often represented in life by such as poor Emma Bovary, shoddily pursuing a shoddy ideal, a piece of imitation jewellery if ever there was one. This bastard Romanticism is what Flaubert is satirizing in *Madame Bovary*. Emma, possessing beauty and some intelligence, lacks one quality which is essential to the genuine Romantic—warmth of heart, which her creator did possess and which he endeavoured to conceal from his readers. Emma's capricious acts of material "generosity" have little significance:

> . . . *elle jetait parfois aux pauvres toutes les pièces blanches de sa bourse, quoiqu'elle ne fût guère tendre cependant, ni facilement accessible à l'émotion d'autrui, comme la plupart des gens issus de campagnards, qui gardent toujours à l'âme quelque chose de la callosité des mains paternelles.*[2]

> [. . . sometimes she would toss all the silver in her purse to the poor, although she was not really of a tender disposition nor easily moved by the plight of others; she was, rather, like most country folk, whose souls always retain something of the callouses on the hands of their ancestors.]

And in fact she is completely selfish. Another of the worst tendencies of the Romantic disposition—the tendency to self-dramatization—is very marked in her. But she has such intelligence and taste that she adapts herself easily to the society of the aristocracy, at La Vaubyessard. The picture of Emma at the ball, dancing with a vicomte, is the one that has to be constantly called to mind if the full measure of her increasing misery and degradation is to be brought home, and if the reader is to feel for her any sympathy at all. Flaubert therefore recalls it, with delicate touches, throughout the book, the last reminder of it coming towards the end, when she is in Rouen making a desperate attempt to find money to pay her debts:

> *Elle s'arrêta pour laisser passer un cheval noir, piaffant dans les brancards d'un tilbury que conduisait un gentleman en fourrure de zibeline. Qui était-ce donc? Elle le connaissait. . . . La voiture s'élança et disparut.*
> *Mais c'était lui, le Vicomte!* [3]

2 Pt. 1, Ch. ix, p. 92.
3 Pt. 3, Ch. vii, p. 412.

[She paused to let a tilbury pass, its black horse prancing between the shafts as a sable-clad gentleman drove it. Who could he be? She knew him. . . . The carriage leaped forward and disappeared.

But, it was the Viscount!]

In the first chapters, Flaubert is mainly concerned with Charles, and with Emma only as she appears to others. His first analysis of Emma is in Chapter 6 of Part I (the dramatic technique of the delayed emergence of the principal character is one that rarely fails in its effect) and here he shows the disastrous results of an upbringing in which every hazard increased an already excessive tendency to sentimentality. By the time she left her convent school, she was corrupted by the nonsense of popular pseudo-Romantic literature and art, but remained hard and independent:

Cet esprit, positif au milieu de ses enthousiasmes, qui avait aimé l'église pour ses fleurs, la musique pour les paroles des romances, et la littérature pour ses excitations passionnelles, s'insurgeait devant les mystères de la foi, de même qu'elle s'irritait davantage contre la discipline, qui était quelque chose d'antipathique à sa constitution.[4]

[Her mind and spirit, very practical even in the midst of her enthusiasms, which had loved the church for its flowers, music for the words of the romances, and literature for the excitement of its love stories, revolted in the presence of the mysteries of the Christian faith, much as she became irritated with its discipline, which was contrary to her nature.]

There is something in the character of Emma which condemns her to be second-rate, in spite of all her struggles; and at the end of Chapter 6 it is perfectly clear that if she had all the good fortune in the world, second-rate as a human being she would be condemned to remain. Thus early in the book the reader finds himself involved in a series of speculations about human nature and destiny that are never openly suggested by Flaubert, and realizes that this is a writer who will actually put into words only about one-fifth of what he has to say.

It is Flaubert's own sensibility that gives to this record of

4 P. 54.

Emma's life and emotions its passages of great beauty, its moments of tension and tragedy, but also its humour. Flaubert's inarticulate sexton Lestiboudois, ringing the Angelus at his own convenience and growing potatoes in a corner of the cemetery, would not be much out of place in the churchyard at Elsinore; and there are many other memorable personalities and situations sketched lightly but ineffaceably on the memory so that the overall impression of *Madame Bovary* is not completely tragic: the *pompiers* and the *garde nationale* at the agricultural show; Charles at the opera; the loquacious guide at the cathedral baulked of his prey; Homais whenever he speaks; and the Homais family, large and small, all enveloped to the chins in white aprons, making jam. Flaubert really had a Shakespearean sense of the ways of interrupting tension and tragedy by humour—in both cases it is sometimes embarrassingly tasteless, but more often its nature and position in the work are instinctively right. Flaubert was a lifelong student and devotee of the works of Shakespeare; but of Thomas Hardy, who also knew how to create overwhelmingly the sense of a mood, and to lighten a predominantly sombre view of life with flashes of humour, he had certainly never heard. Hardy's *The Return of the Native*, published in 1878, two years before Flaubert's death, has certain similarities with *Madame Bovary*; it is set in an English province in the same decade; in both works the tragedy is relieved by humour all provided by provincials and rustics; in both the landscape, constantly presented to the reader in all its aspects, influences the characters; in both a sense of driving fatality hangs over the main characters; in both the heroine is a young woman far superior in intelligence and sensibility to her acquaintances, ambitious, sighing for life in Paris, suffering from frustration, unwisely married, driven by despair to death. Eustacia Vye is of the same race as Emma Bovary, a dramatizer of self:

> To be loved to madness—such was her great desire. Love was to her the one cordial which could drive away the eating loneliness of her days. And she seemed to long for the abstraction called passionate love more than for any particular lover.[5]

5 Thomas Hardy, *The Return of the Native* (London: Macmillan Co., 1954), Ch. vii, p. 79.

An exact description of the desire of Emma Bovary. Eustacia too plans to run away with her "Rodolphe," Damon Wildeve, whose character recalls to a certain extent that of Emma's first lover. Eustacia's husband is the *Native* of the title, unlike Charles Bovary in everything but failure to understand his wife—a hypersensitive, intelligent only son, without worldly ambition. Eustacia's mother-in-law is not merely a source of exasperation to her, but the unwitting cause of the tragic situation that drives the girl to despair. The strongest resemblance between the books is not so much in details of the plots as in the fact that the two novels cover the same gamut of moods with the same intensity. But the approaches of the two authors to their subjects are so very different that a consideration of each may illumine the other.

Hardy is no more given to moral judgments than Flaubert; but he is on the side of his characters. Flaubert himself is the satirist of human weakness. For Hardy, the satirist is the one to whom he refers as the "Supreme Power" or, in *Tess*, as the "President of the Immortals."

> To Eustacia the situation seemed such a mockery of her hopes that death appeared the only door of relief if the satire of Heaven should go much further.[6]

Her beauty and distinction are such that:

> The gloomy corner into which accident as much as indiscretion had brought this woman might have led even a moderate partisan to feel that she had cogent reasons for asking the Supreme Power by what right a being of such exquisite finish had been placed in circumstances calculated to make of her charms a curse rather than a blessing.[7]

The "satire of Heaven" is illustrated by the small coincidences and accidents and misunderstandings that give rise to the tragedy, and even more by the tragedy implicit in the clash of the characters themselves. Eustacia's husband Clym Yeobright is presented fairly, his weakness and strangeness revealed, but also his capacity for love and self-torment. Charles, the husband of Emma, is seen from an angle that ensures that the predominant image of him shall be the most grotesque

6 Book 4, Ch. iii, p. 303.
7 *Ibid.*

possible. His unshakeable devotion to the unworthy Emma is simply made to appear as one example of his lack of intelligence. In Hardy's more charitable view such devotion would create in Charles not, indeed, intelligence, but a kind of sixth sense, an intuition, and would certainly not make him more obtuse than ever. Hardy's humble lovers, aware of their inferiority, all have this delicacy of perception that contrasts movingly with their unpolished speech and plainly furnished minds. But the whole emotional power of Flaubert's work is concentrated in one character, minutely analyzed, one fundamentally incapable of loving, but always pursuing a false image of love; Hardy's power is diffused among several characters, all loving in different ways, each way as true as the others. Eustacia and Clym; Wildeve; the gentle Thomasin, Clym's cousin; Mrs. Yeobright his mother; the strange wanderer Venn, Thomasin's self-effacing lover; even Charley, a slightly older and bolder "Justin"—all love more or less deeply according to their natures, some happily, some unhappily, and each for a time holds the centre of the stage. This spreading of interest among the characters may be why *The Return of the Native* lacks some of the force and cohesion of *Madame Bovary*. Emma is never for a moment out of sight. Eustacia too would have been worth this riveted attention; as it is, her character tends to be partly imagined and completed by the reader. Her end comes too soon, but the ultimate degradation of Emma is unimaginable for her. Her death is an interruption—Emma's a conclusion. One thing Flaubert did with all his main characters was to follow them relentlessly to the end of their story—they might continue to live at the end of the book, as Frédéric Moreau does in *L'Education sentimentale*, but nevertheless they have reached the limits of their destiny as human beings.

Flaubert penetrates in two brilliant paragraphs to the core of Emma's despair as she leaves Rodolphe's house for the last time, describes in detail her death from poisoning, her funeral, its aftermath. At Eustacia's death all is darkness and confusion, and her final thoughts are not revealed. Hardy says quietly:— "She had used to think of the heath alone as an uncongenial spot to be in: she felt it now of the whole world." [8] And of

8 Book 5, Ch. vii, p. 414.

Eustacia dead:

> They stood silently looking upon Eustacia, who, as she lay there still in death, eclipsed all her living phases. Pallor did not include all the quality of her complexion, which seemed more than whiteness; it was almost light. The expression of her finely carved mouth was pleasant, as if a sense of dignity had just compelled her to leave off speaking. Eternal rigidity had seized upon it in a momentary transition between fervour and resignation. Her black hair was looser now than either of them had ever seen it before, and surrounded her brow like a forest. The stateliness of look which had been almost too marked for a dweller in a country domicile had at last found an artistically happy background.[9]

That is all. But brooding over the whole work, and all Hardy's work, is the question that Flaubert never asks—of the meaning of human suffering and destiny. The whole force of Flaubert's work is that in spite of his detachment, his sarcasm, his levity, his apparent denial of souls to his characters, his readers are prompted to ask the question themselves.

In both works the secondary characters emphasize the isolation and superiority of the main one. But Hardy's are rather Shakespearean rustics set down on Egdon Heath in the nineteenth century. Flaubert's, as his sub-title suggests, are essentially of the nineteenth century, destined to represent the creeping tide of bourgeois smugness and complacency, the prosaic materialism that Flaubert saw overwhelming poetry, the triumph of the anti-poet Homais and all his kind. Hardy, though he movingly depicts a vanished rural England, is really more concerned with the human lot in general than with the human beings of one period. But the place, the scene, has greater importance than the period.

The attitudes of the two writers towards places seem at first radically different. Hardy's description of Egdon Heath in *The Return of the Native*, his loving and accurate record of the Dorset of the past, are part of his enduring fame. Flaubert in *Madame Bovary* seems to love Normandy no more than he does its inhabitants; yet for most lovers of Normandy the province is unforgettably evoked in his book. A series of brief

9 Book 5, Ch. ix, p. 446.

studies of outline, colour and sound runs through the whole work—short passages, recording the passing of the seasons with their subdued northern tones. On Charles's first visit to the Roualt farm:

> *La pluie ne tombait plus; le jour commençait à venir, et, sur les branches des pommiers sans feuilles, des oiseaux se tenaient immobiles, hérissant leurs petites plumes au vent froid du matin. La plate campagne s'étalait à perte de vue, et les bouquets d'arbres autour des fermes faisaient, à intervalles éloignés, des taches d'un violet noir sur cette grande surface grise, qui se perdait à l'horizon dans le ton morne du ciel. . . .*[10]

> [The rain had stopped; day was breaking, and on the leafless branches of the apple trees birds perched motionless, fluffing out their little feathers in the morning chill. The flat countryside stretched as far as the eye could see, and the clusters of trees about the farmhouses dotted here and there seemed like splotches of black and purple against this great grey surface, which disappeared at the horizon into the dull tone of the sky. . . .]

As in all Flaubert's writing, the effect is conveyed as much by the sounds as by the sense of the words—here by three or four low-pitched recurring vowels. Each one of the other descriptions rings equally true. Flaubert is not a regional novelist, and scenery takes second place; the most important territories are in the minds of his characters. But for many readers the place and climate are among the strongest memories of *Madame Bovary*.

> *Toutes sortes de bruits joyeux emplissaient l'horizon: le claquement d'une charrette roulant au loin dans les ornières, le cri d'un coq qui se répétait ou la galopade d'un poulain que l'on voyait s'enfuir sous les pommiers. Le ciel pur était tacheté de nuages roses; des lumignons bleuâtres se rabattaient sur les chaumières couvertes d'iris; Charles, en passant, reconnaissait les cours. . . .*[11]

> [All sorts of joyous sounds filled the scene: the clattering of a wagon as it rolled along a distant rut, the repeated crowing of a cock, or the galloping of a foal disappearing through the

10 Part I, Ch. ii, p. 16.
11 Part 3, Ch. x, p. 466.

apple trees. The clear sky was spotted with pink clouds; a bluish glow spread down over the cottages surrounded with iris; Charles recognized the farmyards as he passed them. . . .]

At the beginning of *The Return of the Native* the description of Egdon Heath sets the tone of the whole book, and Egdon is itself an essential part of the story. It gives a sense of dignity and timelessness which contributes much to the greatness of the novel. Flaubert allows himself no such aid as this long, meditative initial description; his picture of Yonville and its surroundings at the beginning of Part II is deliberately prosaic. But one of the usual effects of his shorter descriptions is to give glimpses of the vast, which set in perspective his human beings and their little interests; as for example the passage in Chapter 7 of Part I, quoted by Saint-Beuve and by many critics since:

> *Il arrivait parfois des rafales de vent, brises de la mer qui, roulant d'un bond sur tout le plateau du pays de Caux, apportaient, jusqu'au loin dans les champs, une fraîcheur salée. Les joncs sifflaient à ras de terre, et les feuilles des hêtres bruissaient en un frisson rapide, tandis que les cimes, se balançant toujours, continuaient leur grand murmure. . . .*[12]

> [There were occasional gusts of wind, breezes from the sea which in a single rush would reach the Caux region and even bring the cool smell of salt way out into the fields. The reeds whistled as they bent to earth, and the leaves of the beeches trembled and rustled, while their tops, endlessly swaying, kept up their strong murmuring. . . .]

Which for the sound and rhythm of the lines can be remembered like poetry. By such lines, at fairly long intervals, Flaubert maintains his contact with the universal. In his work no less than in Hardy's the setting is of immense importance. And in most enduring works of fiction there is surely an association of moments of keen psychological observation with memorable places—a coincidence of experience and surroundings that creates the "atmosphere" of the book and makes it remain alive when the physical attributes of the characters, and the story itself, have become blurred in the memory. The important thing is the impression of true human experience given by the

12 P. 63.

novel, and the most intense moments of that experience are associated usually with places. These places the reader himself creates in his imagination with the guidance of the writer, and they become familiar territory. When this happens, and they are associated with feelings recognizably real and profound, the novel endures, whatever its defects may be. The story may be a tissue of improbabilities, the dialogue often absurd, the characters odd—as they are for example in *Jane Eyre*—but the emotions are real, and so are Thornfield and Hay Lane, and the country round Whitcross, and Moor House. In *The Return of the Native* certain accidents and coincidences strain credulity at times, the characterization is uneven—but the emotional force of the book, inseparable from the vast sweep of Egdon, is deep and true. In *Madame Bovary* it is not a case of improbability or oddity—on the contrary the story is banal and the characters depressingly mediocre—but this matters less than it might because La Vaubyessard, Tostes, the house at Yonville and the room in Rouen are bound up with universal and most powerfully evoked emotions of ecstasy, despair, and fear. And in passing it may be said that it is essential that all these places should remain in the imagination—the spell is broken if one is confronted with some actual village or house said to be the scene of an event in fiction. Any reader's imaginary Yonville is nearer to the truth of *Madame Bovary* than the actual village of Ry, for long generally accepted as the model for Flaubert's Yonville.[13] And Hardy's Wessex too, though it is so graphically described, is to some extent a realm of the imagination.[14]

The great difference between Hardy's treatment of Eustacia's story and Flaubert's treatment of Emma's lies, however, less in the approach of each writer to the characters and scenes than in the way each constructs his work. By comparison with Flaubert's, Hardy's novel is shapeless, largely because of the device which he so constantly uses in his works, of taking one character a certain way, and then running back to see what

13 Or Neufchâtel-en-Bray, or more recently Forges-les-Eaux. See René Herval, *Les Véritables Origines de "Madame Bovary"* (Paris: Librairie A. G. Nizet, 1957).

14 In the 1912 preface to *The Woodlanders*, Hardy says of the hamlet of "Little Hintock"—"To oblige readers I once spent several hours on a bicycle . . . in a serious attempt to discover the real spot."

another has been doing in the meantime. Flaubert avoids such awkwardness of construction by never leaving his main character. But his great originality lies in his having given to the form or *outline* an importance comparable with the importance of the form—symphonic, fugal, rhapsodic—in a musical composition. To carry the musical analogy too far would be ridiculous; but the fact remains that for certain readers the form of Flaubert's works gives a pleasure rather like that given by form in music. In *Madame Bovary*, the construction of the three sections, the placing of the *Comices Agricoles* scene, the final sentences of the chapters like strong chords, the variations in tempo and key, and many other features, indicate that Flaubert was a writer whose work literally took shape,[15] and that in his hands the novel assumed the dignity of a work of art.

Hardy, at the end of *The Return of the Native*,[16] admits that he substituted a banal ending for the one that would have been aesthetically fitting. The last short section, *Aftercourses*, interesting as it may be, is artistically superfluous and out of key. This truckling to public taste is absolutely unimaginable in Flaubert. The chapters that follow the death of Emma are essential, for her influence prevails after her death—in the lives of Charles, dying of despair in poverty and degradation, and the wretched little orphan Berthe, sent at the age of six or seven to earn her living in a factory; while the main point of the book comes with the final irony of the triumph of Homais, smug, pompous high priest of the cult of material progress which was already widespread in Flaubert's time and has since come to extend its senseless tyranny over most of the world.

The book is tragic, in spite of the levity with which Flaubert often treats his characters; and part of the tragedy lies in the mediocrity of these characters, all dimly aware of some sub-

15 For a remark on the point where the actual division into chapters took place, see "*Madame Bovary* (nouvelle version précédée des scénarios inédits)," J. Pommier and G. Leleu (Paris, José Corti, 1959), p. xvii.

16 The writer may state here that the original conception of the story did not design a marriage between Thomasin and Venn. . . . But certain circumstances of serial publication led to a change of intent. Readers can therefore choose between the endings, and those with an austere artistic code can assume the more consistent conclusion to be the true one. (*Aftercourses*, footnote to Ch. iii.)

lime notion of Love, Duty, Renown, Joy, towards which they strive as towards remote mountain peaks. Certain chapters in the book seem to emphasize this aspect of the tragedy, turning the reader's attention from a particular to a general dilemma; making him see beyond Emma and her affairs other human beings fruitlessly longing for greatness, falling short in some way. The first of these chapters is Chapter 9 of Part I, one of the most brilliant of Flaubert's analyses of Emma's moods; the second, the *Comices Agricoles* scene, Chapter 8 of Part II; and the third, the very brief Chapter 3 of Part III, the "honeymoon" of Emma and Léon at Rouen.

In Chapter 9 Emma is living on the memory of the ball at La Vaubyessard. On the way home she and Charles had picked up a cigar-case dropped by one of a party of horsemen, and she imagines that it belongs to the Vicomte with whom she danced. She thinks of his life in Paris, and wonders about the city. And at this point Flaubert widens the horizon so that for a moment Emma is almost lost in a universal mood of longing and exile:

> *La nuit, quand les mareyeurs, dans leurs charrettes, passaient sous ses fenêtres en chantant* la Marjolaine, *elle s'éveillait; et, écoutant le bruit des roues ferrées qui, à la sortie du pays, s'amortissait vite sur la terre:*
> *—Ils y seront demain! se disait-elle.*
> *Et elle les suivait dans sa pensée, montant et descendant les côtes, traversant les villages, filant sur la grande route à la clarté des étoiles. Au bout d'une distance indéterminée, il se trouvait toujours une place confuse où expirait son rêve.*[17]

[At night when the fish vendors would pass beneath her windows with their wagons singing *la Marjolaine*, she would waken and listen to the noise of the wheels with their iron rims which would be muffled as they left the village and reached the softer ground:
"They will be there tomorrow!" she would say to herself.
And in her mind's eye she would follow them up hill and down dale, through the villages and moving along the open ground beneath the clear stars. After an indeterminate distance, there would always be a confused region in which her dream would expire.]

[17] P. 80.

On a map of Paris she traces imaginary walks; buys a subscription to a Paris paper; reads novels whose scene is Paris, and reads at meals; dreams of the Vicomte:

> Mais le cercle dont il était le centre peu à peu s'élargit autour de lui, et cette auréole qu'il avait, s'écartant de sa figure, s'étala plus loin, pour illuminer d'autres rêves.[18]

[But the circle of which he was the center grew little by little around him, and the halo which he had, moving out from his face, spread out further and illuminated other dreams.]

Then follows the famous passage beginning:

> Paris, plus vaste que l'Océan, miroitait donc aux yeux d'Emma dans une atmosphère vermeille.

[Paris, wider than the ocean, glittered before Emma's eyes in a rosy haze.]

Impossible here not to recall Balzac (whose books Emma has been reading) and the beautiful lines from the opening pages of Le Père Goriot:

> Mais Paris est un véritable océan. Jetez-y la sonde, vous n'en connaîtrez jamais la profondeur. Parcourez-le, décrivez-le? quelque soin que vous mettiez à le parcourir, à le décrire; quelque nombreux et intéressés que soient les explorateurs de cette mer, il s'y rencontrera toujours un lieu vierge, un antre inconnu, des fleurs, des perles, des monstres, quelque chose d'inouï, oublié par les plongeurs littéraires.

[But Paris is a real ocean. No matter where you take your sounding, you will never learn its depth. Travel about it, describe it? No matter how carefully you travel over it and describe it, no matter how many and how careful explorations you make of this sea, there will always remain an unexplored spot, an unknown cavern, flowers, pearls, monsters, something unheard of, forgotten by the literary divers.]

In fact the picture of Paris which forms in Emma's imagination is obviously derived from the Comédie Humaine.

The falseness of her view of her own situation is stressed, with great shrewdness:

> Tout ce qui l'entourait immédiatement, campagne ennuyeuse, petits bourgeois imbéciles, médiocrité de l'existence,

18 P. 81.

lui semblait une exception dans le monde, un hasard par-
ticulier où elle se trouvait prise, tandis qu'au-delà s'étendait
à perte de vue l'immense pays des félicités et des passions.[19]

[Everything that hemmed her in, the boring countryside,
the idiotic petty bourgeois, the mediocrity of her life, seemed
to her an exception in the world, a special piece of misfortune in which she was trapped, while out beyond as far as
the eye could see there stretched the immense land of felicity
and passion.]

Emma, perpetually contrasting her actual surroundings
with the ideal ones of her imagination, tries to introduce into
her life some of the elegance of which she has read. And she
fritters away her time:

Elle souhaitait à la fois mourir et habiter Paris.[20]

[She longed both to die and to live in Paris.]

The complete contrast of Charles's life with hers is force-
fully made—his hard work, his delight in Emma, who contemptuously watches him as he dozes after dinner, and grows
more and more irritated with his coarse manners. She waits
endlessly for something to happen.

Comme les matelots en détresse, elle promenait sur la
solitude de sa vie des yeux désespérés, cherchant au loin
quelque voile blanche dans les brumes de l'horizon.[21]

[Like sailors in distress, she looked about over the solitude of
her life with despairing eyes, seeking somewhere in the distance
a white sail amidst the mists of the horizon.]

One recalls Baudelaire's "matelots oubliés dans une île,"
and the other exiles of *Le Cygne*.

Behind the half-humourous manner in which Flaubert depicts Emma's suffering, there is a profound seriousness. The
tragic exhaustion of energy in futile longings, the sickness of
heart, are poignantly conveyed. There is no invitation from La
Vaubyessard that year:

L'avenir était un corridor tout noir, et qui avait au fond sa porte
bien fermée.[22]

19 P. 82.
20 P. 84.
21 P. 87.
22 P. 87.

[The future was a black corridor with the door at the end shut tight.]

She becomes more and more idle and languid. At this point Flaubert concentrates the whole mood he is depicting into two sounds—the cracked note of the church bell, and the howling of a dog:

> Au loin, parfois, un chien hurlait: et la cloche, à temps égaux, continuait sa sonnerie monotone qui se perdait dans la campagne.[23]

[In the distance, at intervals, a dog would howl: and with even beat, the bell kept up its monotonous tolling which disappeared out over the countryside.]

It is evident by now that the magic of the chapter lies in the way in which, from point to point, Flaubert places an image of infinite distance, emphasizing Emma's longing for escape; and at the same time constantly brings her back to consciousness of her real surroundings in the village of Tostes, where the same things happen at the same time every day. The climax of this long investigation of her *ennui* comes with the description of the itinerant organ-grinder with his puppets performing a dance in a miniature ball-room. This passage is one of the most Flaubertian in the book, because it so clearly reveals the essential quality of the writer—his extreme sensitivity to shades of feeling, his imagination and carefully controlled sympathy, his power of making the apparently straightforward description of something unremarkable contain whole worlds of meaning and suggest long trains of thought. Any commentary on a passage of this sort tends to be a blundering intrusion. All that is needed is to listen to Flaubert, intently.[24]

From this point onwards the movement of the chapter gains speed, with the self-abandon of Emma to her misery, and her reckless display of it to her father, and to her mother-in-law; the actual physical illness caused by her unhappiness; and Charles's decision to move for her sake away from Tostes. The detailed description of her destruction of her wedding-bouquet,[25] which she discovered by chance in a drawer, suggests

23 P. 88.
24 P. 90.
25 P. 94.

three things particularly—the fixed abstracted gaze of the habit-ual day-dreamer ("Elle le regarda brûler," etc. [She watched it burn . . .]): the end of an unhappy phase of her marriage (the hope of departure from Tostes marks the beginning of a re-awakening interest in life); but also the "Pourquoi, mon Dieu, me suis-je mariée?" [Heavens, why did I get married?] of an earlier chapter [26]—the first words spoken by Emma in the book.

The *Comices Agricoles* scene is a masterpiece of technique. Innumerable critics have commented on the effects of contrast, the dry humour, the passages of description, notably of the charming appearance of Emma, the field of the show, the old servant receiving her medal, the dignitaries on the platform; and the skilfully prepared climax when, at the prize-giving cere-mony, Emma with Rodolphe in the town-hall sees in a kind of dream her past life, and, unknowingly, an indication of what is to come as she watches in the distance the old coach l'Hiron-delle "qui descendait lentement la côte des Leux, en traînant après soi un long panache de poussière" [27] [which came slowly down the Leux hill dragging a long plume of dust behind itself] —the coach which is afterwards to play so great a part in her rendez-vous with Léon at Rouen.

Flaubert has in fact assembled in this chapter all his chief characters; even Léon, who is not at Yonville, is present at one time in Emma's thoughts. The construction of the chapter has an orderliness, a rhythmic movement of its own which com-mand the admiration of the reader. But here the author's style is satirical. Humanity in the mass is repellent to him, and this is obvious from certain comments:

> *Tous ces gens-là se ressemblaient;* [28] . . . *toutes les bouches de la multitude se tenaient ouvertes, comme pour boire ses paroles;* [29] . . . *ces bourgeois épanouis.*[30]

> [All these people looked alike; . . . every mouth in the crowd was open, as if to drink in his words; . . . these complacent bourgeois.]

26 Ch. vii, p. 62.
27 Part 2, Ch. viii, p. 204.
28 P. 195.
29 P. 202.
30 P. 207.

The visiting councillor's speech is a collection of pompous platitudes; the banquet at the close of the festivities, too crowded; the fireworks, damp; Homais's account of the proceedings, written for the *Fanal de Rouen,* frankly ridiculous in its exaggeration. The official banalities of the main speech are equalled by the Romantic ones of the conversation of Emma and Rodolphe. In fact, in this assembly of characters, not one is portrayed as a likeable human being; that is to say, not one of the recurring characters. The two who receive sympathetic treatment from Flaubert do not appear elsewhere in the book; they are the old farm-servant Catherine Leroux, and the youngest son of the mayor, in national guard uniform with a helmet much too large:

> *Il souriait là-dessous avec une douceur tout enfantine, et sa petite figure pâle, où des gouttes ruisselaient, avait une expression de jouissance, d'accablement et de sommeil.*[31]

> [He was smiling beneath it with childish gentleness, and his pale little face covered with drops of perspiration showed his delight, his fatigue, and his drowsiness.]

But such moments of gentleness are rare. At the close of this chapter more than at any other point in the book, perhaps, the reader may find himself longing for a character with some depth and goodness. As Sainte-Beuve wrote when first reviewing the book: "Pourquoi n'avoir pas mis là un seul personnage qui soit de nature à consoler, à reposer le lecteur par un bon spectacle, ne pas lui avoir ménagé un seul ami? . . ."[32] [Why did the author not include a single character who could console the reader and give him some respite by his goodness; why not have allowed the reader at least one friend?] and Matthew Arnold, a few years later: ". . . not a personage in the book to rejoice or console us; the springs of freshness and feeling are not there to create such personages. . . ."[33] Obviously the lack of sympathetic principal characters is a strange feature of the book, and one is tempted to wonder whether, if Flaubert

31 P. 202.

32 *Les Grands Ecrivains Français,* par Sainte-Beuve. XIXe *Siècle. Les Romanciers.* (Paris: Garnier, 1927), II, 181.

33 Matthew Arnold, *Essays in Criticism* (2nd Series) (London: Macmillan Co., 1915), *Count Leo Tolstoi,* p. 276.

had developed differently the character of Charles, he would have given greater force to the tragedy of *Madame Bovary*. But such speculations are part of the pleasure of reading Flaubert; he was obviously quite capable of doing things that he did not choose to do, and that his critics have often considered he should have done. In *Madame Bovary* the two minor characters of the boy Justin and the child Berthe are created with delicacy and compassion. Any minor character is a potential major one, and if he had chosen to make either of them the central figure of a novel, would his attitude towards them have changed? Would his sad and indignant view of humanity have ensured that any major character should be at worst completely selfish and at best rather ludicrous? Perhaps. And yet the curious thing about the *Comices* scene is that behind all the pretentiousness and shallowness and hypocrisy occupying the front of the stage, there is a hint of a world of innocence and enjoyment—the *sourire de béatitude* of Catherine Leroux on many other faces. And there is too, all around crowded Yonville, the peaceful sunlit countryside. Flaubert, writing of this chapter when he was completing it, said: "C'est un dur endroit, j'y ai *tous* mes [sic] personnages de mon livre en action et en dialogue . . . et par là-dessus un grand paysage qui les enveloppe. Mais, si je réussis, ce sera bien symphonique." [34] [It is a difficult passage. I've included all my characters moving about and talking . . . and over against it all a great countryside which envelops them all. But if I can succeed in it, it will be quite symphonic.] One of the delights of analyzing this chapter is to try to see how he has managed to convey the impression of this surrounding countryside without ever describing or even mentioning any aspect of it. And for those readers who were immediately aware of the "symphonic effect" of the chapter, and for whom a later reading of his letters simply confirmed that this was the effect he had been aiming at, the *Comices Agricoles* scene will always be one of the major pleasures of literature.

Chapter 3 of Part III is as brief as the *Comices* scene is long; the most important feature of it is that it evokes for a moment an image of beauty and innocence, bringing home all the more painfully the second-rateness and sordidness of the

34 To Louise Colet, September 7, 1853, *Correspondance*, III, 335.

situation of Emma and Léon. Here is the passage in which
Flaubert achieves this curious effect (they are returning by boat
from an island where they have dined. Emma is singing):

> Sa voix harmonieuse et faible se perdait sur les flots; et le
> vent emportait les roulades que Léon écoutait passer, comme
> des battements d'ailes, autour de lui.
> Elle se tenait en face, appuyée contre la cloison de la
> chaloupe, où la lune entrait par un des volets ouverts. Sa robe
> noire, dont les draperies s'élargissaient en éventail, l'amincis-
> sait, la rendait plus grande. Elle avait la tête levée, les mains
> jointes, et les deux yeux vers le ciel. Parfois l'ombre des saules la
> cachait en entier, puis elle réapparaissait tout à coup, comme
> une vision, dans la lumière de la lune.[35]

[Her voice, harmonious and soft, disappeared over the
waves; and the wind carried off the roulades which Léon heard
pass about him like the beating of wings.
She sat across from him leaning against the bulkhead, into
which the moonlight entered through an open shutter. Her
black dress, its folds spreading fanlike about her, made her
seem slimmer and taller. Her head was raised, her hands joined
and she looked upward toward the sky. Sometimes the shadow
of a willow would hide her entirely, then she would suddenly
reappear, like a vision, in the moonlight.]

Then Flaubert shatters the image, as though throwing a
stone into calm water, by the boatman's reference to a lively
party he took out the other day, of which the gayest member,
according to his description, could have been no other than the
faithless Rodolphe. We return to the little intrigues of Emma's
real life. And though we realize that throughout the chapter
Emma is seen by the romantic Léon who is in turn observed by
a sardonic Flaubert, the impression of a momentary glimpse
of something pure, remains.

The famous chapter in which Flaubert describes at length
the death of Emma from arsenic poisoning has many features
more interesting than the medical detail so carefully collected
by the author. For example, Emma's last meeting with Rodolphe: it is made perfectly clear at the end that her impulse to
kill herself comes from a sense of betrayal in love, and betrayal by Rodolphe—not from the more immediate disasters,

35 Pp. 354-55.

her disappointment with Léon and her desperate financial situation:

> . . . *elle ne se rappelait point la cause de son horrible état, c'est-à-dire la question d'argent. Elle ne souffrait que de son amour, se sentait son âme l'abandonner par ce souvenir, comme les blessés, en agonisant, sentent l'existence qui s'en va par leur plaie qui saigne.*[36]

> [. . . she did not remember the reason for her horrible predicament, that is, the problem of money. She was suffering only in her love and could feel her soul slipping away from her through this memory, as men dying of their wounds feel their life escaping through their bleeding gashes.]

It is almost as though Flaubert were suggesting that Emma had indeed loved Rodolphe profoundly. It is notable that her mental state as she leaves La Huchette for the last time is similar to the one she experienced after Rodolphe first abandoned her. On that occasion, her wild flight to the top of the house, to the empty attics, almost ends in suicide as she leans dizzily out of the window. This time the wild flight is repeated:

> *Puis, dans un transport d'héroïsme qui la rendait presque joyeuse, elle descendit la côte en courant, traversa la planche aux vaches, le sentier, l'allée, les halles, et arriva devant la boutique du pharmacien.*[37]

> [Then, in a sort of heroic ecstasy which made her feel almost joyful, she ran down the slope, crossed the cattle bridge, followed the path and the walk, passed by the marketplace, and ended before the pharmacist's shop.]

But even the great dramatic exit from life is bungled and turns into a sordid, lengthy physical agony.

Another interesting feature of this scene is the sudden appearance, carefully engineered by Flaubert, probably with symbolical intent, of the blind beggar with his hideously diseased face and his bawdy little song. That this unfortunate, whom Emma had so often seen as she returned from Rouen, should appear in Yonville to consult Homais at the very moment of her death is scarcely credible; but it is a coincidence of which

36 Part 3, Ch. vii, p. 432.
37 Pp. 432–33.

one can imagine Hardy approving. For him, the most hideous of earthly realities forming the last image in the mind of one who could not bear very much reality, would be an example of the endlessly inventive cruelty of Heaven. For Flaubert, the horrible apparition signifies more probably the embodiment of Emma's degradation. Flaubert is concerned, too, with departing in a startling way from the conventional, sentimental idea of the death-scene with repentance and consoling foretastes of bliss. But on the whole the introduction of the beggar gives a touch of Romantic melodrama which weakens the end of the scene.

But perhaps the most important thing of all in this chapter is the character of Dr. Larivière, the famous doctor from Rouen. Important because here at last is the "personage . . . to rejoice and console us" supposed by Matthew Arnold not to exist in the book. This is a human being after Flaubert's own heart, and he does not conceal his admiration. Certainly the description of Dr. Larivière occupies only one paragraph, and his visit to Yonville a couple of pages—but as the whole is quintessential Flaubert, the character assumes great dramatic importance. For Larivière stands out in complete contrast to all the other characters in the book.

> *Dédaigneux des croix, des titres et des académies, hospitalier, libéral, paternel avec les pauvres et pratiquant la vertu sans y croire, il eût presque passé pour un saint si la finesse de son esprit ne l'eût fait craindre comme un démon. Son regard, plus tranchant que ses bistouris, vous descendait droit dans l'âme et désarticulait tout mensonge à travers les allégations et les pudeurs.*[38]

> [Scorning medals, titles, and academies, hospitable, generous, fatherly with the poor and practicing virtue without believing in it, he would almost have passed for a saint, had not the keenness of his wit made him feared as a demon. His eye, sharper than his scalpel, cut through to one's soul and laid bare all the lies beneath the claims and fears.]

But he is not too hardened by experience to shed a tear at the despair of Charles. Most critics have commented on this fine description, usually to point out that it was Flaubert's

38 Part 3, Ch. vi, p. 441.

tribute to his father; [39] but the importance of the paragraph in the book can scarcely be over-stressed. It simply sets the whole of the rest in perspective—all the pettiness and stupidity, the hysteria and incompetence, the false emotion and unworthy ambition. It suggests the exacting standard by which Flaubert was inclined to measure other human beings, himself included, and their actions. By writing in this way of Larivière, Flaubert balances his picture of provincial life, for Larivière is a provincial too. The fact that Flaubert could bring so vividly to life, in so short a space, this vital and dominating character suggests that it was with deliberate intent that he turned his gaze upon failures and nonentities and the pathetic or ludicrous weaknesses of human beings, and composed almost entirely in the minor key. Larivière, after all, is an example of the triumph of the good; he occupies a position of importance and is revered and loved.

But the apotheosis of Homais closes the book. "Il vient de recevoir la croix d'honneur." [He has just been made a member of the Legion of Honor.] There he stands, perpetuated by this perfect tense, eternally pleased with himself. Emma and Charles are dead, Berthe condemned to a probably brief life of hardship; but the chemist's family is "florissante et hilare" [flourishing and joyful].

> *Napoléon l'aidait au laboratoire, Athalie lui brodait un bonnet grec, Irma découpait des rondelles de papier pour couvrir les confitures, et Franklin récitait tout d'une haleine la table de Pythagore.*[40]

[Napoleon helped him in the laboratory, Athalie embroidered his caps for him, Irma cut out round pieces of paper to cover the jam pots, and Franklin recited the Pythagorean table all in one breath.]

It is perhaps more disturbing than amusing to imagine what Homais's descendants might be like today, if they inherited his character. But let us hope that by some irony of fate the family produced a poet—indifferent to wealth, reputation or "progress," devoting his whole life to the creation of some-

---

39 In any case certain details of the description, notably the reference to Larivière's hands, would suggest that this was a portrait from the life.
40 Part 3, Ch. xi, p. 477.

thing with no material value at all. But Flaubert was aware of the growing power of the Homais breed; his Homais is too intelligent and enterprising, and above all loquacious, not to be a prominent member of society. Flaubert speaks of "la profondeur de son intelligence et la scélératesse de sa vanité" [41] [his profound intelligence and his criminal vanity], and in fact the two characteristics not infrequently produce a public figure full of sound and fury. Homais, the little tutelary genius of bustling busybodies, with his Gradgrindish passion for collecting and disseminating Facts, would have gloried in the sound, which since the invention of wireless is one of the inescapable conditions of social life, of the human voice perpetually imparting information. But ". . . fermons notre porte, montons au plus haut de notre tour d'ivoire, sur la dernière marche, le plus près du ciel. Il y fait froid quelquefois, n'est-ce pas? Mais qu'importe? On voit les étoiles briller clair et l'on n'entend plus les dindons" [42] [. . . let us lock our doors and climb to the top of our ivory tower, on the last step, as near to heaven as we can reach. It is sometimes cold up there, you know. But what does it matter; you can see the stars shining clearly and you no longer have to listen to the turkeys] wrote Flaubert while he was composing Madame Bovary. And Flaubert from the top of his ivory tower could see more than Homais and his kind ever dreamed existed. ". . . tous mes personnages . . . et par là-dessus un grand paysage qui les enveloppe" [all my characters . . . and over against it all a great countryside which envelops them all].

The words which have seemed to me to come nearest to explaining the peculiar charm of this inexhaustible novel are Coleridge's words about the "power of poetry"; which is, he said, "by a single word, perhaps, to instil that energy into the mind, which compels the imagination to produce the picture." [43] This art of filling a small number of words with great significance, this compulsive power over the imagination of his reader, is remarkably developed in Flaubert's case. And again,

41 P. 473.
42 To Louise Colet, November 22, 1852, Correspondance, III, 54.
43 Coleridge's Shakespearean Criticism, ed. T. M. Rayson (London: Constable, 1903), II, 174.

if one tries to pay tribute to the form of the work, the aspect of it that had so much significance for Flaubert, and which he so much desired should be understood—what would please him more than to say that he had ". . . the sense of musical delight, with the power of producing it" [44] which Coleridge said is a gift of imagination?

44 *Biographia Literaria,* XV.

2 · The Life and Letters of Gustave Flaubert

INTRODUCTION

It is useful in a consideration of Gustave Flaubert and Madame Bovary to establish some of the essential facts of Flaubert's life and the more obvious bases for his theoretical views. Both became available to readers, later authors, and critics through the publication of Flaubert's letters, which rapidly occasioned a considerable number of articles in France and elsewhere. Among the more influential critics in England at the end of the nineteenth century was Walter Pater, author of the following two essays. The theoretical underpinnings of Flaubert's novel, now made explicit by the publication of his letters, Pater seized upon to illustrate and clarify concepts of writing which he himself held and which he felt it important to state for English-speaking people. In these two articles (and in other statements as well) he gave his readers those facts of Flaubert's life which it is convenient to know and a carefully selected sampling of the more important of Flaubert's tenets about the writer, writing, and the novel. The footnotes are my additions.

Prose as a fine art, of which French literature affords a continuous illustration, had in Gustave Flaubert a follower, unique in the decisiveness of his conception of that art and the disinterestedness of his service to it. Necessitated by weak health to the regularity and the quiet of a monk, he was but kept the closer to what he had early recognised as his vocation in life.

From *The Pall Mall Gazette*, Aug. 25, 1888.

By taking care, he lived to be almost sixty years old, in the full use of his gift, as we may suppose, and he wrote seven or eight books, none of them lengthy. "Neglect nothing," he writes to a friend. "Labour! Do the thing over again, and don't leave your work till you feel convinced you have brought it to the last point of perfection possible for you. In these days genius is not rare. But what no one has now, what we should try to have, is the conscience of one's work." To that view he was faithful; and he had, and keeps, his reward. So sparing as a writer of books, he was a voluminous letter-writer. A volume of his letters to George Sand appeared in 1883. In 1887 his niece, for many years his intimate companion, published the first portion of his general correspondence, and it is the purpose of this paper to note some of the lights thrown by it on himself and on his work.

Gustave Flaubert was born at Rouen in 1821. His earliest home was in the old Maison-Dieu,[1] of which his father was surgeon. The surgeon's household was self-respecting, affectionate, refined, liberal in expense; but the inevitable associations of the place—the suffering, white-capped faces at the windows—stayed by the susceptible lad, and passed into his work as a somewhat overbalanced sense of unhappiness in things. More cheerful influences came with the purchase of a country house at Croisset, a few miles down the Seine, on the right bank, "white, and in the old style." In after years Flaubert delighted to believe that Pascal, that great master of prose, had once visited it.[2] It was here, in the large rooms, the delightful garden, with views of Rouen, the busy river, the wooded hills, that the remainder of Flaubert's life was chiefly spent. His letters show that the feeling of vocation to literature came early; oddly enough, for he was no precocious child, and took a longer time than is usual in learning to read. From the first he was abundant in enthusiasm for the literary art of others. In early youth he meets Victor Hugo, and is surprised to find

1 "Maison-Dieu" is the older French word for "hospital."
2 Pater is probably in error here, as the house at Croisset appears to have dated from the eighteenth, not the seventeenth, century. Flaubert did, however, enjoy the probably apocryphal story that the Abbé Prévost wrote *Manon Lescaut* here. There would have been a fine irony in having Manon and Emma Bovary conceived under one roof.

him much like any one else externally, wondering at "the greatness of the treasure contained in so ordinary a casket," fixing
his eyes devoutly "on the right hand which had written so many
beautiful things." He was a singularly beautiful child, and re-
cords that royal ladies had stopped their carriages to take him
in their arms and kiss him. By its vigour and beauty, again, his
youth made people think of the young demigods of Greek
sculpture. Then, somewhere in early manhood, came an alarm
regarding health, both bodily and mental; and from that time
to his death he continued more or less of an invalid, or at
least a valetudinarian, enjoying life, indeed, its work, his gift,
but always with an undercurrent of nervous distress.[3] "To
practical life," he writes at twenty-four, "I have said an ir-
revocable adieu. Hence, for a long time to come, all I ask is
five or six hours of quiet in my own room daily, a big fire in
the winter, and two candles every evening to give me light":
again, "I am well enough, now that I have consented to be
always ill": and again, "My life seems arranged now after a
regular plan with less large, less varied horizons, but the deeper
perhaps, because more restrained. You would not believe what
mischief any sort of derangement causes me." Henceforth a
sort of sacerdotal order is impressed everywhere. In the quiet
house his writing-table is before him, reverently covered with
all its apparatus of work, under a light silken cloth, when a
visitor is announced: his life slides early into even grooves; an
organisation naturally exquisite becomes fastidious. He was still,
at carefully-guarded hours, abundant in friendship, in the
good-humour, and the humour or wit, which attaches and
amuses friends. After all, there was plenty of laughter, not always satiric, in his life. And then an intimate domestic affection,
so largely evidenced in these letters, making heavy demands
from time to time on his patience, his self-denial, and procuring
him in return immense consideration, was a necessity alike of
his personal and his literary life. It is a very human picture,
with average battles and sorrows and joys, quite like those of
the bourgeois he so greatly despised, but for him with all the
joys also, all the various intellectual adventure, of the artistic
life, followed loyally as an end in itself. The quiet people he

3 His illness was temporal lobe epilepsy.

quietly loves are a relaxation from the somewhat over-intent character of his "art," while they supply some of its motives. And the enforced monotony of a recluse life is in their favour. "To take pleasure in a place it is necessary to have lived there long. One day is not enough for warming one's nest."

Yet in spite of bad health, in spite of his love of retirement, of routine, his passion for a recluse life, he had been, at least for a Frenchman, a good deal of a traveller. Foreign travel—mental, and as far as might be physical, journeys—to the old classical lands, the desert, the wondrous East, the very matter of his work was in considerable measure dependent upon that. Rapid yet penetrative notice of the places he visits animates his correspondence. The student of his writings—so brief a list!—is glad to add to them the record of a journey to Brittany in 1847, written in "collaboration" with his travelling companion, M. Maxime du Camp. He visited many parts of France, above all, the grand old Pagan towns of the South, Switzerland, Italy, Corsica, "a brave country, still virgin as to the *bourgeois*, who have not yet arrived to degrade it with their admiration, a country ardent and grave, all red and black." At last, with a thousand daily solicitudes for the poor old mother left at Croisset, came his long journey to Syria and Egypt, the record of which fills the last hundred pages of the volume before us.

Flaubert's first great trouble came in his twenty-fifth year, on the death of his father, quickly followed by that of his favourite sister Caroline:

> It was yesterday at eleven o'clock we interred her—poor damsel! They put her in her wedding-gown, with bunches of roses, violets, and immortelles. I passed the whole night watching beside her. She lay straight, reposed on her couch, in the room where you have heard her play. She looked taller and handsomer than in life, with the long white veil down to the feet. In the morning, when all was ready, I gave her a last kiss in her coffin. I stooped down, placed my head within, felt the lead bend under my hands.—It was I who had the cast taken. I saw the coarse hands handle her and enclose her in the plaster. I shall possess her hand and her face. Pradier [4] will

4 James Pradier, a now forgotten French neoclassic sculptor (d. 1852), who was an intimate friend of Flaubert's. His wife Laura, "Ludovica," was one of Flaubert's models for Emma Bovary.

make the bust for me, to be placed in my own room. I have
kept for myself her large striped shawl, a lock of her hair, the
table, and the desk at which she wrote. And that is all!—all that
remains of those one has loved. . . . When we got up there,
in that cemetery behind the walls of which we used to go out
walking in my school days, the grave was too narrow: the
coffin would not go in. They shook it, pulled it this way and
that, used spade and levers, and at last a gravedigger tramped
upon it—where the head was—to force it into its place. I felt
dried up—like the marble of a tomb—but terribly irritated.
And now, since Sunday, we are at home again at Croisset.
What a journey it was! alone with my mother and the infant,
which cried. The last time I left, it was with yourself, you will
remember. Of the four persons who then lived there two remain. . . . My mother is better than she might be; occupies
herself with her daughter's babe, is trying to make herself
a mother once more. Will she succeed? The reaction has not
yet come, and I dread it. I am crushed, stupefied. If I could
but resume my tranquil life of art, of long-continued meditation!

What notes of dismay, of a kind of frozen grief, of a capacity
for pity, of those resources to be so largely tested by *Madame
Bovary!*

I am prepared for everything. I am like the pavement on the
high road; misfortune tramps over me as it wills. . . . As for
me, my eyes are dry as marble. Strange! The more expansive I
find myself, fluid and abundant, in fictitious griefs, just in that
proportion do the real griefs stay fixed in my heart, acrid and
hard. They turn to crystal, there, one by one, as they come.

It is the daughter of that favourite sister who has now
appeared as the editor of his letters from the year 1830 to 1850.
She has introduced them by a sketch of his life, which the
student of Flaubert's work will value, for she became in her
turn her uncle's intimate companion, and has recorded some
characteristic counsels to herself, the mature experience of his
artistic life applied to the formation of the mind of a young
girl. "When you take up a book," he would say, "you must
swallow it at one mouthful. That is the only way to know it
in its entirety. Accustom yourself to follow out an idea. I don't
wish you should have that loose character in your thoughts
which is the appanage of persons of your sex." The author of
Salammbô taught her ancient history. "I interrupted him sometimes," she tells us, "by the question, 'Was he a good man?—

Cambyses, Alexander, Alcibiades.' 'Faith! they were not very accommodating members of society—*messieurs très commodes.* But what has that to do with you?' " He went to church with her, for the young French girl could not go alone—amazing complaisance it seemed in so marked a Freethinker—awaiting patiently, we must not be too sure with what kind of thoughts, till her duties were over.

La Bovary!—many a time she heard of that before she had any notion what the name meant. "I had a vague belief that it was a synonym for labour, perpetual labour. I assisted, a motionless witness, at the slow creation of those pages so severely elaborated." There he sat, month after month, seeking, sometimes with so much pain, the expression, "the phrase," weighing the retention or rejection of an epithet—his one fixed belief the belief in beauty, literary beauty, with liberal delight at beauty in other men's work, remembering after many years the precise place on the page of some approved form of sentence. He knew his favourite passage in Scripture, "How beautiful upon the mountains are the feet of them that bring glad tidings!" " 'Reflect on that, get to the bottom of it, if you can,' he would say to me, full of enthusiasm."

His "distractions" were limited to certain short absences in Paris for a day or two, about once in three months—*pour me retremper.* On the rare occasion of a longer visit it was necessary that his home companions should go with him; and then, on certain days, his rooms in the Boulevard du Temple were put in flowery array, and he entertained a select party of friends. "Whenever I re-enter Paris," he writes, "I breathe at my ease." But in truth he abhorred change. "Man is so poor a machine that a straw among the wheels spoils it." "I live like a Carthusian," he says; and again, "I am but a lizard, a literary lizard, warming himself all day long at the full sun of the beautiful." "For writing," his niece tells us, "he required extreme tension of mind, and he never found himself in the desired condition save in his own workroom, seated at his great round table, sure that nothing could come to disturb him. He had a passionate love of order, and ate sparingly. His force of will in all that concerned his 'art' was immense." He troubled himself little about "moments of inspiration," the waiting on which he held to be a cause of "sterility." Get the habit of working in ordinary daylight, and then perhaps the ray of heavenly light may come. At times the monotony of his method of life, a monotony likely to continue to the end, weighed on the spirits, especially as the passing footsteps about him grew rarer and memory took the place of sensation: for, in spite of what people say, "memories don't fill one's house, they do but enlarge its solitude. There is now a multitude of places at which my heart bleeds as I pass. It seems to me," he writes—only in his twenty-fifth year—"that the angles of my life are worn down under the friction of all that has passed over it."

So his life continued to the last, as he had foreseen, somewhat painfully disturbed towards the end by the German war. That its barbarities should have been the work of a literary, a scientific people, was but the last expression of a soul of stupidity in things, to his view unmistakable. The invaders in occupation of Rouen made use of his house, but respectfully. The end came in 1880, and found him at work, alone apparently, in his large study, with the five windows and wide views, where he had lived so long.

Madame Commanville has printed these letters, chiefly because she thought they reveal her uncle under a different light from that of his books. A kind of scandal attached to his writings, and the editor of his correspondence is certainly right in thinking that her own reminiscences of his life would, after all, make people esteem him as a man. In truth, life and letters alike reveal him not otherwise than as we divine him through his books—the passionate, laborious, conscientious artist, who had found affection and temperance indispensable to his art, abounding in sympathy for the simple people who came nearest to him, conscious of an immense mental superiority to almost every one, a superiority which kept him high and clean in all things, yet full of pity, of practical consideration for men and women as they must be. Anxious to think him a good man, his niece, with some costly generous acts known to herself in memory, was struck above all by that tranquil devotion to art which seemed to have had about it something of the "seriousness and passion that are like a consecration"— something of religion.

3 · Flaubert's Literary Art

The second volume of Gustave Flaubert's correspondence, just now published, is even richer than the first, alike in those counsels of literary art Flaubert was pre-eminently fitted to give, and in lights, direct and indirect, on his own work. The letters belong to a short period in his life, from his twenty-eighth to his thirty-second year (1850–1854), during which he was an exceptionally expansive correspondent, but otherwise chiefly occupied in the composition of *Madame Bovary*, a work of immense labour, as also of great and original genius. The more systematic student might draw from these letters many an interesting paragraph to add, by way of foot-notes, to that impressive book.

The earlier letters find Flaubert still in the East, recording abundantly those half-savage notes of ancient civilisation which are in sympathy with the fierce natural colouring of the country he loved so well. The author of *Salammbô* and *Hérodias* is to be detected already in this lively vignette from an Oriental square:

> Nothing is more graceful than the spectacle of all those men [the Dervishes] waltzing, with their great petticoats twisted, their ecstatic faces lifted to the sky. They turn, without a moment's pause, for about an hour. One of them assured us that, if he were not obliged to hold his hands above his head, he could turn for six hours continuously.

From *The Athenaeum*, August 3, 1889, there entitled, "Correspondance de Gustave Flaubert."

Even here, then, it is the calm of the East which expresses itself—the calm, perhaps the emptiness, of the Oriental, of which he has fixed the type in the following sketch:

> I have seen certain dancing girls, who balanced themselves with the regularity of a palm tree. Their eyes, of a profound depth, express calm only—nothing but the calm, the emptiness, of the desert. It is the same with the men. What admirable heads! heads which seem to be turning over within them the grandest thoughts in the world. But tap on them! and there will be only the empty beer-glass, the deserted sepulchre. Whence then the majesty of their external form? of what does it really hold? Of the absence, I should reply, of all passion. They have the beauty of the ruminating ox, of the greyhound in its race, the floating eagle—that sentiment of fatality which is fulfilled in these. A conviction of the nothingness of man gives to all they do, their looks, their attitudes, a resigned but grandiose character. Their loose and easy raiment, lending itself freely to every movement of the body, is always in closest accord with the wearer and his functions; with the sky, too, by its colour: and then the sun! There is an immense *ennui* there in the sun, which consumes everything.[1]

But it is as brief essays in literary criticism that these letters are most effective. Exquisitely personal essays, self-explanatory, or by way of confession, written almost exclusively to one person—a perfectly sympathetic friend, engaged like the writer in serious literary work—they possess almost the unity, the connected current of a book. It is to Madame X.,[2] however, that Flaubert makes this cynical admission about women:

> What I reproach in women, above all, is their need of *poetisation*, of forcing poetry into things. A man may be in love with his laundress, but will know that she is stupid, though he may not enjoy her company the less. But if a woman loves her inferior, he is straightway an unrecognised genius, a superior soul, or the like. And to such a degree does this innate disposition to see crooked prevail, that women can perceive neither truth when they encounter it, nor beauty where it really exists. This fault is the true cause of the deceptions of which they so often complain. To require oranges of apple trees is a common malady with them.

[1] Emma Bovary's principal problem is her romantic ennui. Flaubert found it everywhere.

[2] Louise Colet, his mistress for nearly a decade and a model for several aspects of Emma. She was a minor poetess.

Flaubert, as seen in these letters, was undoubtedly a somewhat austere lover. His true mistress was his art. Counsels of
art there are—for the most part, the best thing he has to offer.
Only rarely does he show how he could play the lover:

> Your love penetrates me at last, like warm rain, and I feel
> myself searched through with it, to the bottom of my heart.
> Have you not everything that could make me love you? body,
> wit, tenderness? You are simple of soul and strong of head;
> not poetic, yet a poet in extreme degree. There is nothing but
> good in you: and you are wholly, as your bosom is, white,
> and soft to touch. I try sometimes to fancy how your face
> will look when you are old, and it seems to me I shall love you
> still as much as now, perhaps more.

In contrast with the majority of writers, apt to make a
false pretence of facility, it is of his labour that Flaubert boasts.
That was because, after all, labour did but set free the innate
lights of a true diamond; it realised, was a ministry to, the
great imaginative gift of which he was irresistibly conscious. It
was worth his while!

> As for me, the more I feel the difficulties of good writing,
> the more my boldness grows. It is this preserves me from the
> pedantry into which I should otherwise fall. I have plans for
> books, the composition of which would occupy the rest of my
> life: and if there happen to me, sometimes, cruel moments,
> which well-nigh make me weep with anger (so great do I feel
> my weakness to be), there are others also when I can scarce
> contain myself for joy: something from the depths within me,
> for which voluptuous is no word, overflows for me in sudden
> leaps. I feel transported, almost inebriate, with my own
> thoughts, as if there came to me, at some window within,
> a puff of warm perfumes. I shall never go very far, and know
> how much I lack; but the task I undertake will surely be
> executed by another. I shall have put on the true road some
> one better endowed, better born, for the purpose, than myself.
> The determination to give to prose the rhythm of verse, leaving
> it still veritable prose; to write the story of common life as
> history or the epic gets written (that is to say, without detri-
> ment to the natural truth of the subject), is perhaps impossible.
> I ask myself the question sometimes. Yet it is perhaps a con-
> siderable, an original thing, to have tried. I shall have had my
> permanent value for my obstinacy. And who knows? One day I
> may find a good *motif*, an air entirely within the compass of my
> voice: and at any rate I shall have passed my life not ignobly,

often with delight. Yet still it is saddening to think how many great men arrive easily at the desired effect, by means beyond the limits of conscious art. What could be worse built than many things in Rabelais, Cervantes, Molière, Hugo? But, then, what sudden thrusts of power! What power in a single word!

Impersonality in art, the literary ideal of Gustave Flaubert, is perhaps no more possible than realism. The artist *will* be felt; his subjectivity must and will colour the incidents, as his very bodily eye *selects* the aspects of things. By force of an immense and continuous effort, however, the whole scope of which these letters enable us to measure, Flaubert did keep *Madame Bovary* at a great distance from himself; the author might be thought to have been completely hidden out of sight in his work. Yet even here he transpires, clearly enough, from time to time; and the morbid sense of life, everywhere impressed in the very atmosphere of that sombre history, came certainly of the writer himself. The cruelty of the ways of things—that is a conviction of which the development is partly traceable in these letters.

Provided the brain remains! That is the chief thing. But how nothingness invades us! We are scarcely born ere decay begins for us, in such a way that the whole of life is but one long combat with it, more and more triumphant, on its part, to the consummation, namely, death; and then the reign of decay is exclusive. There have been at most two or three years in which I was really entire—from seventeen to nineteen. I was splendid just then, though I scarce like to say so now; enough to attract the eyes of a whole assembly of spectators, as happened to me at Rouen, on the first presentation of "Ruy Blas." Ever since then I have deteriorated at a furious pace. There are mornings when I feel afraid to look at myself, so worn and used-up am I grown.

Madame Bovary, of course, was a tribute to science; and Flaubert had no dread, great hopes rather, of the service of science in imaginative literature, though the combat between scientific truth—mental physiology and the like—and that perfectly finished academic style he preferred, might prove a hard one. We might be all of us, since Sophocles—well, "tattooed savages!" but still, there was "something else in art besides rectitude of line and the well-polished surface." The difficulty lay in the limitations of language, which it would be the literary artist's true contention to enlarge. "We have too many things, too few words. 'Tis from that comes the torture of the fine literary conscience." But it was one's duty, none the less, to accept all, "imprint all, and, above all, fix one's *point d'appui* in the present." Literature, he held, would take more and more the modes of action which now seem to belong exclusively to science. It would be, above all, *exposante*—by way of exposition; by which, he was careful to point out, he by no means intended *didactic*. One must make pictures, by way of showing nature as she really is; only, the pictures must be complete ones. We must paint both sides, the upper and under. Style—what it might be, if writers faithfully cherished it— that was the subject of his perpetual consideration. Here is a sketch of the prose style of the future:

> Style, as I conceive it, style as it will be realised some day— in ten years, or ten generations! It would be rhythmical as verse itself, precise as the language of science; and with undulations—a swelling of the violin; plumage of fire! A style which would enter into the idea like the point of a lancet; when thought would travel over the smooth surfaces like a canoe with fair winds behind it. Prose is but of yesterday, it must be confessed. Verse is *par excellence* the form of the ancient literatures. All possible prosodic combinations have been already made; those of prose are still to make.

The effort, certainly, cost him much; how much we may partly see in these letters, the more as *Madame Bovary*, on which he was then mainly at work, made a large demand also on his impersonality:

> The cause of my going so slowly is just this, that nothing in that book [*Madame Bovary*] is drawn from myself. Never has my own personality been so useless to me. It may be, perhaps, that hereafter I shall do stronger things. I hope so, but I can hardly imagine I shall do anything more skilful. Here everything is of the head. If it has been false in aim, I shall always feel that it has been a good mental exercise. But after all, what is the non-natural to others is the natural to me —the extraordinary, the fantastic, the wild chase, mythologic, or metaphysic. *Saint Antoine* [3] did not require of me one

3 *The Temptation of Saint Anthony*. Flaubert is here referring to a first version of it, which he finished in 1849. Short selections from a revised or second version he published in 1856. A third and entirely rewritten version of the whole work he published in 1874.

quarter of the tension of mind *Madame Bovary* has caused me. *Saint Antoine* was a discharge: I had nothing but pleasure in writing it; and the eighteen months devoted to the composition of its five hundred pages were the most thoroughly voluptuous of my life, hitherto. Judge, then, of my condition in writing *Madame Bovary*. I must needs put myself every minute into a skin not mine, and antipathetic to me. For six months now I have been making love Platonically; and at the present moment my exaltation of mind is that of a good Catholic: I am longing to go to confession.

A constant reader of Montaigne, Flaubert pushed to the utmost the habit of doubt, as leading to artistic detachment from all practical ends:

Posterity will not be slow in cruel desertion of those who have determined to be useful, and have sung "for a cause." It cares very little for Chateaubriand, and his resuscitation of mediaeval religion; for Béranger, with his libertine philosophy; will soon care little for Lamartine and his religious human-itarianism. Truth is never in the present; and if one attaches oneself to the present, there comes an end of one. At the present moment, I believe that even a thinker (and the artist, surely, is three times a thinker) should have no convictions.

Flaubert himself, whatever we may think of that, had certainly attained a remarkable degree of detachment from the ordinary interests of mankind.

Over and above its weightier contributions to the knowl-edge of Flaubert, to the knowledge and practice of literature at its best, this volume, like its predecessor, abounds in striking occasional thoughts:

There is no imagination in France. If you want to make real poetry pass, you must be clever enough to disguise it.

In youth one associates the future realisation of one's dreams with the existence of the actual people around us. In proportion as those existences disappear, our dreams also depart.

Nothing is more useless than those heroic friendships which require exceptional circumstances to prove them. The great difficulty is to find some one who does not rack your nerves in every one of the various ordinary occurrences of life.

The dimensions of a soul may be measured by its power of suffering, as we calculate the depth of rivers by their current.

Formerly, people believed that the sugar-cane alone yielded sugar; nowadays it is extracted from almost anything. It is the same with poetry. Let us draw it, no matter whence, for it lies everywhere, and in all things. Let us habituate ourselves to regard the world as a work of art, the processes of which are to be reproduced in our works.

To have talent, one must be convinced one has it; and to keep the conscience pure, we must put it above the consciences of all other people.

We retain always a certain grudge against any one who instructs us.

What is best in art will always escape people of mediocrity, that is to say, more than three quarters of the human race.

Let our enemies speak evil of us! it is their proper function. It is worse when friends speak well of us foolishly.

Materialists and spiritualists, in about equal degree, prevent the knowledge of matter and spirit alike, because they sever one from the other. The one party make man an angel, the other a swine.

In proportion as it advances, art will be more and more scientific, even as science will become artistic. The two will rejoin each other at the summit, after separating at the base.

Let us be ourselves, and nothing else! "What is your duty? What each day requires." That is Goethe's notion. Let *us* do our duty; which is, to try to write well. What a society of saints we should be, if only each one of us did his duty!

Margaret Gilman

4 · Two Critics and an Author:
Madame Bovary *Judged by Sainte-Beuve*
and by Baudelaire

INTRODUCTION

Two great contemporaries of Flaubert each wrote a review of his novel: the reigning critic, Sainte-Beuve, and the poet Charles Baudelaire. The two reviews taken together set forth, from the very start, the major concerns which have dominated much of the criticism of Madame Bovary ever since, and upon which readers today are still embroidering variations.

Sainte-Beuve, whose work appeared first, established a number of important points, foremost among them the relationship between Flaubert's writing and the scientific age which was then in full swing. As Pater's critiques suggest, Flaubert's theory of the novel does give enormous importance to scientism, the belief in the great role properly to be attributed to science. Madame Bovary was an immediate and noisy success; hence Flaubert soon knew personally all the major writers of his day. Under his impress and also independently, they too show deeply the influence of science. Shortly all of French realism and still more the slightly later naturalism became dominated by this approach to literature. Emile Zola even proclaimed that he was writing scientific novels. When Flaubert's letters were published after his death, his became the definitive name around which these literary theories clustered and, through the writings of Pater and others, they were spread throughout the reading public of the world. The greatest influence of Flaubert's scientism was perhaps in American and English literature, from William Dean Howells to Sinclair Lewis and beyond. Carol Kennicott of Main Street is a daughter of Emma Bovary.

Sainte-Beuve was interested in a second aspect of Madame Bovary, this one, too, destined to have a long life: he found the tone of the novel pitiless. This point, which he raised at some length, became a commonplace among the gentler sort of critic and is still to be heard today. It was allied to the serious doubts Sainte-Beuve felt about the possibility of an art of unrelieved ugliness, which he felt he detected in the new novel. And there have been readers even since for whom a more consoling type of novel has always seemed preferable. Flaubert was unmoved by the objection, feeling on the one hand that his novel was only apparently pitiless for the most part and, on the other hand, that to the extent that the accusation was justified it should be leveled, not at his novel, but at the way life really was. For that he had no responsibility.

In sharp and important contrast Baudelaire, a craftsman like Flaubert, felt that the novel was in point of fact a highly moral treatise, in no sense ugly, and a triumph of that new art which found beauty in the artist's way of looking at life. For him the truth was, in and of itself, moral. Hence, he urged that the writer could, and indeed must, treat of any and every subject, for it was style and not the subject in itself which was the concern of the writer. Therefore he sought to place the discussion on the level of the theory of the novel and the nature of beauty. This line of approach, too, had great development in English and American literature, in Henry James, Joseph Conrad, James Joyce, William Faulkner, and others.

On the various lines established in these two reviews, later readers and critics have for the most part taken their positions. The two reviews are compared and contrasted in the article which follows.

The criticism which greets a masterpiece on its first appearance is in the main discouraging reading for later generations, whether we choose to pride ourselves on our own less clouded vision or, more modestly, to wonder how future generations will estimate our judgments of our contemporaries.

Reprinted from *The French Review,* XV (1941–1942), 138–46. By permission.

The majority of the first reviews of *Madame Bovary* are no exception to this rule, and well deserve the accumulated dust which only erudition has disturbed.[1] But two of them are well worth re-reading: Sainte-Beuve's and Baudelaire's.[2]

Sainte-Beuve's article was one of the first criticisms of *Madame Bovary*; it appeared in *Le Moniteur* on May 4, 1857, shortly after the publication of the novel in book form.[3] Unlike the numerous critics who were to deplore the lack of structure in the novel, Sainte-Beuve maintains that "*Madame Bovary* est un livre avant tout, un livre composé, médité, où rien n'est laissé au hasard de la plume, et dans lequel l'auteur ou mieux l'artiste a fait d'un bout à l'autre ce qu'il a voulu" (p. 347). [*Madame Bovary* is first of all a book, composed, meditated, one in which nothing is left to chance and in which the author, or better the artist, has from one end to the other done exactly what he wished to do.] Then he notes that Flaubert has lived much in the country, but that, unlike most of those who know nature well, he perceives neither its beauty nor its poetry; he sees it only as a setting for his dreary and vulgar characters. The incorrigible romantic in Sainte-Beuve, the disciple of the Lake Poets, regrets with a kind of nostalgic astonishment that nature is not for Flaubert what she was for an earlier generation: "l'idéal a cessé; le lyrique est tari. On en est revenu. Une vérité sévère et impitoyable est entrée jusque dans l'art comme dernier mot de l'expérience" (p. 348). [The ideal has come to an end; the lyric source has dried up. People have gotten over it. A severe and pitiless truth has entered even art as the last word of experience.] This leads Sainte-Beuve to emphasize

1 For a bibliography of these articles see Descharmes and Dumesnil, *Autour de Flaubert*, Mercure de France, 1912, II, 256–70, and for a discussion of them, "Madame Bovary et son temps," *ibid.*, I, 11–98, and René Dumesnil, *La Publication de "Madame Bovary,"* Edgar Malfère, Amiens, 1928, pp. 103–26. Excerpts from a number of the articles are published in the Conard edition of *Madame Bovary*, pp. 527–39, "Opinion de la Presse sur *Madame Bovary*."

2 Sainte-Beuve, "*Madame Bovary*, par M. Gustave Flaubert," *Causeries du lundi*, Garnier frères, 1851–1862, 15 vols., XIII, 346–63: Baudelaire, "*Madame Bovary*, par Gustave Flaubert," *Oeuvres*, Editions de la Pléiade, 1932, 2 vols., II, 440–50. All the references to the articles are to the pages of these two editions.

3 Many of the ideas in the article are foreshadowed in Sainte-Beuve's letter to Flaubert of April 25, 1857 (*Autour de Flaubert*, I, 53–54).

the complete objectivity of the novel. Then, in about a dozen pages, he tells the story of the book, interspersing his own comments. *Madame Bovary*, he concludes, bears the stamp of its time: "science, esprit d'observation, maturité, force, un peu de dureté. Ce sont les caractères que semblent affecter les chefs de file des générations nouvelles. Fils et frère de médecins distingués, M. Gustave Flaubert tient la plume comme d'autres le scalpel. Anatomistes et physiologistes, je vous retrouve partout" (p. 363) [science, the spirit of observation, maturity, strength, a bit of hardness. These are the characteristics which the leaders of the new generation seem to affect. Son and brother of distinguished doctors, M. Gustave Flaubert wields the pen as others hold the scalpel. Anatomists and physiologists, I find you everywhere].

Baudelaire's article did not appear until several months later, in *L'Artiste* of October 18, 1857. The delay of an article for which Flaubert, as his correspondence shows, was waiting with some impatience, was evidently caused in large measure by Baudelaire's preoccupation with the *Fleurs du Mal* trial, the outcome of which was to be less fortunate than that of the *Madame Bovary* case in January.[4] At the beginning the words of gratitude to the magistrates who acquitted Flaubert recall Baudelaire's own case and are an implicit criticism of less enlightened magistrates, a plea *pro domo suo*, with the affirmation that "tous les écrivains, tous ceux du moins dignes de ce nom, ont été acquittés dans la personne de M. Gustave Flaubert" (p. 441) [all writers, all those at least who are worthy of the name, were acquitted in the person of M. Gustave Flaubert]. Then Baudelaire, after surveying the literary landscape since the death of Balzac, sets himself to imagine how Flaubert must have conceived his novel, choosing with conscious deliberation the most banal of settings, provincial life, the most unbearable of characters, small town people, the most outworn of themes, adultery. He must have said to himself:

Je n'ai pas besoin de me préoccuper du style, de l'arrangement pittoresque, de la description des milieux; je possède

4 See Flaubert's letters to Jules Duplan and Ernest Feydeau (*Correspondance*, IV, 209, 216), and Baudelaire's letter to Flaubert (*Correspondance*, éd. Nouvelle Revue Française, I, 182).

toutes ces qualités à une puissance surabondante; je marcherai appuyé sur l'analyse et la logique, et je prouverai ainsi que tous les sujets sont indifféremment bons ou mauvais, selon la manière dont ils sont traités, et que les plus vulgaires peuvent devenir les meilleurs (p. 445).

[I do not need to worry about style or picturesque arrangements or descriptions of settings; I have a superabundance of all these qualities. I shall go forward supported by analysis and logic, and I shall prove thus that all subjects are equally good or bad, depending upon the way in which they are treated, and that the commonest can become the best.]

Baudelaire concludes: "Dès lors, *Madame Bovary,*—une gageure, une vraie gageure, un pari, comme toutes les oeuvres d'art,—était créée." [From that moment on, *Madame Bovary,*—a wager, a real wager, a bet, like all works of art—was created.] Then, leaving Flaubert's point of view, he goes on to his own impressions of the book, ending with a brief parallel between *Madame Bovary* and the *Tentation de saint Antoine:* "Il m'eût été facile de retrouver, sous le tissu minutieux de *Madame Bovary,* les hautes facultés d'*ironie* et de *lyrisme* qui illuminent à outrance la *Tentation de saint Antoine*" (p. 449). [It would have been easy for me to trace out, beneath the minute fabric of *Madame Bovary,* the remarkable faculties of *irony* and *lyricism* which abundantly illuminate *The Temptation of Saint Anthony.*]

In comparing the two articles one notices first of all a difference in attitude. Sainte-Beuve is judging a book hot from the press, writing with a sense of conscientious responsibility towards the public, with whom, as he is well aware, his judgment will weigh heavily. It is above all a review for those who have not yet read the novel, furnishing them with a nutshell version and a definitive judgment. Baudelaire's criticism is less professional, less arbitrary, based not on a just-finished first reading, but on a slow mulling over of the book. He is writing for readers who at that stage will hardly read his article without having read *Madame Bovary.* Whereas Sainte-Beuve devotes some twelve pages to telling the story of the novel, Baudelaire condenses it into one terse sentence: "le léger et soudain miracle de cette pauvre petite provinciale adultère, dont toute l'histoire, sans imbroglio, se compose de tristesses, de dégoûts,

de soupirs et de quelques pâmoisons fébriles arrachés à une vie
barrée par le suicide" (p. 443). [The light and sudden miracle
of this poor little provincial adulteress, whose entire history,
without any imbroglio, is composed of sorrow, disgust, sighs,
and a few feeble moments of intoxication torn from a life erased
by suicide.]

Sainte-Beuve reproaches Flaubert for his realism, "sa
méthode qui consiste à tout décrire et à insister sur tout ce qui
se rencontre" [his method which consists of describing everything and insisting on everything which he meets]. He declares
that "un livre, après tout, n'est pas et ne saurait jamais être la
réalité même" (p. 360) [a book, after all, is not and can never
be reality itself]. Baudelaire, completely in agreement with the
latter statement, as all his criticism shows, has a different view
of Flaubert's realism. He imagines him saying:

> *Comme nous avons entendu parler d'un certain procédé*
> *littéraire appelé réalisme,—injure dégoûtante jetée à la face de*
> *tous les analystes, mot vague et élastique qui signifie pour le*
> *vulgaire, non pas une méthode nouvelle de création, mais une*
> *description minutieuse des accessoires,—nous profiterons de la*
> *confusion des esprits et de l'ignorance universelle. Nous*
> *étendrons un style nerveux, pittoresque, subtil, exact, sur un*
> *canevas banal. Nous enfermerons les sentiments les plus chauds*
> *et les plus bouillants dans l'aventure la plus triviale. Les*
> *paroles les plus solennelles, les plus décisives, s'échapperont*
> *des bouches les plus sottes* (p. 444).

> [As we have heard of a certain literary procedure called
> *realism*—a disgusting insult thrown in the face of all analysts,
> a vague and elastic word which means to the common herd not
> a new method of creation but a minute description of the ac-
> cessories—we shall take advantage of all the confusion in
> people's minds and the universal ignorance. We shall spread
> a powerful and sensitive style, picturesque, subtle, and exact,
> over a banal canvas. We shall enclose the hottest and most
> boiling of feelings within the most trivial of adventures. The
> most solemn words and the most decisive will issue from the
> most stupid mouths.]

For Sainte-Beuve Flaubert has succeeded in abstracting himself
entirely from his book:

> *Parmi tous ces personnages très-réels et très-vivants, il n'en*
> *est pas un seul qui puisse être supposé celui que l'auteur*

voudrait être; aucun n'a été soigné par lui à d'autre fin que pour être décrit en toute précision et crudité, aucun n'a été ménagé comme on ménage un ami; il s'est complètement abstenu, il n'y est que pour tout voir, tout montrer et tout dire; mais dans aucun coin du roman on n'aperçoit même son profil. L'oeuvre est entièrement impersonnelle. C'est une grande preuve de force (p. 349).

[Among all these very real and very living characters there is not a single one whom the reader can imagine the author would wish to be; no single one has been prepared for any other purpose than to be described in all precision and all crudity; none has been treated gently as one treats a friend; he has held himself completely aloof, he is there only to see everything, to display everything, to tell everything; but in no corner of the novel can we see even his profile. The work is entirely impersonal. It is a great proof of his strength.]

But this very point leads Sainte-Beuve to his most serious criticism of Flaubert: "Tout en me rendant bien compte du parti pris que est la méthode même et qui constitue l'*art poètique* de l'auteur, un reproche que je fais à son livre, c'est que le bien est trop absent; pas un personnage ne le représente. . . . Le livre, certes, a une moralité: l'auteur ne l'a pas cherchée, mais il ne tient qu'au lecteur de la tirer, et même terrible" (p. 362).[5] [Even though I do take account of the deliberate position which is the very method and *ars poetica* of the author, still I should wish to make one objection to his book, which is that the good is too absent; not a single character represents it. . . . The book certainly has a moral; the author has not sought it out, but the reader has only to draw it for himself, and it is even

5 Sainte-Beuve emphasizes this point in a letter to Flaubert, May 10, 1857, enclosing his article (*Autour de Flaubert*, I, 55): "Appliquez cette faculté d'observation et de peinture à d'autres sujets également vrais, et avec cette autre faculté de composition qui est en vous, placez-y quelques-unes de ces figures qui reposent, qui consolent, et vous n'aurez pas seulement des admirateurs, mais des amis, de tout lecteur." [Apply this gift for observation and for depiction to other subjects which are equally true, and with your gift for composition, place within them a few of those characters who bring repose and consolation, and your reader will be not only an admirer but a friend.]

His final word is in a letter to Madame du Gravier, August 6, 1857 (*Autour de Flaubert*, I, 55, n.): "Je ne vous conseille pourtant de lire ce livre. Il est trop cru pour la plupart des femmes et il vous froisserait." [But I don't advise you to read this book. It is too crude for most women and it would irritate you.]

terrifying.] This is evidently one of the passages that Baudelaire had in mind when he wrote: "Plusieurs critiques avaient dit: cette oeuvre, vraiment belle par la minutie et la vivacité des descriptions, ne contient pas un seul personnage qui représente la morale, qui parle la conscience de l'auteur. Où est-il, le personnage proverbial et légendaire, chargé d'expliquer la fable et de diriger l'intelligence du lecteur? En d'autres termes, où est le réquisitoire?" (pp. 445–46) [Several critics had said: although this work is really beautiful for the minuteness and the vivacity of its descriptions, still it contains no character to stand for ethics, no one who may speak for the conscience of the author. Where is the proverbial and legendary character who is supposed to explain the story and to direct the intelligence of the reader? In other words, where is the indictment?] Baudelaire protests at this criticism, which undermines the foundations of his own artistic creed: "Absurdité! éternelle et incorrigible confusion des fonctions et des genres!—Une véritable oeuvre d'art n'a pas besoin de réquisitoire. La logique de l'oeuvre suffit à toutes les postulations de la morale, et c'est au lecteur à tirer les conclusions de la conclusion." [An absurdity! the eternal and incorrigible confusion of functions and genres!—A real work of art needs no indictment. The logic of the work suffices for all the postulations of ethics and it is up to the reader to draw the conclusions from the conclusion.] In opposition to Sainte-Beuve's statement that the novel is completely impersonal, with no character that represents the author, Baudelaire returns to the point he has already made, that Madame Bovary is really Flaubert himself: "malgré tout son zèle de comédien, il n'a pas pu ne pas infuser un sang viril dans les veines de sa créature, et . . . Madame Bovary, pour ce qu'il y a en elle de plus énergique et de plus ambitieux, et aussi de plus rêveur, Madame Bovary est restée un homme" (p. 445). [Despite all his actor's zeal, he has not been able to avoid infusing a man's blood into the veins of his creation and . . . Madame Bovary, because of what is most energetic and most ambitious and also most full of dreams in her, has remained a man.] Baudelaire reiterates: "Quant au personnage intime, profond, de la fable, incontestablement c'est la femme adultère; elle seule, la victime déshonorée, possède toutes les grâces du héros.—Je disais tout à l'heure qu'elle était presque mâle, et que l'auteur l'avait ornée (inconsciemment peut-être) de toutes les qualités viriles" (p. 446). [As for the intimate, profound personage of the story, beyond a doubt this is the adulterous woman; she alone, the dishonored victim, possesses all the graces of a hero.—I said a moment ago that she was almost a man and that the author had embellished her (perhaps without realizing it) with all the virile qualities.] Sainte-Beuve also had dwelt at length on Emma's character, but emphasizing her feminine quality: "Comment le définir? elle est femme; elle n'est que romanesque d'abord, elle n'est nullement corrompue" (p. 352). [How can we define it? She is a woman, she is only romantic at the start; she is in no way corrupted.] The essence of her character is that she has "une qualité de trop, ou une vertu de moins: là est le principe de tours ses torts et de son malheur" [one good quality too many, or one virtue too few: this is the basis of all her faults and all her misfortune]:

> La qualité qu'elle a de trop, c'est d'être une nature non pas seulement romanesque, mais qui a des besoins de coeur, d'intelligence et d'ambition, qui aspire vers une existence plus élevée, plus choisie, plus ornée que celle qui lui est échue. La vertu qui lui manque, c'est de n'avoir pas appris que la première condition pour bien vivre est de savoir porter l'ennui, cette privation confuse, l'absence d'une vie plus agréable et plus conforme à nos goûts (pp. 352–53).

> [Her good quality which is one too many is that in addition to being a romantic she has emotional and intellectual needs and ambitions which lead her to aspire to a more elevated and choice existence, a more embellished life than the one which it is her lot to live. The virtue she lacks is that she has not learned that the first prerequisite for a good life is to accept boredom, that strange feeling of deprivation over the absence of a life which we would find more agreeable and according to our tastes.]

Later Sainte-Beuve adds: "elle a un défaut grave, elle n'a pas beaucoup de coeur; l'imagination de bonne heure a tout pris et absorbé [she has a grave defect, she has not much heart; her imagination early absorbed everything], and he has an admirable phrase, "le regret qui s'augmente chez elle par le souvenir et qui s'exalte après coup à l'aide de l'imagination" (p. 358) [her regret which her recollections increase and her imagination raises to a fever pitch]. Sainte-Beuve sees in Emma a thoroughly feminine character, created objectively by a detached observer; "Toutes ces bizarreries, ces inconséquences de la nature féminine sont d'une observation excellente" (p. 359). [All these peculiarities and lack of logic in feminine nature are admirably observed.] Baudelaire notes in Emma certain of the characteristics Sainte-Beuve had emphasized, notably the domination of the heart by the imagination. But for him this is one of the indications that Flaubert, perhaps unconsciously, had endowed his heroine with masculine characteristics:

> *Qu'on examine attentivement:*
> 1° *L'imagination, faculté suprême et tyrannique, substituée au coeur, ou à ce qu'on appelle le coeur, d'où le raisonnement est d'ordinaire exclu, et qui domine généralement dans la femme comme dans l'animal;*
> 2° *Energie soudaine d'action, rapidité de décision, fusion mystique du raisonnement et de la passion, qui caractérise les hommes créés pour agir;*
> 3° *Goût immodéré de la séduction, de la domination et même de tous les moyens vulgaires de séduction, descendant jusqu'au charlatanisme du costume, des parfums et de la pommade—le tout se résumant en deux mots: dandysme, amour exclusif de la domination* (p. 446).

[Let the reader consider carefully:
1° The imagination, a supreme and tyrannical faculty, substituted for the heart, or for what is called the heart, from which reasoning is ordinarily excluded and which is generally dominant in women as in animals:
2° A sudden energy in action, a rapidity in decision, a mystical fusion of reason and passion, which characterizes men born for action;
3° An immoderate enjoyment of seduction and of domination, even of all the vulgar means of seduction, descending even to charlatanism in her costume, her perfumes, her pomade—all of which is summed up in two words: dandyism, and exclusive love of domination.]

And Baudelaire concludes: "Cette femme, en réalité, est très-sublime dans son espèce, dans son petit milieu et en face de son petit horizon" (p. 447).[6] [This woman is in reality sublime in her species, in her petty milieu and in the face of her petty horizon.]

After all this one asks with some curiosity what Flaubert himself thought of the two articles. He has only a somewhat slighting mention of Sainte-Beuve's, early in May 1857: "L'article de Sainte-Beuve a été bien bon pour les bourgeois; il a fait à Rouen (m'a-t-on dit) grand effet" (*Correspondance*, IV, 176). [Sainte-Beuve's article was a good thing for the bourgeois; I am told it had quite an effect in Rouen.] A few days later, speaking of the articles which had appeared up to that time, he says: "je n'en ai pas encore trouvé *un* qui me gratte à l'endroit sensible, c'est-à-dire qui me loue par les côtés que je trouve louables et qui me blâme par ce que je sais défectueux" (*Correspondance*, IV, 177). [I haven't found *a single one* which really hits the spot, which praises me where I think I should be praised and blames me for the defects I know are there.] But when Baudelaire's article appears Flaubert writes to him: "Je vous remercie bien, mon cher ami. Votre article m'a fait le plus *grand* plaisir. Vous êtes entré dans les arcanes de l'oeuvre, comme si ma cervelle était la vôtre. Cela est compris et senti *à fond*" (*Correspondance*, IV, 229). [Thank you very much, my dear friend. Your article gave me the *greatest* pleasure. You penetrated to the heart of the work, as if you had read my mind. You understood and felt *completely* what I wanted.] The letter, with

---

6 It is amusing to note that Baudelaire finds something of himself as well as of Flaubert in Madame Bovary; her unfortunate conversation with the abbé Bournisien awakens memories of his own: "quel est celui de nous qui, dans un âge plus naïf et dans des circonstances troublées, n'a pas fait forcément connaissance avec le prêtre incompétent?" (p. 449) [Who among us, at a more naive age and under difficult circumstances, has not come to know the incompetent priest?] The shadow of Jeanne Duval falls across another sentence: "emportée par les sophismes de son imagination, elle se donne magnifiquement, généreusement, d'une manière toute masculine, à des drôles qui ne sont pas ses égaux, exactement comme les poètes se livrent à des drôlesses" (p. 446). [Carried away by the sophistries of her imagination, she gives herself magnificently, generously, in a wholly manlike way, to wretches who are not her equals, just as poets give themselves to women of the same sort.] And in concluding his analysis he says: "voilà le poète hystérique!" [There is the hysterical poet!] His penetration and understanding of Emma's character is certainly increased by his personal experience, and he too is saying in some measure, "Madame Bovary, c'est moi."

its emphatic underlinings, rings true; Flaubert was not one to write a hypocritical letter of thanks for an article that had not really pleased him.

One might think at first that Sainte-Beuve's insistence on the complete impersonality of the book would have been to Flaubert's liking. For while he is writing *Madame Bovary* he never tires of reiterating: "Nul lyrisme, pas de réflexion, personnalité de l'auteur absente." [7] [No lyric outbursts, no reflections; the personality of the author must be absent.] And after the publication of the novel he maintains: "*Madame Bovary* n'a rien de vrai. C'est une histoire *totalement inventée*; je n'y ai rien mis ni de mes sentiments ni de mon existence" (*Correspondance*, IV, 164). [*Madame Bovary* has no models from real life. The story is *totally invented*; I put nothing of my feelings or my existence into it.] Against these repeated affirmations we can set only the somewhat doubtful legend of Flaubert's having said, when asked where he had got the character of Emma: "Madame Bovary, *c'est moi—d'après moi.*" [8] [*I am* Madame Bovary; she is patterned *after me.*] There is no record of when this was said, and one is tempted to wonder whether perhaps Baudelaire's article had revealed to Flaubert a truth he had not admitted even to himself. Or had the article merely driven him to state publicly what he very well knew already? At all events the letter to Baudelaire implies that Flaubert in no way questioned his assumption. Moreover Sainte-Beuve's easy classification of *Madame Bovary* among realist novels had little appeal for the author who had written: "On me croit épris du réel, tandis que je l'exècre; car c'est en haine du réalisme que j'ai entrepris ce roman" (*Correspondance*, IV, 134). [People think I am mad about the real, whereas actually I hate it; in fact I undertook this novel from hatred of reality.] But Baudelaire's praise of the lyricism and irony veiled in *Madame Bovary*, shown unreservedly in the *Tentation de saint Antoine*, recalls Flaubert's own words: "Toute la valeur de mon livre, s'il en a une, sera d'avoir marché droit sur un cheveu, suspendu entre le double abîme du lyrisme et du vulgaire" (*Correspondance*,

---

7 *Correspondance*, II, 361, to Louise Colet, February 1, 1852. See also II, 365; III, 155–56; and *passim*.
8 René Descharmes, *Flaubert*, Ferroud, 1909, p. 103, n. 3.

II, 372) [All the value of my book, if it has any, will be to have walked a tightrope between the two chasms of lyricism and vulgarity], and: "Si la *Bovary* vaut quelque chose, ce livre ne manquera pas de coeur. L'ironie pourtant me semble dominer la vie" (*Correspondance*, II, 407). [If the *Bovary* is worth something, it will be because the book has warmth. But irony seems to me to be dominant in life.]

Baudelaire's conception of art and morality was close to Flaubert's, and his outburst against the "moral" critics recalls Flaubert's declaration: "La morale de l'art consiste dans sa beauté même, et j'estime par-dessus tout d'abord le style et ensuite le Vrai. Je crois avoir mis dans le peinture des moeurs bourgeoises et dans l'exposition d'un caractère de femme naturellement corrompu, autant de littérature et de *convenances* que possible, une fois le sujet donné, bien entendu" (*Correspondance*, IV, 136). [The ethics of art consists specifically in its beauty, and I value style above everything else and, next in order, the Truth. I think I have displayed in the portrayal of bourgeois customs and a naturally corrupt woman as much literature and propriety as possible, given the subject, of course.]

Finally, Flaubert had little use for Sainte-Beuve's critical method in general; in 1871 he writes to George Sand: "Est-ce que la critique moderne n'a pas abandonné l'Art pour l'Histoire? La valeur intrinsèque d'un livre n'est rien dans l'école Sainte-Beuve, Taine. On y prend tout en considération, sauf le talent" (*Correspondance*, VI, 295). [Hasn't contemporary criticism abandoned Art for History? The intrinsic value of a book counts for nothing in the school of Sainte-Beuve and Taine. They take everything into consideration except talent.] But Baudelaire's criticism is true to the opinion Flaubert expressed in his preface to Bouilhet's *Dernières Chansons*: "On simplifierait peut-être la critique si, avant d'énoncer un jugement, on déclarait ses goûts; car toute oeuvre d'art enferme une chose particulière tenant à la personne de l'artiste et qui fait, indépendamment de l'exécution, que nous sommes séduits ou irrités. Aussi notre admiration n'est-elle complète que pour les ouvrages satisfaisant à la fois notre tempérament et notre esprit." [Criticism would perhaps be simplified if, before giving his judgment, the critic stated his preferences; for any work of art contains something highly individual coming from the personality of the artist and which means that, quite independently of its execution, it appeals to us or irritates us.] This is too often forgotten by critics: "au lieu d'entrer dans l'intention de l'auteur, de lui faire voir en quoi il a manqué son but et comment il fallait s'y prendre pour l'atteindre, on le chicane sur mille choses en dehors de son sujet, en réclamant toujours le contraire de ce qu'il a voulu." [9] [Instead of entering into the aims of the author, or showing him how he failed and how he should have gone at it to succeed in what he wished, the critic quibbles with him over dozens of details which are unrelated to his subject and which are the opposite of what he intended to do.]

Flaubert recognized in himself "deux bonshommes distincts" [two separate people]. Sainte-Beuve sees the one "qui fouille et creuse le vrai tant qu'il peut, qui aime à accuser le petit fait aussi puissamment que le grand, qui voudrait vous faire sentir presque *matériellement* les choses qu'il reproduit" [who digs and probes into the true as deeply as he can, who delights in bringing out the little fact as much as the important one, who would like to make you feel almost *materially* the things which he reproduces], while Baudelaire's admiration is for the one "qui est épris de *gueulades*, de lyrisme, de grands vols d'aigle, de toutes les sonorités de la phrase et des sommets de l'idée" (*Correspondance*, II, 343–44) [who loves to shout, who admires lyricism, the great flights of eagles, all the sonorities a sentence is capable of, and the heights of the world of ideas]. Sainte-Beuve, one might say, judges the novel according to its sub-title, "Moeurs de Province," whereas for Baudelaire it is, in spite of all its deliberate objectivity, the legitimate heir of the long line of novels named for a hero or heroine who is always the author in more or less illusory disguise. And Flaubert himself, who had so harped on the impersonality and objectivity of the novel, recognized that Baudelaire, a critic after his own heart, had penetrated into the secret places of his thought.

[Editor's note: When Miss Gilman wrote this article, Flaubert's warm and appreciative letter of thanks to Sainte-Beuve

9 Louis Bouilhet, *Dernières Chansons*, avec une préface par Gustave Flaubert, 2ème éd., Charpentier, 1874, pp. 3–4.

for his article had not yet come to light. He was in fact deeply gratified by much in Sainte-Beuve's review and asked if he might call on the critic to get his advice, which he said he would treat as a "lesson." The letter was published in an article of mine in the *Revue d'histoire littéraire de la France*, LXIV (1964), 427-35.

It is also demonstrably true that Emma is Flaubert; if in fact he never said it—and one cannot now be sure—he certainly could easily have done so. I have made the point at some length in my general study noted above.]

5 · Gustave Flaubert

INTRODUCTION

The American novelist Henry James knew Flaubert's work well and had in fact met the Frenchman in his Paris apartment. James had a major role in establishing—for English speakers—the concept of the novel as a conscious art form. At one stage in his career he was delighted by the precepts and practice of Flaubert and did much to further their spread. It was not so much a matter of "influence" as—to use the phrase of Howells earlier—that he "felt authorized" to continue in his own vein by what he found here. James played an important part in carrying forward the efforts of critics like Pater to establish an understanding of the chaftsmanship of Flaubert and to clarify its importance for all later novelists. In this regard he stems from Baudelaire's original position.

This attitude on James's part appears in an occasional comment in the selection which follows and is essentially the same as Pater's approach. But there was another James, the fastidious novelist who was repelled by the inelegant subjects of the realists and who belonged instead to the genteel tradition, which he did so much to foster. An attitude such as this—which one does not have to share in order to allow—must lead infallibly to a distaste for Flaubert: Madame Bovary is simply not a nice novel about nice people. And there was a major revolt against Flaubert, against both his subjects and his style, shortly after the turn of the century. This revolt, insofar as it stemmed from Philistines and the good bourgeois whom Flaubert flayed in Homais, is unimportant. But it was not in fact confined to such

readers, and this and the following selection suggest how novelists who are great in their own right have raised serious questions which it is well for even the most sympathetic of Flaubert's
readers to ponder.

Everything in France proceeds by "schools," and there
is no artist so bungling that he will not find another to call
him "dear master." Gustave Flaubert is of the school of Balzac;
the brothers De Goncourt and Emile Zola are of the school of
Flaubert. This last writer is altogether the most characteristic
and powerful representative of what has lately been most
original in the evolution of the French imagination, and he has
for ourselves the farther merit that he must always be strange
and curious. English literature has certainly been doing some
very odd things of late, and striving hard to prove she is able to
be anything that individual writers choose to make her. But
at the best we are all flies in amber, and however furiously we
may buzz and rattle, the amber sticks to our wings. It is not
in the temper of English vision to see things as M. Flaubert
sees them, and it is not in the genius of the English language
to present them as he presents them. With all respect to *Madame Bovary*, *Madame Bovary* is fortunately an inimitable
work.

Madame Bovary was M. Flaubert's first novel, and it has
remained altogether his best. He has produced little and his
works bear the marks of the most careful preparation. His
second work of fiction was *Salammbô*, an archaeological novel
of the highest pretensions. Salammbô is a Carthaginian princess,
the elder sister of Hannibal. After this came, at a long interval,
L'Education sentimentale, a tale of the present day, and lastly
appeared *La Tentation de St. Antoine*—archaeology, but in the
shape of something that was neither novel nor drama; a sort
of free imitation of the mediaeval "mystery." *Madame Bovary*
was a great success—a success of merit, and, as they say in
France, a success of scandal; but the public verdict has not been
flattering to its companions. The mass of the public finds them
dull, and wonders how a writer can expend such an immensity

From *French Poets and Novelists* (1878).

of talent in making himself unreadable. To a discriminating taste, however, M. Flaubert can write nothing that does not repay attention.

The "scandal" in relation to *Madame Bovary* was that the book was judicially impeached and prosecuted for immorality. The defence was eloquent, and the writer was acquitted; the later editions of the book contain, in an appendix, a full report of the trial. It is a work upon which it is possible to be very paradoxical, or rather in relation to which sincere opinion may easily have the air of paradox. It is a book adapted for the reverse of what is called family reading, and yet we remember thinking, the first time we read it, in the heat of our admiration for its power, that it would make the most useful of Sunday-school tracts. In M. Taine's elaborate satire, *The Opinions of M. Graindorge,* there is a report of a conversation at a dinner party between an English spinster of didactic habits and a decidedly audacious Frenchman. He begs to recommend to her a work which he has lately been reading and which cannot fail to win the approval of all persons interested in the propagation of virtue. The lady lends a sympathetic ear, and he gives a rapid sketch of the tale—the history of a wicked woman who goes from one abomination to another, until at last the judgment of Heaven descends upon her, and, blighted and blasted, she perishes miserably. The lady grasps her pencil and note-book and begs for the name of the edifying volume, and the gentleman leans across the dinner table and answers with a smile—"*Madame Bovary; or The Consequences of Misconduct.*" This is a very pretty epigram and it is more than an epigram. It may be very seriously maintained that M. Flaubert's masterpiece is the pearl of "Sunday reading." Practically M. Flaubert is a potent moralist; whether, when he wrote his book, he was so theoretically is a matter best known to himself. Every out-and-out realist who provokes serious meditation may claim that he is a moralist; for that, after all, is the most that the moralists can do for us. They sow the seeds of virtue; they can hardly pretend to raise the crop. Excellence in this matter consists in the tale and the moral hanging well together, and this they are certainly more likely to do when there has been a definite intention—that intention of which artists who cultivate "art for art" are usually so extremely mistrustful; exhibiting thereby, surely, a most injurious disbelief in the illimitable alchemy of art. We may say on the whole, doubtless, that the highly didactic character of *Madame Bovary* is an accident, inasmuch as the works that have followed it, both from its author's and from other hands, have been things to read much less for meditation's than for sensation's sake. M. Flaubert's theory as a novelist, briefly expressed, is to begin on the outside. Human life, we may imagine his saying, is before all things a spectacle, an occupation and entertainment for the eyes. What our eyes show us is all that we are sure of; so with this we will at any rate begin. As this is infinitely curious and entertaining, if we know how to look at it, and as such looking consumes a great deal of time and space, it is very possible that with this also we may end. We admit nevertheless that there is something else, beneath and behind, that belongs to the realm of vagueness and uncertainty, and into this we must occasionally dip. It crops up sometimes irrepressibly, and of course we do not positively count it out. On the whole we will leave it to take care of itself and let it come off as it may. If we propose to represent the pictorial side of life, of course we must do it thoroughly well—we must be complete. There must be no botching, no bungling, no scamping; it must be a very serious matter. We will "render" things—anything, everything, from a chimney-pot to the shoulders of a duchess—as painters render them. We believe there is a certain particular phrase, better than any other, for everything in the world, and the thoroughly accomplished writer ends by finding it. We care only for what is—we know nothing about what ought to be. Human life is interesting, because we are in it and of it; all kinds of curious things are taking place in it (we do not analyse the curious— for artists it is an ultimate fact); we select as many of them as possible. Some of the most curious are the most disagreeable, but the chance for "rendering" in the disagreeable is as great as anywhere else (some people think even greater), and moreover the disagreeable is extremely characteristic. The real is the most satisfactory thing in the world, and if we once fairly advance in this direction nothing shall frighten us back.

Some such words as those may stand as a rough sketch of

the sort of intellectual conviction under which *Madame Bovary* was written. The theory in this case at least was applied with brilliant success; it produced a masterpiece. Realism seems to us with *Madame Bovary* to have said its last word. We doubt whether the same process will ever produce anything better. In M. Flaubert's own hands it has distinctly failed to do so. *L'Education sentimentale* is in comparison mechanical and inanimate. The great good fortune of *Madame Bovary* is that here the theory seems to have been invented after the fact. The author began to describe because he had laid up a great fund of disinterested observations; he had been looking at things for years, for his own edification, in that particular way. The imitative talents in the same line, those whose highest ambition is to "do" their Balzac or their Flaubert, give us the sense of looking at the world only with the most mercenary motives—of going about to stare at things only for the sake of their forthcoming novel. M. Flaubert knew what he was describing—knew it extraordinarily well. One can hardly congratulate him on his knowledge; anything drearier, more sordid, more vulgar and desolate than the greater part of the subject-matter of this romance it would be impossible to conceive. *Moeurs de Province*, the sub-title runs, and the work is the most striking possible example of the singular passion, so common among Frenchmen of talent, for disparaging their provincial life. Emma Bovary is the daughter of a small farmer, who has been able to send her to boarding-school, and to give her something of an "elegant" education. She is pretty and graceful, and she marries a small country doctor—the kindest, simplest, stupidest of husbands. He takes her to live in a squalid little country town, called Yonville-l'Abbaye, near Rouen; she is luxurious and sentimental; she wastes away with ennui, loneliness, and hatred of her narrow lot and absent opportunities, and on the very first chance she takes a lover. With him she is happy for a few months, and then he deserts her, brutally and cynically. She falls violently ill and comes near dying; then she gets well and takes another lover, of a different kind. All the world—the very little world of Yonville-l'Abbaye—sees and knows and gossips; her husband alone neither sees nor suspects. Meanwhile she has been spending money remorselessly and insanely; she has made promissory notes and she is smothered in debt. She has undermined the ground beneath her husband's feet; her second lover leaves her; she is ruined, dishonoured, utterly at bay. She goes back as a beggar to her first lover, and he refuses to give her a sou. She tries to sell herself and fails; then, in impotence and desperation, she collapses. She takes poison and dies horribly, and the bailiffs come down on her husband, who is still heroically ignorant. At last he learns the truth, and it is too much for him; he loses all courage, and dies one day on his garden-bench, leaving twelve francs fifty centimes to his little girl, who is sent to get her living in a cotton-mill. The tale is a tragedy, unillumined and unredeemed, and it might seem, on this rapid and imperfect showing, to be rather a vulgar tragedy. Women who get into trouble with the extreme facility of Emma Bovary, and by the same method, are unfortunately not rare, and the better opinion seems to be that they deserve but a limited degree of sympathy. The history of M. Flaubert's heroine is nevertheless full of substance and meaning. In spite of the elaborate system of portraiture to which she is subjected, in spite of being minutely described, in all her attitudes and all her moods, from the hem of her garment to the texture of her finger-nails, she remains a living creature, and as a living creature she interests us. The only thing that poor Charles Bovary, after her death, can find to say to her lovers is, "It's the fault of fatality." And in fact, as we enter into the situation, it is. M. Flaubert gives his readers the impression of having known few kinds of women, but he has evidently known intimately this particular kind. We see the process of her history; we see how it marches from step to step to its horrible termination, and we see that it could not have been otherwise. It is a case of the passion for luxury, for elegance, for the world's most agreeable and comfortable things, of an intense and complex imagination, corrupt almost in the germ, and finding corruption, and feeding on it, in the most unlikely and unfavouring places—it is a case of all this being pressed back upon itself with a force which makes an explosion inevitable. Madame Bovary has an insatiable hunger for pleasure, and she lives in the midst of dreariness; she is ignorant, vain, naturally depraved; of the things she dreams about not an intimation ever reaches her; so she makes her *trouée*, as the French say, bores her opening, scrapes and scratches her way out into the light, where she can. The reader may protest against a heroine who is "naturally depraved." You are welcome, he may say, to make of a heroine what you please, to carry her where you please; but in mercy do not set us down to a young lady of whom, on the first page, there is nothing better to be said than that. But all this is a question of degree. Madame Bovary is typical, like all powerfully-conceived figures in fiction. There are a great many potential Madame Bovarys, a great many young women, vain, ignorant, leading ugly, vulgar, intolerable lives, and possessed of irritable nerves and of a high natural appreciation of luxury, of admiration, of agreeable sensations, of what they consider the natural rights of pretty women; who are more or less launched upon the rapid slope which she descended to the bottom. The gentleman who recommended her history to the English lady at M. Taine's dinner-party would say that her history was in intention a solemn warning to such young women not to allow themselves to think too much about the things they cannot have. Does M. Flaubert in this case complete his intention? Does he suggest an alternative —a remedy? Plenty of plain sewing, serious reading, general house-work? M. Flaubert keeps well out of the province of remedies; he simply relates his facts, in all their elaborate horror. The accumulation of detail is so immense, the vividness of portraiture of people, of places, of times and hours, is so poignant and convincing, that one is dragged into the very current and tissue of the story; the reader himself seems to have lived in it all, more than in any novel we can recall. At the end the intensity of illusion becomes horrible; overwhelmed with disgust and pity he closes the book.

Besides being the history of the most miserable of women, *Madame Bovary* is also an elaborate picture of small bourgeois rural life. Anything in this direction more remorseless and complete it would be hard to conceive. Into all that makes life ignoble and vulgar and sterile M. Flaubert has entered with an extraordinary penetration. The dullness and flatness of it all suffocate us; the pettiness and ugliness sicken us. Every one in the book is either stupid or mean, but against the shabby-coloured background two figures stand out in salient relief. One is Charles Bovary, the husband of the heroine; the other is M. Homais, the village apothecary. Bovary is introduced to us in his childhood, at school, and we see him afterwards at college and during his first marriage—a union with a widow of meagre charms, twenty years older than himself. He is the only good person of the book, but he is stupidly, helplessly good. At school "he had for correspondent a wholesale hardware-merchant of the Rue Ganterie, who used to fetch him away once a month, on a Sunday, send him to walk in the harbour and look at the boats, and then bring him back to college, by seven o'clock, before supper. Every Thursday evening he wrote a long letter to his mother, with red ink and three wafers; then he went over his copy books, or else read an old volume of *Anacharsis* which was knocking about the class-room. In our walks he used to talk with the servant, who was from the country like himself." In Homais, the apothecary, M. Flaubert has really added to our knowledge of human nature—at least as human nature is modified by French social conditions. To American readers, fortunately, this figure represents nothing familiar; we do not as yet possess any such mellow perfection of charlatanism. The apothecary is that unwholesome compound, a Philistine radical—a *père de famille*, a freethinker, a rapacious shopkeeper, a stern moralist, an ardent democrat and an abject snob. He is a complete creation; he is taken, as the French say, *sur le vif*, and his talk, his accent, his pompous vocabulary, his attitudes, his vanities, his windy vacuity, are superbly rendered. Except her two lovers, M. Homais is Madame Bovary's sole male acquaintance, and her only social relaxation is to spend the evening with his wife and her own husband in his back shop. Her life has known, in the way of recreation, but two other events. Once she has been at a ball at the house of a neighbouring nobleman, for whom her husband had lanced an abscess in the cheek, and who sends the invitation as part payment—a fatal ball, which has opened her eyes to her own deprivations and intolerably quickened her desires; and once she has been to the theatre at Rouen. Both of these episodes are admirably put before us, and they play a substantial part in the tale. The book is full of expressive

Douglas W. Alden

6 · *Proust and the Flaubert Controversy*

INTRODUCTION

In France the attack on Flaubert broke out perhaps later than in England and America; but it had long been smoldering. It was partly a matter of an evolution which the history of every great work has shown. If any art is to continue to develop, it must break those bonds from the past which are proving shackles instead of supports. This has been the fate of all great authors; and it has happened to authors greater than Flaubert. Dante and Shakespeare were both for long periods, and even in their own countries, looked upon as far less than great and sometimes even as inferior authors.

The controversy in France over Flaubert erupted just after World War I. It centered, at least in considerable measure, upon an issue which is largely foreign to English speakers: the critical role in France (and in other countries where the romance languages are spoken) of the notion of correctness in the handling of the language. This is not merely, in France, a matter of following accepted and fundamental rules of basic structure or the dictionary meaning of words. Rather it is a delight in and a fascination with every detail of language. It is as though there could be, among English speakers, passionate quarrels over preferences in a particular situation for saying "I am going in town—or to town—this morning." While those who do not read French cannot weigh the details of the argument, the following article suggests enough of it for any reader to understand this major concern of the French, which has existed since the

65

seventeenth century. Flaubert was found to have sinned in this regard.

The quarrel rapidly expanded beyond these bounds, which the English speaker may leave to the French to resolve. Marcel Proust enlarged it, raising first the whole question of how Flaubert handled the metaphor, the key to so much of modern writing. Since Proust himself renewed the whole domain of the metaphor in French writing, his views on Flaubert's use of this rhetorical device are particularly interesting. Moreover, Flaubert was himself entirely persuaded that no writing can be great unless it is based on a great command of metaphor. Proust's comments and attitude illustrate the interesting phenomenon of criticism that certain great authors have been great critics but that, in their criticism, they are always limited by their own strong feelings about the creative act. Flaubert was, Proust to the contrary, a great creator of images, but only in ways diametrically opposed to the supple and fluid use envisaged by the later novelist. The attack on him which Proust made was in part, then, the complaint that he had not produced Proustian images. Literature proceeds by devouring its own forebears. Nonetheless Proust is important for drawing attention, not merely to his own limits, but to those of Flaubert in this crucial matter. And no reader of Proust's observations can fail to be impressed with the fact that Flaubert's metaphors do have a massive, stationary, and sometimes frozen quality, to which Proust was quite right to object, however great the metaphors may be in other ways.

After this perhaps biased attack, Proust turned to another area of Flaubert, which he was especially suited to perceive: the handling of time. Proust, the novelist who more than any one else showed what a Bergsonian preoccupation with time could add as dimensions to a novel, was sensitive to this in Flaubert and was essentially the first to point to Flaubert's use of verb tenses to manipulate the reader's sense of time as he moves through a paragraph. The observation stimulated a whole line of discussion which keeps reappearing in the later essays of this collection.

Before attempting to reduce Proust's thought to a few formulae, it will be necessary to consider first the circumstances which gave rise to the article on Flaubert. The controversy in which Proust became engaged did not originate with him but had its genesis in an article by Louis de Robert in the *Rose Rouge*[1] headed "Flaubert écrivait mal" [Flaubert wrote badly]; in his treatment of the subject, this novelist turned literary critic contended, apparently with intentions of sensationalism, that Flaubert at times wrote incorrect French. The "bull dog" of *Le Temps*,[2] Paul Souday, rose to Flaubert's defense, insisting that the so-called mistakes were admissible variants or intentional misuse with the purpose of conveying the peculiar flavor of a character's speech. Countering this, Louis de Robert wrote an irreverent letter[3] which began: "Je suis *sur* ma porte. Je réfléchis *à* vous. Je viens de me promener dans mon jardin *à lire* votre article. . . ." Every sentence was a parody of Flaubert's unorthodox expressions. Souday's reply[4] this time was more malicious, and, as was frequently the case with this critic, more factual than that of his adversary, although it was no more than a reiteration of points already made. If Proust's correspondence reveals no particular interest in this stage of the controversy, it is nevertheless certain that he read Souday's articles since he refers to them in a letter[5] to that critic, proffering excuses for his failure to mention them in his own discourse on Flaubert.

The second stage of the controversy began when Albert Thibaudet, who was shortly to undertake a lecture series on Flaubert at the University of Upsala, devoted his column in the *Nouvelle Revue Française*[6] to the problem. Not only did Flaubert write incorrect French, says this critic, but he was not a

Extract from an article originally published in *Romanic Review*, XXVIII (1937), 232–36. Copyright © 1937 by Columbia University Press.

1 August, 1919. To be sure, there were previous discussions of Flaubert's inadvertencies; cf. Faguet's *Flaubert*, 1899, and a note in the "bulletin bibliographique" published in the *Revue des Deux Mondes* a few days after the appearance of *Madame Bovary*.

2 Aug. 29, 1919.

3 *Le Temps*, Sept. 5, 1919.

4 *Ibid.*

5 *Correspondance générale*, III, 74.

6 "Sur le style de Flaubert," Nov., 1919.

"grand écrivain de race" [a great writer by native genius] inasmuch as his mistakes were not the inadvertencies of a genius but rather the residue of an inherently unliterary style made literary by dint of much polishing. Thibaudet expressed it thus: ". . . la pleine maîtrise verbale ne lui était pas donnée dans sa nature même." [. . . full mastery of words was not a part of his nature.]

At this point Marcel Proust entered the discussion. In the letter to Paul Souday already mentioned, he explains the circumstances of this article: ". . . quand le numéro de la *Nouvelle Revue Française* a été prêt, il n'était pas assez long, Jacques Rivière était malade (moins que moi pourtant); pour alléger sa tâche, j'ai bâclé, sans un livre sous la main, un article sur le style de Flaubert." [. . . when the issue of the *Nouvelle Revue Française* was ready, it was not long enough. Jacques Rivière was sick (though less so than I); to make things easier for him, without having a single book at hand I put together an article on Flaubert's style.] This claim of last-minute improvisation, repeated at the outset of the article itself in the guise of an excuse for its imperfections, seems entirely plausible, if we remember that Proust had already given thought to the subject when he composed his pastiche of Flaubert [7] and that, as we shall see, he was applying preconceived general notions to his problem. Exaggeration probably occurs in the boast of having consulted no sources; as a matter of fact, the references are sufficiently definite to lead us to believe that he at least opened one volume of Flaubert, the *Education sentimentale*, to refresh his mind on uncertain passages. Furthermore the article was more than a favor to Rivière; the occasion must have appealed to him as an excellent chance to publicize his work, a legitimate consideration for any artist and especially justified in the case of one whose esthetic tenets prescribe that his own salvation shall depend upon the ultimate survival of his work.

When Thibaudet said Flaubert was not a born artist, he offered Proust the opportunity of saying once more what an artist should be. Proust's entire article is then primarily an excuse to propound his theories even though the subject in hand

7 *Figaro*, March 14, 1908; republished in *Pastiches et mélanges*, 1919.

is not of the best, for, as Proust himself admits, he does not like Flaubert, which is another way of saying that this writer does not completely fit his definition of an artist. This definition, the key to the article, is to be found at the beginning: "J'ai été stupéfait . . . de voir traiter de peu doué pour écrire, un homme qui . . . a renouvelé autant notre vision des choses que Kant. . . ." [8] [I was amazed to find a man who has renewed our vision of things as much as Kant did being treated as having little in the way of a gift for writing.] The revelation is what counts and artistic perfection, while desirable, is not the first criterion. Once Proust has made this declaration, it is not surprising that he should immediately discount the entire discussion of Flaubert's mistakes and turn to the central accusation that Flaubert is not a natural artist. To Proust's way of thinking, it is the metaphor which best interprets the originality of the artist's vision; Flaubert, weak in imagination and therefore devoid of metaphors, must compensate for this deficiency in another way: by his very special use of verb tenses. The bubble seems pricked; from the poetic level of metaphors we descend precipitously to the prosaic level of verb tenses. But no, says Proust, "il y a une beauté grammaticale qui n'a rien à voir avec la correction" [there is a type of grammatical beauty which has nothing to do with correctness]. While defending his own work in this somewhat insidious fashion, Proust is getting at his own fundamental truth, time in a Bergsonian sense. His "beauté grammaticale" has nothing to do

8 An elaboration of Proust's esthetic doctrine seems unnecessary, since it has been very adequately treated by so many commentators, notably by Arnaud Dandieu, *Marcel Proust: sa révélation psychologique*, 1930, and by Eméric Fiser, *L'Esthétique de Marcel Proust*, 1933. However, it is interesting to note the similarity between this quotation and certain texts of *A la recherche du temps perdu*. In the *Côté de Guermantes* (II, 20) we read of "le monde . . . qui n'a pas été créé une fois, mais aussi souvent qu'un artiste original est survenu" [the world . . . which was not created a single time but as often as an original artist has appeared]. Another text from the *Prisonnière* (II, 235): "Cette qualité inconnue d'un monde unique et qu'aucun autre musicien ne nous avait jamais fait voir, peut-être est-ce en cela, disais-je à Albertine, qu'est la preuve la plus authentique du génie, bien plus que dans le contenu de l'oeuvre elle-même." [This unknown quality of a unique world and which no other musician had ever demonstrated to us is perhaps the most authentic proof of genius, I said to Albertine, far more than the content of the work itself.]

with geometrical and arithmetical patterns in the sentence; it refers to the ideas which grammar succeeds in conveying, perhaps in spite of itself.

For Proust, the highest type of criticism is intuitive understanding and, in the particular case of style, such understanding would manifest itself in an ability to reproduce instinctively the style of the author studied. When he protests that, in composing his pastiche of Flaubert, he was not conscious of grammatical peculiarities, the implication seems to be that this vivisection of his is a concession made to his readers much against his will. Although that may be the case, another interpretation seems indicated. Professor Feuillerat [9] sees fit to make of Proust a rationalist. Even admitting, on the contrary, the more tenable thesis that Proust is basically an irrationalist and the outstanding exponent of the so-called "modern" literary school which glorifies the sensation, no one can deny that Proust has a predilection for "ideas" and takes immense pleasure in following them through their various ramifications. But he is not a man of one idea; like Montaigne, Proust cannot be reduced to a formula.[10] In the case of the Flaubert article, therefore, it is certain that Proust enjoys reasoning for the sheer pleasure it produces; another day, in another mood, he might approach the problem in a different way. For a true rationalist, this is heresy; and yet Proust's universality is no more impaired by his attitude than was Montaigne's.

Intentionally or otherwise, Proust is here demonstrating his ability to reason with the best of critics, going so far as to introduce into his remarks many issues quite tributary to the main thesis; what he gives us is a complete study of Flaubert's style. These minor issues might be catalogued as: the improper use of pronouns in very obvious places and the correct use of them elsewhere when the rhythmic continuity of a complicated sentence must be kept intact; the almost complete absence of the conjunction "et" in its usual function and a special use when

9 *Comment Marcel Proust a composé son roman*, 1934.
10 Charles Blondel, *La Psychographie de Marcel Proust*, 1932, has attempted to relate Proust's solipsism to his "universal" generalizations, a simplification which Proust never makes.

it marks a "pause dans une mesure rythmique et divise un tableau" [a pause in a rhythmic measure and divides a tableau]; a similar use of "tandis que"; a willfully heavy and sonorous style, heavy to the point of awkwardness and massively sonorous to react against a more ethereal literature, a style which best interprets Flaubert's own inner reality and which, by reason of this honesty, produces the result that, as Proust says, ". . . nous les aimons ces lourds matériaux que la phrase de Flaubert soulève et laisse retomber avec le bruit intermittent d'un excavateur." [. . . we like these heavy materials which Flaubert's sentence lifts and drops again with the intermittent noise of a pile-driver.] For the *flaubertisant* these are all remarks of prime importance; for our purposes they demonstrate Proust's ability to develop common logical arguments in a way that is convincing to the most confirmed rationalist.

But Proust's most lasting revelations respecting Flaubert, and most significant to us, as already noted, are in regard to the latter's use of tenses, especially the imperfect. Proust defines: "Un état qui se prolonge est indiqúe par l'imparfait." [A state which is prolonged is indicated by an imperfect.] Furthermore: ". . . souvent le passage de l'imparfait au parfait est indiqué par un participe présent, qui indique la manière dont l'action se produit, ou bien le moment où elle se produit." [. . . often the passage from the imperfect to the perfect is indicated by a present participle, which indicates the way in which an action is produced or else the moment when it is produced.] The next remark has a wider implication: ". . . cet imparfait, si nouveau dans la littérature, change entièrement l'aspect des choses et des êtres, comme font une lampe qu'on a déplacée, l'arrivée dans une maison nouvelle, l'ancienne si elle est presque vide et qu'on est en plein déménagement." [. . . this imperfect, which is so new in literature, completely changes the look of things and of people, as a lamp does when you move it, or arriving in a new house, or the former one if it is almost empty and you are in the midst of moving.] If the end of the quotation reminds us of the narrator's anguish in the strange hotel room at Balbec or of Proust's own wanderings from the boulevard Haussmann to the rue Hamelin at this very time, its beginning reminds us all the more of numerous passages [11] in Proust's work where he discourses on the purpose of art. The imperfect, says Proust, is used by Flaubert to express the continuity of time which is for Proust, although he is careful to leave it in the form of an implication, the super-verity; even if he never expressly says it, he sees in Flaubert a precursor, since that author has preëminently the sense of *la durée*. "A mon avis la chose la plus belle de l'*Education sentimentale*, ce n'est pas une phrase, mais un blanc" [In my opinion the most beautiful thing in the *Sentimental Education* is not a sentence but a blank space], he says, referring to a passage in which the action stops in mid air, the scene and cadence change but the character Frédéric remains, aged and altered from traversing the blank which represents elapsed time: time as continuity but time as change. Occasionally the present springs forth to check the flow of imperfects and to distinguish "des choses qui passent une réalité durable" [things which exist for a durable reality]. In the last quotation we discover an echo of the familiar "essence of things" which, as is fitting, conjures up memories of "madeleines," irregular paving blocks and the like. On the heels of this we expect a reference to the subconscious, and indeed there is one; this "vision nouvelle" [new way of looking at things], arising from Flaubert's subconscious, finds its expression in the abundant use of the imperfect. Proust has indeed secreted all of his cherished notions in this one article.

11 See note 8.

7 · Art, Energy, and Aesthetic Distance

INTRODUCTION

Proust's discussion of Flaubert depended upon close textual analysis. Other critics continued this approach, which had not been used by either Sainte-Beuve or Baudelaire, and studied the paragraphs and sentences and even the specific words of the novel, seeking thereby to ground their critical judgments more solidly. The method risks being wrong, in specific cases, because the passage in question may be unrepresentative; but it has the advantage of putting all the data before the reader so that he can make his own judgment. Many excellent French scholars have followed this lead; but it seems unfortunate to compound the problems of reading a work in translation by then reading critical articles also in translation. I have therefore ventured to include an article of my own of this type in this collection.

In evaluating Flaubert—or any author—it is often convenient to find some point outside him upon which one may stand to view him. I have compared him to Balzac in an effort to find out what Flaubert gains and what he loses by the polished excellence of his prose, which Balzac lacks. Balzac is a valid vantage point, for Flaubert felt great admiration for his predecessor; but he was sure that he could surpass him precisely because of his own artistry. Hence the interest of the comparison.

This approach led other critics to make certain fruitful suggestions for further directions of investigation. One of the results was the second part of the essay, in which, returning to the same passage, I have examined it from another point of view and *then gone on to consider further passages and to raise the broader issue of the role of tragedy in Madame Bovary and in the novel in general. I have made great use of Proust's insight into Flaubert's imperfects, a topic carefully examined by a number of critics once Proust had drawn attention to it.*

I

Flaubert discovered upon publishing *Madame Bovary* how much his work invites comparison with the novels of Balzac. The setting, the subject, even the characters seem to belong to the *Comédie humaine*; his contemporaries were immediate in their reaction and lost no time in informing Flaubert of it. Writing a note intended to please and flatter the hermit of Croisset, Léon Gozlin told him that he had never thought of Balzac so much as he had in reading *Madame Bovary*. The reviewers, too, noticed the resemblance and succeeded finally in infuriating him,[1] for he had striven to write a book of sharply contrasting tone. It is that contrast which I wish to evaluate here by an examination of parallel passages from the two men which treat the same subject: romantic dreams in which a young woman, in flights of fancy, identifies herself with other ages, other people. The contrast between the two treatments is as illuminating of Balzac's strength as it is of Flaubert's preoccupation with form. Which has proved the more satisfactory approach?

Balzac's passage is near the beginning of the *Illusions perdues*.[2] He is depicting the early life of Mme de Bargeton, a provincial like Emma Bovary, our other subject. Fortunately

---

This essay combines, with a little rewriting, two essays separately published: "Balzac and Flaubert: Energy Versus Art," reprinted from *Romanic Review*, XLII (1951), 198–204 (copyright © 1951 by Columbia University Press); and "Aesthetic Distance in *Madame Bovary*," reprinted by permission of the Modern Language Association of America from *PMLA*, LXIX (1954), 1112–26.

1 Letter to Jules Duplan, No. 537 in the *Correspondance*, dated by the editors "derniers jours de mai 1857."

2 First published by Werdet (1837) and then by Furne (1843) with minor changes, one of which I shall discuss below. The modern Conard edition (*Oeuvres complètes*, Paris, 1913, XI, 214–15) follows the Furne edition, except that it italicizes the proper names as I have done.

the difference of a few decades in the setting of the stories is not crucial to our examination, for Mme de Bargeton is a typical character from the *Comédie humaine*[3] and the vigorous, emotive description is thoroughly representative of Balzac. With him we are caught up in her swirling, palpitating emotions when she was a young woman in her late teens and early twenties, full of vibrant imagination and enthusiasm:

> *Le dithyrambe était dans son coeur et sur ses lèvres. Elle palpitait, elle se pâmait, elle s'enthousiasmait pour tout événement: pour le dévouement d'une soeur grise et l'exécution des frères Faucher, pour l'Ipsiboé de monsieur d'Arlincourt comme pour l'Anaconda de Lewis, pour l'évasion de Lavalette comme pour une de ses amies qui avait mis des voleurs en fuite en faisant la grosse voix.*

> [She had a dithyramb in her heart and on her lips. Her heart beat faster, she felt faint, she was moved to enthusiasm by all sorts of things: by the devotion of a grey sister and the execution of the Faucher brothers, for Monsieur d'Arlincourt's *Ipsiboé* as for Lewis's *Anaconda*, for Lavalette's escape as for one of her women friends who had frightened off thieves by shouting at them.]

In these first two sentences the high pitch of her emotion is already clear, nor is it harmed by the cascade of unfamiliar names. The various nouns contribute to the effect: "dévouement . . . exécution . . . évasion . . . voleurs." But the key lies elsewhere, in the verbs, which serve more than any other element to illumine the contrast with Flaubert. Balzac goes directly to the emotions of his heroine: "Elle palpitait, elle se pâmait, elle s'enthousiasmait. . . ." [Her heart beat faster, she felt faint, she was moved to enthusiasm.] We feel her responses; we can watch their physical manifestations. And we join with her, sharing her tensions.

3 Mme de la Baudraye (*Muse du département*), for instance, shares many of Mme de Bargeton's traits. Modeste Mignon's readings and general state of mind offer a third use of this type of character. The latter two (1843 and 1844) are symptomatic of Balzac's practice of grounding a new character in elements of earlier ones. Indeed, in *Modeste Mignon* this provides one of the few sound aspects of an otherwise weak potboiler. These "reappearing character traits" are brilliantly and sympathetically discussed in Jean Hytier, "Un Chef-d'oeuvre improvisé: *La Cousine Bette*," *Romanic Review*, XL (1949), 81–92.

He continues in a vein reminiscent of Rabelais in its violent outpourings of language. The words tumble forth in a torrent which rushes us onward with its headlong advance. As we give in to it, we continue not so much to observe as to experience Mme de Bargeton's exaltation:

> *Pour elle, tout était sublime, extraordinaire, étrange, divin, merveilleux. Elle s'animait, se courrouçait, s'abattait sur elle-même, s'élançait, retombait, regardait le ciel ou la terre; ses yeux se remplissaient de larmes.*

> [To her everything was sublime, extraordinary, strange, divine, marvelous. She grew excited, angry, despondent, she soared and fell back again, looked up at heaven or down at the earth; her eyes filled with tears.]

We have experienced a complete drama with her, but it is a play without a plot. We are still dealing with her sublimations: but this time only the emotions are given us. In their varied and successive forms they have become so exclusively our concern that we do not even know what it is that has evoked them . . . nor do we care.

Balzac shares with Rabelais more than a vigorous joy in the play of words. Both can always find a new way to turn an idea in order to display new facets. Now he puts in the objects which arouse her emotions or, better, he gives them foci upon which they may converge to gain greater intensity:

> *Elle usait sa vie en de perpétuelles admirations et se consumait en d'étranges dédains. Elle concevait le pacha de Janina, elle aurait voulu lutter avec lui dans son sérail, et trouvait quelque chose de grand à être cousue dans un sac et jetée à l'eau. Elle enviait lady Esther Stanhope, ce bas-bleu du désert. Il lui prenait envie de se faire soeur de Sainte-Camille et d'aller mourir de la fièvre jaune à Barcelone en soignant les malades: c'était là une grande, une noble destinée! Enfin, elle avait soif de tout ce qui n'était pas l'eau claire de sa vie, cachée entre les herbes.*

> [She wore herself out in endless admirations and consumed herself in strange contempts. She could imagine the pasha of Janina, she would have liked to wrestle with him in his harem; and she found something grandiose in the idea of being sewn up in a sack and thrown into the water. She envied Lady Esther Stanhope, the desert bluestocking. She wanted to be a

Sister of Saint Camille and go die of yellow fever in Barcelona taking care of the sick: that was a great and noble fate! All in all, she thirsted for everything that was not the limpid pool of her existence hidden amongst the reeds.]

Balzac has allowed us no pause for calm analysis: the unimpeded flow of the fantasy life, turbulent, irrational, convincing, has forced us to take part in Mme de Bargeton's life.

But there is an observation which surely Flaubert would have made.[4] The pronoun "elle" turns up four times in three sentences. And "Elle enviait" is much too close to "Il lui prenait envie": the first has not stopped echoing before the second intrudes. A classicist—Flaubert was one where form is concerned —a classicist is going to object that this repetition is unharmonious. If one gives first allegiance to form, as Flaubert did, then these sentences must be recast at whatever cost to their impact. But the force of Balzac's phrasing comes from the constant return to "elle." The reader is brought back, over and over again, to Mme de Bargeton. As for *envie—enviait,* despite Flaubert's objections would not Balzac maintain them precisely for their powerful reiteration? Péguy would have understood and approved.

Balzac rapidly completes the description with the same continuing vitality and with a nicely balanced alternation between generalized emotions and particularized reactions. Again the verbs are dominant and in each case the description is from within the character so that our contact is direct and immediate:

> *Elle adorait lord Byron, Jean-Jacques Rousseau, toutes les existences poétiques et dramatiques. Elle avait des larmes pour tous les malheurs et des fanfares pour toutes les victoires. Elle sympathisait avec Napoléon vaincu, elle sympathisait avec Méhémet-Ali massacrant les tyrans de l'Egypte.[5] Enfin elle revêtait les gens de génie d'une auréole, et croyait qu'ils vivaient de parfums et de lumière.*

4 ". . . comme il s'inquiète peu de l'Art!" [. . . how little he worries about Art!] Flaubert writes contemptuously to his niece Caroline (Letter of Dec. 3, 1876. Comment repeated in the letters from about the same date numbered 1631 and 1691.)

5 The reference to Mohammed-Ali is an addition of the edition of 1843, a cogent example of Balzac's feeling for the contemporary event. Around 1840, with growing tensions in the eastern Mediterranean, French

[She adored Lord Byron, Jean-Jacques Rousseau, and all poetic
and dramatic lives. She had tears for every misfortune and ap-
plause for every victory. She sympathized with Napoleon when
he was conquered, she sympathized with Mehemet-Ali when
he was massacring the tyrants of Egypt. Finally, she clothed
men of genius with a halo and thought they lived on perfume
and light.]

So much for Balzac, whose dynamic approach has led to
a tense and dramatic passage. What happens if a writer decides
to place other concerns uppermost? What is the result if he
allows form to become so dominant that it is no longer the
mere vehicle in which a thought is contained but becomes instead the ultimate purpose of writing? It will be my contention
that he risks losing the very dynamism which we have admired
in Balzac.

Flaubert's parallel passage, early in *Madame Bovary*, describes Emma's readings in the convent and their tremendous
grip upon her imagination.[6] The similarities are obvious; it is
the divergences which matter here. First, however, an understanding of Flaubert's theories is essential to a comparison of
our two passages. He knew clearly what he wanted and it was
emphatically not to be a reworking of Balzac, however much his
subject may have recalled those of his predecessor. Immediately
after beginning the *Bovary* he wrote:

*J'entrevois maintenant des difficultés de style qui m'épou-
vantent. Ce n'est pas une petite affaire que d'être simple. J'ai
peur de tomber dans le Paul de Kock ou de faire du Balzac
chateaubrianisé.[7]*

---

interest in the area revived. Balzac took advantage of his readers' new
preoccupations by adding this comment. Conveniently Mohammed-Ali
had carried out a massacre of the Mamelukes in 1811, during the period
when Mme de Bargeton was enjoying her flights of fancy.

We may note that the *Enfin*, added at the start of the next sentence,
repeats one only a few lines above, a further slip Flaubert would not have
tolerated.

6 P. 51. There can be no question here of imitation, conscious or unconscious. Flaubert's scruples on this subject were most delicate. Cf. his
letter to Louise Colet, Dec. 27, 1852. Here he notes similarities to *Louis
Lambert* and to the *Médecin de campagne* in his own book, ". . . à croire
que j'ai copié, si ma page n'était infiniment mieux écrite, sans me vanter"
[. . . to the point where you would think that I had copied, if it weren't
that my page is infinitely better written, if I may say so without bragging].
Note how conscious he is of what marks him off from Balzac!

7 Letter to Louise Colet, undated, No. 287 in the *Correspondance*.

[I can glimpse now difficulties of style which terrify me. It is no easy matter to be simple. I am afraid of falling into the style of Paul de Kock or of turning out Chateaubrianized Balzac.]

He means, obviously, that he does not wish to take the material of Balzac and clothe it with the forms of Chateaubriand, whose style aroused his exuberant enthusiasm, particularly for its "poésie." [8] Nor does he care for what makes the strength of Balzac, whose lack of style, he proclaims elsewhere, means that "son oeuvre restera plutôt curieuse que belle, et plutôt forte qu'éclatante" [9] [his work will remain curious rather than beautiful, and strong rather than striking]. What are the difficulties which terrify him in the style he is seeking for his own work? He clarifies them in a further letter: [10]

Ce qui me semble beau, ce que je voudrais faire, c'est un livre sur rien, un livre sans attache extérieure, qui se tiendrait de lui-même par la force interne de son style . . . un livre qui n'aurait presque pas de sujet ou du moins où le sujet serait presque invisible. . . .

[What seems to me beautiful and what I would like to do would be a book about nothing, a book without external ties, which would stand on its own by the internal strength of the style . . . a book which would almost have no subject or at least in which the subject would be almost invisible. . . .]

"A book in which the subject would be almost invisible": if the thought seems paradoxical, one must remember that Flaubert never hesitates to exaggerate his concepts. How literally should he be taken? Already in 1846 he had come to feel that beauty of thought and beauty of form were inseparable; [11] but as he struggled with *Madame Bovary*, he found that he was no longer content with this position. The Goncourt *Journal* for 1857 [12] shows that he has established a definite hierarchy and

8 Letter to Louise Colet, Oct. 14, 1846.

9 Letter to Louise Colet, June 28–29, 1853. Flaubert felt real admiration for Balzac (Letter to Louis Bouilhet, Nov. 14, 1850) and does note once (Letter to Louis Bouilhet, Aug. 5, 1854) that *Eugénie Grandet* is "réellement beau." But adverse comments on Balzac's lack of style are far more common in Flaubert's Correspondence.

10 Letter to Louise Colet, Jan. 16, 1852. Our passage was written in March, only a few weeks subsequent to this declaration.

11 Letter to Louise Colet, Sept. 18, 1846.

12 9 vols. (Paris: Charpentier, 1888). Cf. I, 164 and 178.

that form is now supreme. The good brothers would have Flaubert say that, "de la forme naît l'idée" [from the form is born the idea], and they revolt against his theories: ". . . enfin, tant d'importance donnée au vêtement de l'idée, à sa couleur, à sa trame, que l'idée n'est plus que comme un patère à accrocher des sonorités" [. . . finally, so much importance accorded to the clothing of the idea, to its color, its fabric, that the idea is no longer any more than a peg on which to hang sonorities]. Even with allowance for the somewhat odd attitude of the Goncourts toward literary doctrines not wholly their own, the tendency still remains and Flaubert has invited this objection by his approach. He could easily slip into the pitfall of saying well rather than saying something, of allowing the subject to become almost invisible. I do not wish to exaggerate this: *Madame Bovary* stands as the peer of *Père Goriot* and is magnificent for its substance quite as much as for its form. Yet the danger will remain, and its incidence upon our passage will be clear.

Part of the harmony in the description of Emma's readings depends, of course, upon the totality of the passage. But in such an examination as this something must be sacrificed, and I shall comment upon it a section at a time in order to introduce material from the published drafts and preliminary manuscripts: [13] the transition from them to the final form reveals Flaubert's principles most clearly at work.

Originally he opened with a sentence which immediately recalls Balzac: "Elle lut de l'histoire palpitant d'un plaisir tout nouveau, au récit d'aventures dont elle était sûre de la réalité." [She read history, her heart beating with a wholly new pleasure at the account of adventures of whose reality she was sure.] In the "palpitant" we have a typical Balzac word; in fact he had used it himself in opening his description. It is good because it gives us her feeling directly and far more powerfully than the later clause, "dont elle était sûre de la réalité." But to Flaubert other considerations must be more important. The alliteration of "palpitant d'un plaisir" is not a meaningful one; and,

---

13 The drafts are given in Mlle Gabrielle Leleu, *Ebauches et fragments inédits recueillis d'après les manuscrits de Mme Bovary* (Paris: Conard, 1936). Cf. I, 157–58.

immediately, he crosses out the participle. Form has intervened at the expense of vividness.

Ultimately the whole sentence was struck out and the idea was remolded into a clause in the sentence which now opens the description:

> *Avec Walter Scott, plus tard, elle s'éprit de choses historiques, rêva bahuts, salle des gardes et ménestrels. Elle aurait voulu vivre dans quelque vieux manoir, comme ces châtelaines, au long corsage, qui, sous le trèfle des ogives, passaient leurs jours le coude sur la pierre et le menton dans la main, à regarder venir du fond de la campagne un cavalier à plume blanche qui galope sur un cheval noir.*

> [With Walter Scott, later, she became fascinated with history, dreamed of ancient cabinets, guardrooms, and minstrels. She would have liked to live in some old manor, like those long-waisted chatelaines, who spent their days beneath trefoiled arches, an elbow on the stone ledge and chin in hand, watching a white-plumed knight galloping toward them from the distant horizon on a black horse.]

This is certainly Flaubert at his best. The visual image is clear; illustrations from books on medieval subjects come to mind at once. One suspects that Flaubert may even have had a picture before him. But was this the most important thing to bring before us? What has happened to the dynamism of Balzac, the immediate contact with the raw emotions of the heroine? In part Flaubert is hampered by a psychological hazard implicit in his choice of subject: his distaste for Emma made it notably more difficult for him to live his character. His repugnance is clear in a letter to Louise Colet referring to our passage and bearing its imprint:

> *Voilà deux jours que je tâche d'entrer dans des rêves de jeunes filles et que je navigue pour cela dans les océans laiteux de la littérature à castels, troubadours à toques de velours à plumes blanches.*[14]

> [For two days now I have been trying to enter into the *dreams of young ladies* and for that I've been navigating in the milky

14 Dated March 3, 1852. He continues: "Fais-moi penser à te parler de cela. Tu peux me donner là-dessus des détails précis qui me manquent." [Remind me to speak about that to you. You can give me precise details about it which I lack.] One wonders what details Louise Colet provided!

ocean of castle literature, with troubadours wearing velvet toques with white plumes.]

To be sure, "Elle aurait voulu vivre . . ." in our text again suggests one of Balzac's phrases. But thereafter the reader finds his attention shifted to the chatelaines, who are allowed to crowd Emma off stage. This was not so in the first draft, where it was a chateau rather than a manor; it had its drawbridge, lake and woods. And then Flaubert had written: ". . . elle enviait la vie des châtelaines . . ." [she envied the life of the chatelaines], bringing us back to Emma by another verb which we have approved in Balzac. Why did he abandon it? Partly, perhaps, because he had an "elle" only a few words earlier, but far more because of the uneuphonious "enviait la vie." If these were the considerations then here, too, formal elements have been allowed to predominate at the expense of presenting a living experience to the reader.

Flaubert continues, using a turn of phrase which marks him as belonging to the second half of the century. Balzac had written of Mme de Bargeton: "Elle adorait lord Byron, Jean-Jacques Rousseau, toutes les existences poétiques et drama-tiques." [She adored Lord Byron, Jean-Jacques Rousseau, and all poetic and dramatic lives.] Madame Bovary was to feel the same emotions, but Flaubert will phrase them quite differently, preferring the use of *avoir* and a noun to the more vital verb "adorait." "Elle eut dans ce temps-là le culte de Marie Stuart, et des vénérations enthousiastes à l'endroit des femmes illustres ou infortunées." [During this period she worshipped Mary Stuart and revered other illustrious or unfortunate women.] Here he is following the general trend of the language . . . or guiding it along what will be its path. But the analytic quality of the result lacks the impact of the earlier form. We, as readers, lose by it.

Nowhere thus far has Flaubert used the device so effec-tively employed by Balzac, the direct notation of his heroine's emotion without pausing to give it an object. Nor does he try it in the remainder of our passage. He turns instead to a list of characters, just as did Balzac. But unfortunately he neglects the core of the matter, Emma. The focus, as with the chatelaines, will be upon the figures, not upon the girl reacting to them:

> *Jeanne d'Arc Héloïse, Agnès Sorel, la belle Ferronnière et Clémence Isaure, pour elle se détachaient comme des comètes sur l'immensité ténébreuse de l'histoire, où saillissaient encore çà et là, mais plus perdus dans l'ombre et sans aucun rapport entre eux, Saint-Louis avec son chêne, Bayard mourant, quelques férocités de Louis XI, un peu de Saint-Barthélemy, le panache du Béarnais, et toujours le souvenir des assiettes peintes où Louis XIV était vanté.*

> [Joan of Arc, Heloise, Agnes Sorel, the Belle Ferronnière, and Clemence Isaure stood out like comets for her against the dark immensity of history; and here and there, but more lost in the shadows and wholly unrelated to each other, were Saint Louis with his oak tree, Bayard at the moment of his death, a few ferocious acts of Louis XI, details from the Saint Bartholomew Massacres, the white plume of Henry IV, and always the set of plates with scenes from the life of Louis XIV.]

The passage is a sonorous example of the prose Flaubert wished to write, its very melodies telling the story, the rhythms moving along majestically. And the drafts show us with what labors Flaubert attained his result. Taking only those that have been published, we find Flaubert trying four different forms for one phrase before he was satisfied. Numerous little details had to be wrestled with: "Saint-Louis avec son chêne" was originally the sibilant monstrosity, "Saint-Louis sous son chêne," for instance. And six or eight similar problems had to be cared for.

Was this necessarily the right aspect of the problem to occupy him so greatly? Balzac, unquestionably, would have written "le panache blanc du Béarnais." This is the way everyone thinks of it; and it is the way Flaubert first wrote it. But "blanc" had to go: the galloping knight earlier in the passage had worn a "plume blanche" and Flaubert needed to keep that to contrast with his "cheval noir." These questions of form are important, of course, and not to be ignored. But when the last adjective has been smoothed into place, the last clause balanced against the others about it, has the author perhaps polished the basic vitality out of his subject? Has the subject

disappeared into the form . . . never fully to reappear again?
The drafts show Flaubert writing a style halfway between
Balzac's and that of his own finished novel. But his effort, as
we have seen, is to work ever farther from the problem of the
reader perusing the novel and ever more toward the difficulties
of presenting a work perfect in itself.[15]

Perhaps it is a matter of temperament. Flaubert has interesting comments on hallucinations; he experienced them himself as did Balzac. Yet I have never been able to feel that they
were of the character of Balzac's. Both men suffered from extreme tensions which drove them away from reality into hallucinations.[16] But when Balzac plunged into the world of the
Comédie humaine, it was with a feeling of hyperreality, of a
greater joy to be gained. When Flaubert turned to art, it was
for consolation, for assuagement, for relief from a world he
loathed and despised. This may be some explanation for the
odd phenomenon that his rewriting, his effort to improve upon
his first draft, has moved the passage ever further from Emma
and from us, however much it may have rendered its harmonies
more perfect, its melodies more suave. With Balzac, on the
contrary, there was no drawing back from life. The France
of his period had its vices, its shortcomings; Balzac was well
aware of them, anxious to do his part to correct them. But it
was still a dynamic, vigorous place and period in which to live.
When he depicted it for his readers, that dynamism and vigor
infused the sentences and have penetrated his readers ever since.

15 Flaubert glimpsed the difficulty himself; but he dismissed it: "Quel
homme eût été Balzac, s'il eût su écrire. Mais il ne lui a manqué que cela.
Un artiste, après tout, n'aurait pas tant fait, *n'aurait pas eu cette ampleur.*"
[What a man Balzac would have been had he known how to write! But
that is all he lacked. An artist, after all, would not have done so much,
would not have had that breadth.] (Letter to Louise Colet, Dec. 17, 1852.
Italics mine.)

16 Professor Edward B. Ham of the University of Michigan raises here
the interesting query: "Could this have been a factor in the Swedenborgian
fad in several stories, the mesmerism (*Ursule Mirouet*) and even the almost
longing to take Mme Fontaine seriously (*Cousin Pons*)? Mme Fontaine
is, of course, trimmed to size in the *Comédiens sans le savoir.*" It is a
pleasure to acknowledge here my debt to Mr. Ham, not only for this but
also for other suggestions about this paper.

II

As novelists in nineteenth-century France grew more familiar with their medium through practice in handling it, it became ever more possible for them to conceive of incorporating into it many of the qualities hitherto sought only in poetry or in the theater: the grandeur of the epic, the penetration of comedy, the sublimity of tragedy. The novel, relatively new in comparison with other forms, required the development of new techniques and new understandings which force the critic regretfully to abandon many criteria made comfortable through long use; but some of the basic problems remain and carry over with them some at least of the older canons. An enquiry into the meaning of *Madame Bovary* may properly raise the familiar question of tragedy or pathos and, although the question is posed in terms foreign to the older forms, the criteria for them may be restated to meet the new issues. One such canon is the matter of "aesthetic distance," which has recently been defined as "an implicit set of directions concerning the distance from the object at which the reader must stand if he is to see it for what it is." [17] Studied in this light, *Madame Bovary* shows constantly shifting distances which lead to a richness and variety prohibited in the shorter compass of most of the older forms but which also proportionately increase the difficulties for the novelist, who must bring unity and meaning into this complex.

Flaubert strove for an impartiality which would allow the facts, presented in a style in harmony with them, to determine the reader's reaction and his final judgment. One critical element in that reaction and judgment is the aesthetic distance for the reader, which is in turn a reflection of Flaubert's own attitude toward the material. His attitude governed his selection and guided his presentation, whether by conscious act of literary creation or in response to unconscious factors the

17 David Daiches, *A Study of Literature for Readers and Critics* (Ithaca: Cornell Univ. Press, 1948), p. 63. I shall also be drawing on the analysis offered in E. Bullough, " 'Psychical Distance' as a Factor in Art and Aesthetic Principle," *British Jour. of Psych.*, V (1912), 87–118. Bullough relates his suggestions for a new criterion to the older Aristotelian catharsis, precisely the sort of radical restatement I have in mind.

more potentially dangerous because he was unaware of them and hence not alert to distinguish the relevant and valid from the irrelevant or actually detrimental. The various aspects of the problem are typified in a recurrent theme of the novel (already examined from another point of view in Part I), the effect upon Emma of her readings in the convent in her youth and the parade of romantic visions which she created from them. The various treatments applied successively to this theme are indices of Flaubert's shifting approach, which in turn determines the constantly changing impact upon the reader as the aesthetic distance from which he sees Emma increases or diminishes. An examination of these shifts suggests an explanation for the reader's alternations between irony and pity and ultimately affords a basis for posing the question of pathos or tragedy in the book.

It is crucial to Flaubert's intent in *Madame Bovary* that the reader remain aloof from Emma's dreams in the convent. If one were fully to ally himself with her, then the irony which informs the novel would be diminished: it is difficult to be ironic toward what one wholeheartedly accepts! Flaubert brings to bear all his harmonious artistry to keep the reader distant from Emma as she turns to the shoddy excitement she found in her reading in the convent:

> *Avec Walter Scott, plus tard, elle s'éprit de choses historiques, rêva bahuts, salle des gardes et ménestrels. Elle aurait voulu vivre dans quelque vieux manoir, comme ces châtelaines, au long corsage, qui, sous le trèfle des ogives, passaient leurs jours, le coude sur la pierre et le menton dans la main, à regarder venir du fond de la campagne un cavalier à plume blanche qui galope sur un cheval noir. Elle eut dans ce temps-là le culte de Marie Stuart, et des vénérations enthousiastes à l'endroit des femmes illustres ou infortunées. Jeanne d'Arc, Héloïse, Agnès Sorel, la belle Ferronnière et Clémence Isaure, pour elle se détachaient comme des comètes sur l'immensité ténébreuse de l'histoire, où saillissaient encore çà et là, mais plus perdus dans l'ombre et sans aucun rapport entre eux, Saint-Louis avec son chêne, Bayard mourant, quelques férocités de Louis XI, un peu de Saint-Barthélémy, le panache du Béarnais, et toujours le souvenir des assiettes peintes où Louis XIV était vanté.[18]*

(See the translation, pp. 81 and 83.)

18 P. 51.

His intent is perfectly clear, at least in this passage. The reader's attention is on Emma's visions, not on her. The ironic clash between them and a more sober reality stands forth unclouded by any effort to understand what in Emma might explain (and thus perhaps excuse) the dreams. Flaubert provokes a cool evaluation by not distracting our attention from the visions to her, even in the details of the phrasing, which bear out the general impression as do the careful textual revisions.[19] Thus the original form, "elle enviait la vie des châtelaines" [she envied the lives of the chatelaines], disappeared when Flaubert reworked the passage; it would have served to return us to Emma by giving her emotions directly, instead of confining us to her imaginings alone; the bitter irony implicit in the passage would have been diminished.

Many years later Flaubert again described the impact of a first reading of Scott, in *Bouvard et Pécuchet*. The ambivalence of his attitude toward his two *copistes* enormously complicates the general question of aesthetic distance in the book, but the particular passage exemplifies a much more sympathetic portrayal. The use of present tenses, and certain phrases which I have italicized for emphasis, invite the reader to share the experience and diminish the irony:

> *Ils lurent d'abord Walter Scott.*
> *Ce fut comme la surprise d'un monde nouveau.*
> *Les hommes du passé, qui n'étaient* pour eux *que des fantômes ou des noms, devinrent des êtres vivants, rois, princes, sorciers, valets, garde-chasses, moines, bohémiens, marchands et soldats, qui délibèrent, combattent, voyagent, trafiquent, mangent et boivent, chantent et prient, dans la salle d'armes des châteaux, sur le banc noir des auberges, par les rues tortueuses des villes, sous l'auvent des échoppes, dans le cloître des monastères. Des paysages artistement composés entourent les scènes comme un décor de théâtre. On suit des yeux un cavalier qui galope le long des grèves. On aspire au milieu des genêts la fraîcheur du vent, la lune éclaire des lacs où glisse un bateau, le soleil fait reluire les cuirasses, la pluie tombe sur les huttes de feuillages. Sans connaître les modèles,* ils trouvaient *ces peintures ressemblantes, et* l'illusion *était complète. L'hiver s'y passa.*[20]

19 The quotations from the drafts are drawn from Gabrielle Leleu, *Ebauches et fragments inédits recueillis d'après les manuscrits de Mme Bovary* (Paris: Conard, 1936). For this passage, see I, 157–58.
20 *Bouvard et Pécuchet* (Paris: Conard, 1923), p. 164.

[At first they read Walter Scott.
It was like the discovery of a new world.

The people of past ages, who had been only phantoms
or names *to them,* became living beings, kings, princes,
sorcerers, valets, gamekeepers, monks, gypsies, merchants, and
soldiers, who deliberate, fight, travel, trade, eat and drink,
sing and pray, in the fencing rooms of castles, on the black
benches of inns, through the winding streets of cities, under
the pent roofs of booths, in monastery cloisters. Artistically
composed landscapes surround the scenes like stage sets. *One's
eyes follow* a rider galloping along the strand. *One breathes in*
the freshness of the breeze in the midst of the gorse, the
moonlight falls on lakes where boats glide, the sun shines on
armor, rain falls on huts made of boughs. Without knowing the
originals, *they found* these depictions faithful reproductions,
and *the illusion* was complete. They spent the winter thus.]

A contrasting treatment of similar material (cited in Part I
to compare Balzac's "strength" to Flaubert's "preoccupation
with form"), by Balzac, this time points up the "distance" in
Flaubert's approach in *Madame Bovary:*

*Le dithyrambe était dans son coeur et sur ses lèvres. Elle
palpitait, elle se pâmait, elle s'enthousiasmait pour tout
événement: pour le dévouement d'une soeur grise et l'exécution
des frères Faucher, pour l'Ipsiboé de monsieur d'Arlincourt
comme pour l'Anaconda de Lewis, pour l'évasion de Lavalette
comme pour une de ses amies qui avait mis des voleurs en fuite
en faisant la grosse voix. Pour elle, tout était sublime, extraordinaire, étrange, divin, merveilleux. Elle s'animait, se cour-
rouçait, s'abattait sur elle-même, s'élançait, retombait, regardait
le ciel ou la terre; ses yeux se remplissaient de larmes. Elle usait
sa vie en de perpétuelles admirations et se consumait en
d'étranges dédains. Elle concevait le pacha de Janina, elle aurait
voulu lutter avec lui dans son sérail, et trouvait quelque chose
de grand à être cousue dans un sac et jetée à l'eau. Elle
enviait lady Esther Stanhope, ce bas-bleu du désert. Il lui
prenait envie de se faire soeur de Sainte Camille et d'aller
mourir de la fièvre jaune à Barcelone en soignant les malades:
c'était là une grande, une noble destinée! Enfin, elle avait soif
de tout ce qui n'était pas l'eau claire de sa vie, cachée entre les
herbes. Elle adorait lord Byron, Jean-Jacques Rousseau, toutes
les existences poétiques et dramatiques. Elle avait des larmes
pour tous les malheurs et des fanfares pour toutes les victoires.
Elle sympathisait avec Napoléon vaincu, elle sympathisait avec
Méhémet-Ali massacrant les tyrans de l'Egypte. Enfin elle*

revêtait les gens de génie d'une auréole, et croyait qu'ils vivaient de parfums et de lumière.[21] (See the translations on pp. 75 and 76–77).

The effective use of *enviait* [envied], abandoned by Flaubert in his passage, is but one suggestive detail. The absence of any important distance between reader and heroine makes for a strikingly different reaction: since we have shared Mme de Bargeton's feelings, the irony is both gentler and broader. While we do recognize the discrepancy between her dreams and reality, our participation in the scene facilitates the admission that this is no more than a normal human feeling. We smile, but tolerantly. It is that gentle irony which arises when the reader accepts the actions of the heroine, only to realize a moment later that both he and she have been displaying their common human frailty.

Conveniently, Emma's readings are one of the guideposts in her life, one of those points of reference to which she frequently returns for orientation. As she does so, she poses for Flaubert new problems of evaluation and new questions of aesthetic distance. Whether he ever viewed the matter in this fashion or would even have accepted the term is less relevant than the clear and meaningful shifts in aesthetic distance which accompany each of these returns. The varying impact of Emma's recollection reveals incisively the meaning he wishes to attribute to the scene. When the distance remains considerable, irony is usually present and bitter. The distance sometimes narrows, however, and the irony becomes gentler or even disappears. At two crucial moments of her life, Emma was to recall the books surreptitiously brought into the convent by the old seamstress: first, immediately after giving herself to Rodolphe and second, much later, as she sat outside the convent and came to realize the folly of her dreams. As irony strengthens or fades in these two scenes and in the death scene, the aesthetic

21 *Illusions perdues* (*Oeuvres complètes,* Paris: Conard, 1913, XI, 214–15). I compared these two passages more fully from another point of view in Part I. An excellent correction and expansion of the points there proposed was presented by W. M. Frohock in his "Energy vs. Art: A Suggested Alternative," *Romanic Review,* XLIII (1952), 155–56. I am glad to take this opportunity to indicate my acceptance of his objections and additions.

distance clarifies their significance and reveals the delicacy of shading in Flaubert's writing.

Emma came back from her fateful ride with Rodolphe, passed through dinner almost in a trance, and was at last alone in her room, able to repeat deliciously to herself: "J'ai un amant! un amant!" (pp. 225–26) [I have a lover! a lover!] She was now to live the dream she had so long caressed:

> *Alors elle se rappela les héroïnes des livres qu'elle avait lus, et la légion lyrique de ces femmes adultères se mit à chanter dans sa mémoire avec des voix de soeurs qui la charmaient.*

> [Then she recalled the heroines of the books she had read, and the lyric legion of these adulterous women began to sing in her memory with sisterly voices which charmed her.]

The marked change in phrasing corresponds to a changed situation. This is no idle dream; it is a very certain reality. Each link in the sentence is forged to bind it to Emma. We start from her recollections; we shift away for an instant to mention the legion of adulterous women, but it is her memory; they are her sisters, she is charmed by them. The paragraph continues, riveting our attention always to Emma. We are invited, not to analyze it, but to live it:

> *Elle devenait elle-même comme une partie véritable de ces imaginations et réalisait la longue rêverie de sa jeunesse, en se considérant dans ce type d'amoureuse qu'elle avait tant envié.*

> [She herself was becoming a part of these imaginings and was carrying out the long dream of her youth, as she contemplated herself in this model of a woman in love that she had so envied.]

Flaubert has so infused his prose with the feelings of his heroine that the reader is forcibly drawn in, much as he was in the Balzac passage. For the moment, Flaubert wishes us to feel with Emma, and we do. Moreover, he has been able to retain the verb *envié*, the elimination of which diminished the force of the earlier passage. He has shown that he appreciated its aptness: it will recur. Similarly, he has recognized the contrasting aesthetic distances for irony and for sympathetic participation. A more dynamic form has reduced the aesthetic distance and made the account more captivating, more like Balzac.

The drafts for the passage support this view, as in one of them there is a further sentence, which Flaubert later removed:

> *Elle ne pensait pas à l'avenir: elle ne cherchait pas si Rodolphe l'aimerait; elle ne songeait qu'à elle-même, et l'idée de son bonheur lui absorbait sa conscience aussi complètement qu'eût fait une sensation brutale.*[22]

> [She was not thinking of the future; she was not wondering whether Rodolphe would love her; she was thinking only of herself, and the idea of her happiness occupied her mind as fully as a brutal sensation would have.]

Why was this deleted? In part perhaps because of its rather clumsy negative, but more because of its effect on the aesthetic distance of the passage. Emma did not herself think of the future; to bring it in would have destroyed for us the illusion now gripping her and would have revived the basic irony by permitting us to stand off and judge her. Flaubert's handling of the readings themselves indicated that that was his intent there. The new approach may reflect his desire to have us participate somewhat more in this scene, which thereby becomes more dramatic and, also, more understandable.

But there is more. The narrowed aesthetic distance has made us partners with Emma. The cause for the altered attitude is not far to seek: while Flaubert may have had no patience with Emma's earlier reveries, he himself felt strongly the "poetry of adultery" and is reacting to it.[23] The change from irony to the evocation of a sympathetic response marks a major shift in the emphasis. Balzac, too, evoked such a response, but he knew that Mme de Bargeton was wrong. Flaubert's position was precisely the opposite. His paragraph is the vivid amplifica-

---

22 The drafts are given in Leleu, II, 21–23. In them, the sentence which did remain had the further notation that these voices which charmed her also used to speak to her. The disappearance of this thought from the final form causes no loss; the possible reminiscence of Jeanne d'Arc could add nothing.

23 E.g., in the *Oeuvres de jeunesse inédites*, II, 193; *Notes de voyages*, I, 60; *Par les champs*, pp. 268–69. Flaubert's relation to his mistress, Louise Colet, would also be a factor; it will be recalled that she was married.

tion of his original sketch for it: "après la baisade avec Rodolphe elle a l'amour vrai, complet—le bonheur—longtemps il a cuvé, s'est préparé" [24] [after intercourse with Rodolphe she has true, complete love—happiness—for a long time it has been fermented, prepared]. His pen has not betrayed him, for the reader, sensing this, accepts Emma's feelings as valid and joins with her. Irony has disappeared.

The full import of this change becomes clearer later in the book when, again, Flaubert's own feelings come close to the surface. It stems, not so much from formal aesthetic considerations, as from the basic stimuli leading Flaubert to write of Emma in the first place. The shorter his own "distance" from the subject, the more difficult it is for a writer to consider it from the point of view of the artist and to strip from it considerations extraneous and even alien to aesthetics. In his account of Emma's reaction to having a lover, Flaubert benefits by his "proximity"; the technique is in marked contrast to the passage on the readings in the convent and is, for my taste, superior. The subjective or personal quality is not absolute and conscious as in the case of the romantics; it does not necessarily stand in formal opposition to Flaubert's canon of impersonality. Rather, Emma has naturally and logically come to a position in which certain of her views and reactions coincide with his. So long as the aesthetic requirements remain identical with Flaubert's personal ones, there is no loss; quite on the contrary, there is a potential gain. The pitfall lies in the possibility that the two aspects of Flaubert, the artist and the man, may not necessarily be concordant. He fought heroically over the years against what he hated in Emma and her milieu; he was not on his guard against elements with which he sympathized. Yet, despite the personal appeal of Emma's reaction to Rodolphe, Flaubert was able in writing of it to maintain sufficient distance to ensure its aesthetic appeal.

Many months pass before Emma once more recalls her readings. The affair with Rodolphe has gradually turned bitter and soured; Léon has taken his place, offering a new brief incarnation of her dreams. That, too, is now withering. One

24 J. Pommier and G. Leleu, *Madame Bovary, Nouvelle Version précédée des scénarios inédits* (Paris: Corti, 1949), p. 101.

afternoon in Rouen, after taking leave of him, she is walking
alone toward the inn to board the Hirondelle for the trip back
to Yonville. Suddenly she realizes that she is passing the convent; she sits down on a bench in the shade of the elms, remembering her earlier days:

> *Quel calme dans ce temps-là! Comme elle enviait les ineffables
> sentiments d'amour qu'elle tâchait, d'après des livres, de se
> figurer!* [25]
>
> [How calm things were then! How she envied the ineffable
> feelings of love which she used to try to imagine from her
> reading!]

Here, and again subsequently, Flaubert will report indirectly
thoughts which represent direct discourse in her mind. His use
of the imperfect tense for such passages of "mental discourse"
is familiar; its importance for aesthetic distance lies in the
feeling of immediacy and close personal contact which it imparts. It suggests to the reader that he is, as it were, present
while the thought is in the very act of becoming. This technique
alternates with the direct statement of the thought itself, an
even closer and more immediate device. The alternation is
not merely for variety; the interplay between the two becomes
particularly significant for the shifts in aesthetic distance.
Flaubert phrased directly Emma's recollection of the calmness of
those days; her longing for the emotions described in her books
is only a shade less immediate and neither feeling is accom-

---

25 Page 392. The second sentence was far clearer in the drafts (Leleu,
II, 422–25), where it read: "Comme elle enviait *alors* les ineffables sentiments d'amour." [How she *then* envied the ineffable feelings of love.] In
context it is not immediately clear in the final form whether she envied
them in the past or still envies them. The *alors* was removed when
Flaubert decided that a further one was indispensable in a preceding
sentence. As the deleted *alors* remained through most of the drafts, it is at
least possible that, when Flaubert removed it, he may not have noticed the
slight ambiguity which arose.

This scene, in which Emma recalls her earlier dreams in the convent,
was among the earliest to occur to Flaubert as he planned his book. In the
very first of the published scenarios, it is noted on the opening sheet as an
interlinear addition to the fact of her being brought up at the convent:
"souvenir de ses rêves quand elle repasse devant le couvent" [recollection
of her dreams when she passes again in front of the convent] (Pommier
and Leleu, p. 3). Its intimate structural relationship to the original scene
is thus further guaranteed.

panied by a verb of thinking or reflecting. It would have moved us away and weakened the effect of the passage, here reinforced by *enviait*. The direct impression, not analysis of it, is appropriate and Flaubert has so treated it.

Replacing the sentences in their context explains the change. Emma, long deluded, is coming slowly to the awful revelation; she is about to face the unreality of her dreams and the concomitant shattering of everything she wanted to live for. As at the moment of her exultation over having a lover, so here Flaubert wishes the vivid remembrance of the experience to be dominant. There, no place needed to be reserved for irony; here, it is in temporary abeyance. The drafts again show a typical Flaubert suppression: he had had her recall her envy of these "sentiments d'amour *qui ne servent qu'à composer des livres*" [feelings of love *which are useful only for writing books*]. This would be to analyse and state the falseness of the feelings. Instead of this analytic approach, he will have her experience their hollowness in the next paragraph:

> *Les premiers mois de son mariage, ses promenades à cheval dans la forêt, le vicomte qui valsait, et Lagardy chantant, tout repassa devant ses yeux. . . . [sic] Et Léon lui parut soudain dans le même éloignement que les autres.*[26]

> [The first months of her marriage, her horseback rides in the forest, the viscount waltzing, and Lagardy singing, all passed before her eyes again. . . . (sic) And Léon suddenly appeared before her, as distant as the others.]

Once again Flaubert has moved back from Emma. The list of experiences and even the tense of the verbs mark a return to the aesthetic distance of the original passage on the readings. The purpose, however, is different this time, for Emma, too, is standing off from her visions and is about to evaluate them.

The few portentous moments on the bench outside the convent are filled with the tension of strain and counter-strain.

---

26 For similar reasons, I imagine, he also deleted from his draft the further statement: "Elle les [these dreams] avait eus pourtant et les examinait à présent comme on s'amuse à tenir dans ses mains des coquilles brisées." [She had had these dreams and was examining them now as one amuses himself by holding broken seashells in his hands.]

Long-inhibited promptings have placed the key incidents in her past in a perspective which permits her sad appraisal of their worth: small wonder that she tries hard to cling to her old view. Perhaps consciously, and surely with utmost sensitivity, Flaubert varies his technique, quoting her directly, but using an imperfect tense for the verb of saying: "Je l'aime pourtant! se disait-elle." [But I love him! she said (was saying) to herself.] The thought —counter to what she divined a moment before—we cannot accept with her for we know that it is false, yet the relative intimacy of the phrasing does let us understand and sympathize with her melancholy desire that this be true. Irony is present, but our nearness keeps it sympathetic and gentle.

A final paragraph ends the rapid drama and the bell of the convent brings Emma back to present reality. In this paragraph she makes a frenzied effort to revive her old illusions (and we remain distant from her), before she faces directly the frightening conclusions which her life has been forcing upon her. When she does so, Flaubert will again close the gap between her and us and will invite us to share directly in her thoughts.

He opens with her bitter reflection; it arises from her self-pity, which is in part justified, to be sure, but not so fully that we accept it wholly. The nuance is important, for each shade of meaning is echoed in the form. The reflection is in the imperfect again to revive the feeling of intimacy: "N'importe! elle n'était pas heureuse, ne l'avait jamais été." [Never mind! She was not happy, she never had been.] Her petulance pierces in the staccato phraseology. She continues in similar fashion, skirting the truth she is soon to face; the tense keeps the distance slight: "D'où venait donc cette insuffisance de la vie, cette pourriture instantanée des choses où elle s'appuyait. . . ?" [Whence came this inadequacy of life, this instant rotting of whatever she sought to lean upon?] Contrast the more distant phrasing: "Elle se demandait d'où venait . . ." [She wondered whence came. . . .]

Again suspension-points in the text break the chain of thought. The dream has been challenged; Emma wonders vaguely if it has any reality. After the pause a change of rhythm and a dithyrambic tone signal her reversion to her old illusion and suggest her desperation.[27] As we have learned to recognize these indices, we draw back and irony at once intervenes, despite the tenses:

> *Mais, s'il y avait quelque part un être fort et beau, une nature valeureuse, pleine à la fois d'exaltation et de raffinements, un coeur de poète sous une forme d'ange, lyre aux cordes d'airain, sonnant vers le ciel des épithalames élégiaques, pourquoi, par hasard, ne le trouverait-elle pas?*

> [But if there were somewhere a man strong and handsome, a valiant nature both exalted and refined, with the heart of a poet in the body of an angel, a lyre with strings of brass sounding forth to heaven elegiac nuptial songs, why should she not by chance meet him?]

It is in truth only a wraith of a dream which must depend upon chance ("par hasard") for its realization; earlier she had been sure that injustice of fate alone kept her from happiness. Now melancholy sweeps over her and she knows the worst: a change of tempo again helps us as the phrasing lengthens, and the words themselves allow us to draw closer. Irony, evoked a moment before, is now suspended and we join with her in her disabused view of life. It is her own thoughts which we read, the imperfects continuing to mirror them:

> *Oh! quelle impossibilité! Rien, d'ailleurs, ne valait la peine d'une recherche; tout mentait! Chaque sourire cachait un bâillement d'ennui, chaque joie une malédiction, tout plaisir son dégoût, et les meilleurs baisers ne vous laissaient sur la lèvre qu'une irréalisable envie d'une volupté plus haute.*

---

27 Melodically speaking, we now return to the tempo and discordant harmonies of the fantasies which used to charm her as she lay in bed about to go to sleep beside Charles: "Au galop de quatre chevaux, elle était emportée depuis huit jours vers un pays nouveau, d'où ils ne reviendraient plus. Ils allaient, ils allaient, les bras enlacés, sans parler. Souvent, du haut d'une montagne, ils apercevaient tout à coup quelque cité splendide avec des dômes, des ponts, des navires, des forêts de citronniers et des cathédrales de marbre blanc, dont les clochers aigus portaient des nids de cigognes. . . ." (p. 271) [For a week she had been being carried away to the gallop of four horses toward a new country, whence they would never return. They were going forward, ever forward, arm in arm, without talking. Often from a mountain top they would suddenly perceive below them a splendid city with domes, bridges, ships, forests of lemon trees, and cathedrals of white marble, whose bell towers bore storks' nests.]

[Oh! How impossible! Nothing, moreover, was worth the effort of hunting for it; everything was a lie! Each smile concealed a yawn of boredom, each joy a curse, every pleasure its distaste, and the best of kisses left on your lips only an impossible desire for greater voluptuousness.]

The bell breaks off the train of thought; it could not profitably go further.[28] An earlier Emma, seen from a distance, had aroused scorn, contempt, even condescension on our part. Now, with the gap narrowed between us and her, she is more likely to elicit our sympathy, perhaps our pity. The gentler aura of the previous passage has strengthened, foreshadowing some of the mood of the ending.

Two questions clamor for attention: Why is Flaubert enlisting our sympathy for Emma here, and are we to be dealing with pathos or tragedy? The latter question must await a consideration of the end of the book; the matter of sympathy can be answered at once. It is Flaubert himself who is speaking; it is his own conclusion on life to which Emma has come. The thought and even her phrases come directly from him and may be found over and over again in his letters or in the autobiographical juvenile works. No writer will use irony when a character is phrasing the author's own, intimate beliefs: it would destroy the point he is trying to make. Were we not to draw closer to Emma as she discovers the validity of Flaubert's thesis, we should be less likely to accept it and the passage would risk failing of its effect. Irony is very naturally being displaced by intimacy here. Flaubert feels sympathy and invites

28 In one of the drafts Flaubert had allowed us to understand more clearly that Emma was not committed to this view that all is vanity; in the final form the reader wonders for several pages whether Emma has perhaps now achieved a fuller understanding. The confusion was not possible in the draft, which carried: "Elle se cramponna pourtant, et de toute la force d'un désir soudain, à cet idéal d'amant qui venait de passer. Elle ne pouvait le saisir, tant il était vague et magnifique. Mais il lui en fallait un puisqu'elle ne pouvait se passer d'aimer, et que l'amour était insuffisant." [She clung, however, with all the strength of sudden desire to this ideal of a lover which had just flashed before her mind. She could not manage to grasp it, it was so vague and magnificent. But she had to have one since she could not live without loving, and love was insufficient.] In the final version it is only some pages later (p. 399), when Emma again hopes for the realization of her dreams, that we can be sure how transitory is this mood: another typical suppression.

the reader to feel it, too; that sympathy could, moreover, lead to pity and to an aura of pathos in which the aesthetic distance would narrow, perhaps to the vanishing point. There is a potentially dangerous conflict here between two moods, a possible clash between a sentence whose phrasing evokes contemptuous irony and the succeeding one, which is intended to call forth approval. Once more the varying "distances" of the passage for the reader are the direct result of their varying distances for Flaubert. How could it be otherwise? The danger inherent in this disparateness is that Flaubert, for all his scrupulous artistry, is not the master of it. Here the discord emphasizes an inconsistency in Emma which is in full accord with the internal logic of the book thus far. Only when that logic requires consistency will these variations become damaging.[29] The recollections outside the convent are as delicately handled as were those on her return from the ride with Rodolphe and both gained from Flaubert's personal involvement in them.

If the book is to achieve towering stature, it must in the end forthrightly elect either irony or pity as its foundation and erect thereon a structure which will be conditioned by that basis. Within the shorter compass of a play it had long been clear that the choice had to be made at the outset: if tragedy were sought, aesthetic distance had to be maintained and a sympathetic pity evoking pathos had to be eschewed. The longer forms, the epic for instance, gave ample proof that a greater compass permitted wider ranges in aesthetic distance during the course of the work; for the conclusion, however, the requirements were as rigid as for drama. The novel, for which Flaubert was trying to establish new molds, seems to me equally rigid. The complementary polarities, irony-pity and tragedy-pathos, must be resolved during Emma's last moments. It is there that Flaubert must finally hammer out in unmistakable terms the meaning he finds in her life: inconsistency will mean a book which falters at the end, when it should rather be rising to a

29 I should wish here to depart from the analysis suggested by Bullough, in which he appears to me to lay too great emphasis upon consistency of "distance." A subject such as Emma seems to lend itself to constant variations in the distance; it is only Flaubert's practice at the end of the book that I shall wish to challenge and call vacillation rather than enrichment.

clear conclusion. Her romantic illusions dead, she herself lies dying:

> *Emma, le menton contre sa poitrine, ouvrait démesurément les paupières; et ses pauvres mains se traînaient sur les draps, avec ce geste hideux et doux des agonisants qui semblent vouloir déjà se recouvrir du suaire* (p. 446).

> [Emma, her chin on her breast, opened her eyes very wide; and her poor hands dragged across the sheets with that hideous and gentle gesture of those who are about to die and who seem to be seeking already to cover themselves with their shroud.]

The adjectives *pauvres* and *doux* set a new tone. On the one hand, we do stand apart from Emma, observing her actions, but not sharing them: there is a palpable distance between us and her, for we are forced to resort to simile to divine the meaning of her actions. On the other hand, the appeal of her actions ("pauvres," "doux") breaks down the distance by calling directly upon our emotions and seeking to make us personally involved in the scene.[30] A tempting explanation lies ready to hand: Flaubert is here envisioning not Emma but his sister Caroline: If this be so, then once more Flaubert's personal involvement has narrowed the distance.[31] What was earlier an aura of gentleness tinged occasionally with irony has now become unconcealed tenderness. It invites pathos; it is not

[30] This was deliberate on Flaubert's part and thereby—in terms of his aesthetic of impassivity—dangerous. Long before he came to the actual drafting of these paragraphs, he wrote to Louise Colet: "Dans ma 3e partie . . . je veux qu'on pleure" [In my 3rd part . . . I want my reader to weep] (letter of Oct. 9, 1852). Cf., much later in connection with Félicité of *Un Coeur simple*: "Je veux apitoyer, faire pleurer les âmes sensibles, en étant une moi-même" [I want to move sensitive people to weep, being one myself] (letter to George Sand, June 19, 1876). Félicité's death scene, however, is in marked contrast to Emma's; the method of portrayal, serene and dignified, leaves the reader always sufficiently close to be deeply moved, yet sufficiently distant for an aesthetic, not a personal, feeling of loss.

[31] His sister, to whom he was devoted, had died in childbirth in 1846. My hypothesis cannot be categorically proved, but the *Correspondance* does offer some confirmation: Flaubert wrote to Du Camp on March 20, 1846, speaking of his sister on her deathbed: "Quelle grâce il y a dans les malades, et quels singuliers gestes!" [What grace ill people have and what odd gestures!] So far as I know, he never described these gestures more closely.

consonant with the severity of tragedy. The appropriate aesthetic distance here is a matter of great delicacy.[32] Tenderness is permissible and may indeed heighten the tragedy, as when Horatio addresses the dead Hamlet:

> Good night, sweet prince;
> And flights of angels sing thee to thy rest!

But dignity and restraint have marked these lines; they have not guarded Flaubert's pen. This time the shifting distances from which we must view Emma can no longer be credited as an enrichment of her character. Lamartine's anguish in reading this passage is no more than an exaggeration of what anyone must feel.[33] Art is giving place to sentiment, however valid and natural it was in the man as opposed to the artist.

Emma is approaching the climactic moment when she will give to the figure of Christ on the curé's cross the most deeply felt kiss she has ever given. A paragraph leads up to it, in which Flaubert, and we, continue to observe her from without and, as it were, to guess at her feelings:

> *Elle tourna sa figure lentement, et parut saisie de joie à voir tout à coup l'étole violette, sans doute retrouvant au milieu d'un apaisement extraordinaire la volupté perdue de ses premiers élancements mystiques, avec des visions de béatitude éternelle qui commençaient.*

> [She turned her face slowly and seemed full of joy on seeing the purple stole, no doubt discovering once again in the midst of an extraordinary peacefulness the lost voluptuousness of her first mystic flights, along with visions of eternal bliss which were beginning.]

The priest, Bournisien, is about to administer the last rites of the Church. Emma has returned in memory to the time before her romantic readings, to that period of vague religiosity which had preceded them. She is now seeking in religion both relief and a surer type of ecstasy. As the reader wonders whether this is meant to be the key which will finally unlock the meaning

---

32 It is delicate for both author and reader. No critic can escape being subjective in this matter and my remarks should be read in this light.

33 ". . . vous m'avez fait mal aux nerfs" [. . . you have upset me very much], cited by Sénard in his defense of Flaubert, reproduced in the Conard edition of *Madame Bovary*, p. 588.

of life for Emma, Flaubert answers unequivocally by continuing
to keep us at a distance from her. However closely we observe,
we still do not share with her:

> *Le prêtre se releva pour prendre le crucifix; alors elle allongea
> le cou comme quelqu'un qui a soif, et, collant ses lèvres sur le
> corps de l'Homme-Dieu, elle y déposa de toute sa force
> expirante le plus grand baiser d'amour qu'elle eût jamais
> donné.*

> [The priest rose to get the crucifix; then she raised her head
> like someone who is thirsty and, pressing her lips on the body
> of the Man-God, she placed there the most passionate kiss she
> had ever given.]

Flaubert was well aware that the Church authorized such
a fusion of love with religion, of passion with devotion to
Christ; no doubt it was he who placed in his lawyer's hands the
passage from Bossuet which justified this sentence before the
tribunal which judged the book.[34] But, although the action is
compatible with dogma, this is less important than its aesthetic
value. In describing the kiss, Flaubert returns to the greater
distance of his earlier passages and thereby revives the irony.
To what purpose? He has woven easily into the fabric of his
novel the most potent of western symbols. He has Emma accept
it in the fullest way she knows, but he is not yet attempting
to generalize beyond the restricted confines of his novel: Emma
remains entirely herself. She has brought the symbol of the
Cross down to her level.[35] Flaubert is continuing the conflict
he initiated in the scene outside the convent: we know Emma's
longing, and we are saddened that here, too, she must be
frustrated; but we are not yet to be at one with her, for she
has not yet perceived what is to Flaubert the true meaning of
life. In the earlier scene she had first to make a detour through

34 *Ibid.*, p. 618.
35 This fusion of passion and religion Flaubert understood as characteristic of Emma. His intentions are most obvious in the scenarios. In
one of them he defines the inner quality of her religious experiences while
still in the convent: "Catholicisme amoureux mais en tire plus de propen-
sion à l'amour qu'à la religion, car n'est pas mystique mais po-é-tique (et
sensuelle plus tard)" [Sentimental Catholicism but she draws from it more
propensity to love than to religion, for she is not a mystic but po-e-tic
(and later sensual)] (Pommier and Leleu, p. 42; see also p. 45). *Po-é-tique*
or *pohétique* is a familiar term of opprobrium in his vocabulary.

a shoddy concept of an ideal lover before coming to Flaubert's view. In the death scene, this detour has its parallel in her snatching at religion. Here, however, the conflict and her illusion are much more dangerous: Flaubert started from a narrow framework, his own period and his own small corner of France. He has just made Emma tenderly appealing on her deathbed. If his novel is to achieve broader meaning, it must ultimately expand its scope and convert its parochial significance into one of universality. If Flaubert is to succeed, he must make Emma become a symbol of mankind.[36] She may well continue to meet frustration, but in so doing she must be felt as incarnating man. Emma may properly be viewed from a distance as her life closes; such a post could lend her symbolic grandeur. If instead irony intervenes and she falls beneath the stature of the symbols surrounding her, then the distance has served only to demean her. She, not mankind, is dominant; and she lacks nobility. It is her personal and partial understanding which we have witnessed, nor are there yet any overtones which carry beyond her. But there remain a few more moments before the end.

She relaxes serenely after her experience ("avec une expression de sérénité, comme si le sacrement l'eût guérie" [with a serene expression, as if the sacrament had cured her]). The anguish and doubt which permeate the first version of *Saint-Antoine* are warrants that this cannot be Flaubert's message. Her serenity, too, must be an illusion, however cherished. That is why we have kept our distance despite the pity we have felt. Emma, wholly absorbed in her new-found peace, sends for her mirror, looks long at her face, and weeps. The death agony begins, her breathing becomes rapid and noisy . . . and the loathsome Blindman is heard outside the window. She starts up, recognizing the song he used to sing as the Hirondelle was leaving Rouen:

Et Emma se mit à rire, d'un rire atroce, frénétique, désepéré, croyant voir la face hideuse du misérable qui se dressait dans les ténèbres éternelles comme un épouvantement.[37]

36 Cf. Daiches, loc. cit.

37 Note how her visions have twisted from "béatitude éternelle" to "ténèbres éternelles" [eternal bliss—eternal shadows]. Flaubert's efforts to find the adjectives to convey the meaning of the *Aveugle* are further evidence of his attempt to capture the overtones of his symbol. One of

[And Emma began to laugh, with an atrocious, frenzied, despairing laugh, as she thought she saw the wretch's hideous face rising up in the eternal shadows to terrify her.]

Two more lines of his song, and a convulsion seizes Emma; she falls back dead.

The laugh, atrocious, frenzied, despairing, was her last act in life; it arose because she believed that the scrofulous Blindman was to be with her for eternity. The symbol gives forceful statement to Flaubert's meaning: religion cannot preserve man from having to face his own nature, nor can it save him from his sins. Emma's laugh bears dramatic relation to an earlier one in Flaubert's works and its import is the same: as he drew his *Saint-Antoine* to a close he had the Devil laugh in the same fashion, while the tortured desert saint turned again to prayer. In Emma's case, the meaning is implicit and derives from the symbolism; in *Saint-Antoine* the Devil states it explicitly:

> *Adieu! l'enfer te laisse. Eh! qu'importe au Diable après tout? sais-tu où il se trouve, le véritable enfer?*
> *lui montrant son coeur*
> *Là! Tant que tu ne l'auras pas arraché de dessous tes côtes, tu le porteras avec toi; les péchés sont dans ta poitrine, la désolation dans ta tête, la malédiction est ta nature. . . .*[38]

[Farewell! Hell leaves you. Well! After all, what does it matter to the Devil? Do you know where the real hell lies?
pointing to his heart
There! So long as you have not torn it from beneath your ribs, you will bear it with you; the sins are in your breast, sorrow in your head, a curse on your nature. . . .]

The meaning of the Blindman, the final, mocking message of Satan and Emma's bitter reflections on life as she sat outside

---

the drafts has "un rire atroce, strident, enragé" [an atrocious, strident, mad laugh] (Leleu, II, 533). The "strident" remains too close to the physical sound; "enragé" is less strong than "frénétique." Neither has the force of "désespéré."

Flaubert had not originally envisaged this return of the Blindman. In a long succession of the scenarios it is the coach (the Hirondelle) which is to pass under Emma's window (e. g., Pommier and Leleu, pp. 19 and 32). The greater emotive and symbolic power of the Blindman is the obvious explanation of Flaubert's later preference for him. The new idea seems to be mentioned first in a letter of Sept. 20, 1855, to Bouilhet.

38 P. 494.

the convent, all express Flaubert's view of man's ultimate fate. If Saint Anthony found solace in prayer, it was only because the rising sun was driving away the darkness; with its setting, night and Satan would return. For Emma, no more suns could rise: she faced man's eternal meaning and found there eternal darkness, *malédiction*.[39]

The clear symbolic intent renews the problem of the aesthetic distance. The account is essentially from the point of view of the onlooker. But, just as a painter may emphasize vivid three-dimensionality to heighten drama and realism, so Flaubert has used powerful and emotive adjectives to gain an effect similar to that of the Balzac passage. The technique is similar to that of the death-bed description though the effects are dissimilar. If Emma remains distant, her appeal is gripping and immediate. Flaubert has drawn back to allow his symbols to achieve their full stature, but the words he has chosen have made them dynamic and emotive. Emma can now stand forth stripped of her personal attributes and adequate as a symbol.

Any summing up must be a report of personal reactions, an analysis of highly subjective responses, which one hopes to find matched in other readers. It is my belief that Flaubert strove for the aesthetic distance necessary to make his novel symbolic and to lend it the overtones of tragedy; yet my own reaction is that, despite this closing scene, he did not achieve it.[40] If the book does fail of its mark (a mark and a failure

---

39 If this meaning is ultimate, as I have suggested, it is not thereby total. Flaubert's religion of art offered him a haven and salvation; this, however, he explicitly denied to Emma (e. g., "Il fallait qu'elle pût retirer des choses une sorte de profit personnel; et elle rejetait comme inutile tout ce qui ne contribuait pas à la consommation immédiate de son coeur— *étant de tempérament plus sentimental qu'artiste . . .*" [She had to get a sort of personal profit from everything; and she rejected as useless anything which did not directly provide nourishment for her emotions—*being of a temperament which was more sentimental than artistic*] (p. 50; italics mine); for similar notations in the scenarios, see Pommier and Leleu, pp. 6, 8, and 23.

40 A possible difficulty arises in the contrast between this aura or mood which I have been suggesting and an earlier categoric statement of Flaubert's in 1853: "La *hideur* dans les sujets bourgeois doit remplacer le *tragique* qui leur est incompatible" [Hideousness in bourgeois subjects must replace the *tragic*, which is incompatible with them] (letter to Louise Colet, Nov. 29, 1853; italics present in the original). In line with this dictum, the adjective *hideux* occurs twice in these last pages ("geste hideux," "face

which may both exist only in my imagination), the causes are multiple. Was pathos permissible so close to the end? Was the vantage-point of irony wise here? [41] Were these consonant with the overtones of that final, satanic laugh? Or could Emma achieve full stature as a symbol immediately after being so completely herself in the kiss she gave the crucifix? The questions may be phrased as ones of timing; I suspect that they are better put as matters of consistency in aesthetic distance: we alternately stood off and drew near, we were torn between sympathy and irony. We may have shared her physical anguish from the poison (as Flaubert did), but we did not identify ourselves with her mental anguish and so do not see her as symbolic of ourselves and mankind till this last instant. The clash between the points of view is resolved here, perhaps, but we are unprepared for our new attitude toward her. We have stood off to condemn her too often for it to be entirely satisfactory to accept her now as one with us, and a book which might have pointed the way toward a form for tragedy in the modern novel closes without achieving that stature.

---

hideuse"). The final test, however, must be the tone of the novel itself. Significantly, the letter considerably antedates the writing of the conclusion; it is quite common to find Flaubert gradually drawing closer to his heroines as he came to know them better through long creative association (e. g., his change of attitude during the writing of the final *Education sentimentale*). I should maintain that when writing the end of the *Bovary*, he had markedly altered his point of view and was striving for tragedy: he was no longer trying to treat it as merely a *sujet bourgeois*. At most the letter would point to a possible ambivalence in his attitude, which might underlie some of the conflict to which I have been drawing attention.

41 Flaubert felt no opposition between irony and pathos. Speaking of his *scène d'auberge*, he wrote to Louise Colet: "L'ironie n'enlève rien au pathétique; elle l'outre au contraire" [Irony removes nothing from pathos; on the contrary it increases it] (letter of Oct. 9, 1852). I cannot agree. A similar question, though with other characters, arises over the common, almost stupid irony applied to Bournisien and Homais in these same pages. The tone here, which sets the "distance," is one of contempt: we are above them, but are forced to look down and see them. They remain so true to themselves as to bind us to their individualities and to seem petty and out of place, if tragedy is our mark. We lose by having to observe them. Their prominence could indicate that Flaubert was not striving for tragedy in *Madame Bovary*; against this argument it may be urged that they mirror a flaw in Flaubert's taste and could, in him, easily coexist with an intention to portray tragedy.

8 · The Female Quixote

INTRODUCTION

One of the most perceptive American critics of European literature is the author of the following section drawn from a study of the French novel throughout the nineteenth century. This passage will serve to put Flaubert into the larger context in which he belongs, the tradition of the novel in his own country and, more broadly still, in the general tradition of European letters.

The general stand is a return to the position of Baudelaire in an effort, after accepting his contentions, to see what more lies beyond them. The moral objections of a long line of critics are here incisively rejected, although of course—and properly—readers of a different temperament will continue to make them. In addition, the excerpt returns to a number of passages in the novel with which earlier selections have dealt in order to bring new insights to bear on them. I have omitted only the bibliographical footnotes which accompany the original text.

As if to put the finishing touches on Flaubert's self-portrait of the artist as a saint, Anatole France likened him to the gigantic and unswerving figure of Saint Christopher, painfully leaning upon an uprooted oak, and stoutly bearing French literature from the romantic to the naturalistic bank of the stream. The quarrel between his two selves—or, perhaps more precisely, the adaptation of temperament to discipline—fitted him uniquely for that mission. His youth, as he recalled it, seemed like some flamboyant cathedral, interposing its stained-glass windows between him and the world. The fact that his native habitat had been a hospital, in all actuality, sanctioned his later efforts to attain a clinical view. This did not entail a rejection of poetry, since he maintained that disillusion was a hundred times more poetic than illusion. The best way of detaching the one from the other was that which he had learned from our classic source; and to it, to *Don Quixote*, he attributed his artistic origins. To it he returned again and again, smitten with its Spanish malady, savoring its gay melancholy, praising its "perpetual fusion of illusion and reality." The generous streak of quixotry in his own nature did not go unremarked by such friends as Alphonse Daudet. Critics have not been remiss in underlining the close analogy between his masterwork and that of Cervantes. Surveying the state of the novel in 1876, an article by Emile Montégut made Flaubert blush by commenting: "Just as Cervantes dealt the death-blow to the chivalric mania with the very weapons of chivalry, so with the very devices of the romantic school Gustave Flaubert has demolished the false ideal that it brought into the world." The doughty deed would not have been committed, in either of these cases, if the time had not conjoined with the talent. Shortly before 1843, in reviewing a play by Scribe, the prophetic Soren Kierkegaard had paused for a footnote to wonder: "It is remarkable that the whole of European literature lacks a feminine counterpart to *Don Quixote*. May not the time for this be coming, may not the continent of sentimentality yet be discovered?"

Heroines were certainly not lacking, and their scope had somewhat widened since the eighteenth century. Marriage was not so much their happy ending as it was the precondition of their unhappiness and an incentive to their emancipation. Delphine or Corinne, the *femme fatale* of Madame de Staël, was presented as the feminine counterpart—and, consequently, the moral superior—to the *homme fatal* of Byron and Chateaubriand. The trousers, the cigars, and the masculine pseudonym of George Sand were the badges of an upsurging feminism, which met with its travesty in the transvestism of Théophile Gautier's *Mademoiselle de Maupin*. Emerging from the domestic incompatibilities of her *Indiana*, George Sand lived through the adventurous passions of her subsequent protagonists, stopping just short of *Lélia's* unhappy denouement. Her wholehearted involvement in her heroine fostered a special empathy with her feminine readers. Transported from their everyday lives to her romanticized sphere, they could view themselves in the role of *la femme incomprise*, the unappreciated wife, the misunderstood woman. That vogue had its *cause célèbre* in 1840, when the pampered and well-connected Madame Lafarge was tried and found guilty of poisoning her vulgar provincial husband. Her defense and her memoirs, clearly nourished by sentimental fiction, gained devout support among the public, and were read by Flaubert on the advice of Louise Colet. They moved such moralists as Alfred Nettement to suggest that the veritable poison must have been an immoral novel. A prize-winning discourse by Menche de Loisne extended this logic by accusing Eugène Sue of fomenting the revolution of 1848. The February uprising was also described by Saint-Marc Girardin as "a scene from *Les Mystères de Paris*." The Second Empire, with its tighter controls and its philistine party-lines, made such reactions official; while Flaubert was completing *Madame Bovary*, the Academy of Moral and Political Sciences was calling for an inquiry into the demoralizing influence of the *roman-feuilleton* [serialized novel]. The incidence of adultery is not subject to computation; but crimes of passion seemed to be breaking out more and more shockingly; while the suicide rate more than tripled during the years between 1830 and 1880 in France. How much had literature done to spread the moral contagion?

Flaubert's novel, though it won no prizes, could have been construed as another inquest into this critical problem. His persistent theme, according to Paul Bourget, was the hazard of thought; the reading habit itself was his principle of social disequilibrium; and Bourget retrospectively endeavored to summon Flaubert as a witness for his own anti-intellectualism. On his side Bourget could indeed count the elder Madame Bovary, who seeks to cancel her daughter-in-law's subscription to a circulating library, denouncing the librarian as a poisoner. She is volubly seconded by the opinionated M. Homais in Flaubert's original manuscript, wherein the book trade is similarly denounced by a reactionary aristocrat. But these denunciations were retrenched, and the denouncers were never Flaubert's spokesmen. Bad novels merely reflected that narcissistic indulgence which occupied him more seriously as a target. To set forth what Kierkegaard had spied out, to invade the continent of sentimentality, to create a female Quixote—mock-romantic where Cervantes had been mock-heroic—was a man's job. Jane Austen might have done it, but not George Sand, whose *Elle et lui* was reversed when Alfred de Musset retold their romance *Lui et elle*. The act of detachment had to be incisive and virile, the gesture of a crusty bachelor interrupting the banns to point out the impediments. The first word of the title proclaims a change of status: instead of *La Princesse* or *La Religieuse*, plain *Madame* without the ennobling *de*. Housewives had rarely played title-roles before, except in the raffish tales of Paul de Kock; Balzac's *Madame Firmiani* stresses its heroine's misalliance; and *Madame Angot*, the revolutionary operetta, is about a parvenu fishwife. *Madame Bovary!* the appellative warns us that our heroine is married, and to a bourgeois—a premise not for romance, but for complications, if she happens to be romance-minded. The latent romanticist within Flaubert had been suppressed when Maxime Du Camp and Louis Bouilhet had advised him to burn the original draft of his *Tentation de Saint-Antoine*. These friends had advised him to discipline himself by taking up a modern subject, something down to earth, such middle-class stuff as Balzac had just been handling in *Les Parents pauvres*.

Bouilhet, who had studied medicine under Flaubert's father, proposed the local and recent case of another former student. In 1848 at the town of Ry, the second wife of a Dr. Delamare, after a series of adulteries and extravagances, was rumored to have poisoned herself and precipitated her husband's suicide, leaving an orphan daughter. Flaubert acknowledged this suggestion, and the years of critical midwifery that supported it, when he dedicated *Madame Bovary* to Bouilhet. To Du Camp, we are informed by the latter, Flaubert's acknowledgments were appropriately medical: "I was ridden by the cancer of lyricism, and you operated; it was just in time, but I cried out in pain." Part of the cure was their Mediterranean voyage, which left Flaubert bored with the exotic and homesick for the commonplace. From a French hotel-keeper in Cairo, a M. Bouvaret, he picked up a name for his bovine country doctor: *forum bovarium* is a cattle-market. Among his *Notes de voyage* he jotted down occasional reflection upon his future theme: "The poetry of the adulterous wife is only true to the extent that she is at liberty in the midst of fatality." To the heroine of George Sand, resisting the prose of her environment, such poetry may be subjectively true. But to the extent that she is caught in the network of objective circumstance, that free will is subjected to determining necessity, the truth about her is bound to be unpoetic; what seems beautiful must prove false. To the extent that her intimate fantasies are exposed by the light of external realities, that sense undercuts sensibility, Flaubert's treatment is like that of other realists. But where the fantasy of *Don Quixote* took on the guise of a vanishing heroism, which the heroine did not jeopardize with her presence, the feminine outlook of *Madame Bovary* is consistently belied by its masculine characters. Where romance, to Cervantes, signified knightly adventure, to Flaubert—more narrowly and intensively—it signifies passionate love. The means of exposure, which put Cervantes' realism on a solid and genial basis, was an appeal to the common sense of the bourgeoisie. That would have been, for Flaubert, almost as delusive and fantastic as romanticism itself. Hence he often seems to have taken the realistic method and turned it inside out. "Realism seems to us with *Madame Bovary* to have said its last word," commented Henry James, with a sigh of somewhat premature relief.

In sharpest contradistinction to Don Quixote, whose vagaries were intellectual, Emma Bovary's are emotional. Hence they are counterweighted by no earthbound Sancho Panza, but by the intellectually pretentious M. Homais. The comic relief that he injects into Emma's tragedy is later to be elaborated into the unrelieved comedy of *Bouvard et Pécuchet*. Because it is herself that she misconceives, where Don Quixote's misconception of actuality could be corrected by reference to his fellow

men, she remains incorrigibly tragic. This paranoiac attitude of
Emma's, this self-hallucination induced by overreading, this
"habit of conceiving ourselves otherwise than as we are," is so
epidemic that Jules de Gaultier could diagnose the weakness of
the modern mind as *Bovarysme*. The vicarious lives that film
stars lead for shop-girls, the fictive euphoria that slogans promise
and advertisements promote, the imaginary flourishes that sup-
plement and garnish daily existence for all of us, are equally
Bovaristic. If to Bovarize is simply to daydream, as everyone
does to a greater or lesser extent, the criterion is not how much
we do so, but whether our daydreams are egoistic like Emma's
or altruistic like Don Quixote's. Every epoch depends upon
some verbal medium for its conception of itself: on printed
words and private fictions, if not on public rituals and collective
myths. The trouble came when, instead of the imitation of
Christ or the veneration of Mary, readers practised the emula-
tion of Rastignac or the cult of Lélia. Yet, whatever their
models, they were romanticizing a reality which would otherwise have been formless and colorless; for when nature has established norms of conduct, art is called upon to publicize
them. "There are people who would not fall in love if they
had never heard of love," said La Rochefoucauld. Denis de
Rougemont has tried to substantiate that epigram by arguing
that the erotic motive was superimposed upon the West
through medieval romance. Paolo might never have loved
Francesca, in Dante's memorable episode, had not the book of
Galeotto acted as a go-between.

But the writer, if not the reader, cannot afford to be swept
off his feet by emotions involved in a given story. Thus Flaubert,
in his first *Education sentimentale*, describes the youthful reading of his poet, Jules:

> He reread *René* and *Werther*, those books of disgust with life;
> he reread Byron and dreamed of the solitude of his great-
> souled heroes; but too much of his admiration was based on
> personal sympathy, which has nothing in common with the
> disinterested admiration of the true artist. The last word in
> this kind of criticism, its most inane expression, is supplied
> to us every day by a number of worthy gentlemen and charming
> ladies interested in literature, who disapprove of this character
> because he is cruel, of that situation because it is equivocal and

rather smutty—discovering, in the last analysis, that in the place of such a person they would not have done the same thing, without understanding the necessary laws that preside over a work of art, or the logical deductions that follow from an idea.

It follows that Emma Bovary and her censors, though their ethics differed, shared the same esthetic approach. Jules on the other hand would learn, as did Flaubert, to differentiate a work of art from its subject-matter and the artist from his protagonist. The anecdote of Cervantes on his deathbed, identifying himself with his hero, has its much quoted Flaubertian parallel: *Madame Bovary, c'est moi*. But this equivocal statement was not so much a confession as a cautious disclaimer of certain resemblances which Madame Delamare's neighbors, without indulging in unwarranted gossip, might have suspected. Insofar as Flaubert lived the part, as any novelist enters into his fully realized characterizations, it was a *tour de force* of female impersonation. The identification was not nearly so close as it had been with Saint-Antoine or would become with Frédéric Moreau. It is true that, on summer days, he worked in the arbor where he stages trysts between Emma and Rodolphe; that the cigar-case, the seal inscribed *Amor nel cor*, and other relics actually commemorate his own affair with Louise Colet; that Louise may well have suggested aspects of Emma, and Emma's lovers and husband may have embodied aspects of Gustave. But the very first premise of the books was the suppression of his own personality, and his later pronouncements adhere with stiffening conviction to the principle of *ne pas s'écrire* [not writing about oneself]. Empathy is seasoned with antipathy whenever he writes about Emma to Louise; he repeatedly complains that the bourgeois vulgarity of his material disgusts and nauseates him. He would much prefer to write a book without a subject; or rather, he would like to abolish the transitions and obstacles between thought and expression; and he prophesies that literary convention, like the Marxian concept of the state, will some day wither away.

Flaubert had chosen the legend of *La Tentation de Saint-Antoine* in accordance with his personal predilections. Baudelaire, who preferred the more imaginative work, explained

Madame Bovary as a sort of wager. "The budding novelist found himself facing an absolutely worn-out society—worse than worn-out, brutal and greedy, fearing nothing but fiction and loving nothing but property." Deliberately choosing the drabbest setting, the pettiest characters, the most familiar plot, he undertook to create a masterpiece out of them, to turn their shapeless ugliness into formal beauty. He did not quite succeed in assimilating the psychology of his heroine, in the opinion of Baudelaire: "Madame Bovary has remained a man." Now it may be—in fact, it would be Dorothy Richardson's hypothesis—that no masculine novelist can ever quite penetrate the feminine mentality. Nevertheless, as Matthew Arnold perceived, Tolstoy's portrayal of Anna Karenina could be more warmly sympathetic than the "petrified feeling" that went into Flaubert's portraiture. Insofar as he attached his narration to his heroine, Flaubert was detaching himself from those whom she repudiated and from those who repudiated her. Thereby he ostensibly gave up, to the indignation of his critics, the moralistic prerogatives of the narrator. He replaced sentiment, so Brunetière charged, with sensation. He developed the technical device that handbooks term point of view by adapting the rhythms of his style to the movement of his character's thoughts. By limiting what has more precisely been termed the center of consciousness to the orbit of a single character—and, with Henry James, a peculiarly limited character—purists could intensify the focus of the novel still further. Nonetheless *Madame Bovary* begins, as if with a prologue, in the first person; then it switches from an anonymous classmate, of whom we learn no more than that, to Charles Bovary; through Charles's eyes we first glimpse Emma's fingernails, and gradually experience his delayed reaction; thereafter the action is mainly, though by no means exclusively, circumscribed within her range of perception. But toward the end the perspective opens up and detaches itself from Emma more and more; her pantomime interview with the tax-collector is reported as witnessed by a chorus of townswomen; and Flaubert's account of her funeral terminates with the various night-thoughts of the men who have loved her.

And there are such moments as when, having escorted his lovers into a curtained cab, Flaubert draws back a tactful distance and projects a rapid sequence of long-range shots, so that—instead of witnessing their embrace—we participate in a tour of the city of Rouen, prolonged and accelerated to a metaphorical climax. The invisible omnipresence that stage-manages these arrangements is normally expressed by *on*, initially by *nous*, but never by *je*. The author's commentary is to be inferred from his almost cinematographic manipulation of detail: the close-up of a religious statuette, for example, which falls from the moving-wagon into fragments on the road between Tostes and Yonville. Such comment is transposed to a scientific key when, after the unsuccessful operation, Emma slams the door on Charles and breaks his barometer. Henceforth the incongruous memento of his failure is the patent-leather shoe affixed to the artificial limb of his patient, the no longer club-footed stableboy. A silly cap which characterizes Charles on his first appearance, a pocket-knife which betokens his coarseness in Emma's eyes—nothing is mentioned that does not help to carry the total burden of significance. Hence every object becomes, in its way, a symbol; the novelist seeks the right thing, as well as the right word; and things are attributes which define their owners, properties which expedite the stage-business. Charles's first marriage is tellingly summed up by a bouquet of withered orange blossoms in a glass jar, while a handsome cigarcase retains the aroma of fashionable masculinity that Emma has inhaled at the ball. Such effects are governed by a rigorous process of selection, far removed from the all-inclusive collection by which Balzac accumulated background. The atmosphere, for Flaubert, is the story; the province is both his setting and his subject—the colorlessness of local color. The midland that he depicts is a bastard territory, somewhere along the borders of Normandy, Picardy, and Ile-de-France, where the speech has no accent, the landscape no character, the soil no richness. Even the cheese thereabouts is lacking in savor. Everything seems like Charles's conversation, "as flat as a sidewalk."

To render flatness flatly, however, is to risk the stalemate that confronted Pope when he tried to excoriate dullness without becoming dull. Flaubert, deploying his full stylistic resources, relieves the ennui by colorful allusion and invidious comparison. What is literally boring he renders metaphorically interesting. The river quarter of Rouen, at first sight, is "a small, ignoble Venice." The names of famous surgeons are mock-heroically sounded in connection with Charles's professional activities. Similes, ironically beautiful, frequently serve to underline ugly realities: thus the pimples on the face of his first wife had "budded like a springtime." Occasionally Flaubert seems to set thousands of miles between himself and the situation at hand, as when—with the anthropological objectivity he had shown at his niece's baptism—he notes the similarity between a statue of the Virgin in the village church and an idol from the Sandwich Islands. The gap between the heroine and her chronicler opens wide with a Shakespearean simile, linking her amorous intoxication to the butt of Malmsey in which the Duke of Clarence was drowned. Despite Flaubert's more usual closeness to his dramatis personae, he austerely dissociates himself from their subjective opinions, and italicizes certain expressions which their lack of fastidiousness has forced him to cite. He manages to approximate their points of view, while retaining the detachment of the third person and avoiding the formality of indirect discourse, through his mastery of *le style indirect libre*. Though this term seems to have no English equivalent, it denotes the kind of grammatical figuration, the modulation of tenses, the dropping of pronominal antecedents, and the resulting internalization of narrative which, thanks primarily to Flaubert, are now employed in most of our novels and short stories.

> She gave up music. Why play? Who would listen?
> What sunny days they had had! What fine afternoons, alone in the shade at the depth of the garden!
> Never before had he come across such grace of speech, such good taste in attire, such supple, dovelike poses. He admired the exaltation of her spirit and the lace of her petticoat.

Through the first two quotations we catch the lilt of Emma's internal monologue. In the third, for a sentence, the voice of Léon echoes the naïveté of her previous responses to Rodolphe, and then yields to the voice of Flaubert, with a clear-cut dissociation which makes manifest Léon's confusion. Meaningful juxtaposition is Flaubert's signature, where Balzac's was miscellaneous accretion. Where Balzac's descriptions were

like introductory stage-directions, Flaubert introduces objects
as they swim into the ken of his personages. His personages,
since they are the fluid receptacles of sense-impressions, are
much less numerous than the sharply moulded types from the
Balzacian mint. In the English novelist's sense, says Elizabeth
Bowen, Emma is not a character at all: "She consists in sentiments and sensations, in moments for their own sake." Flaubert's technique of characterization, as he formulated it to
Taine, was "not to individualize a generality, like Hugo or
Schiller, but to generalize a particularity, like Goethe or Shakespeare."

He forwarded this large intention by deciding to portray
a particular individual who also happened to be a universal type
—who, as he put it, suffered and wept in twenty French villages.
She had actually existed in the ill-fated Madame Delamare;
and, as Zola remarked, her sisters went on existing throughout
France. Even while Flaubert was writing his novel, her mis-
adventures were being enacted by the wife of his friend, the
sculptor Pradier; and some of Louise Pradier's confidences became Emma Bovary's indiscretions. Strangely enough, the
latter's fate was to be paralleled by that of the novel's first
English translator, Karl Marx's daughter, Eleanor Marx-Aveling.
American readers recognize Emma's kinship with Carol Kennicott, the capricious wife of Sinclair Lewis' country doctor in
Main Street, and are struck by recurring features of small-town
subsistence which abridge the spatial and temporal intervals
between Gopher Prairie and Yonville-l'Abbaye. Flaubert's preoccupation with his heroine's environment is emphasized by his
subtitle, *Moeurs de province*—how far a cry from the sympathetic overview that subtitles *Middlemarch, A Study of Provincial Life!* His social observation, which of course is more
precise and analytic than Balzac's, concentrates upon a much
smaller terrain and thoroughly exhausts it. His fiction starts
from, and returns to, fact; when in a newspaper he came across
the very phrase that he had put into his imaginary orator's
mouth, he congratulated himself that literature was being reduced to an exact science at last. When *Madame Bovary* appeared, it was saluted by the magazine *Réalisme* as "a literary
application of the calculus of probabilities." Though that is a

far cry from any classical doctrine of probability, it looks beyond
mere particularizing toward some meaningful pattern into
which all the particulars must fit, a result which is predictable
from the data, the logical deductions that follow from an idea.
The concrete details that Flaubert selects, we have noticed,
are always typical and often symbolic. We notice too his
tendency to multiply the specific instance into a generalization.
In his treatment of crowds, at the wedding or the exhibition,
traits which were individually observed are collectively stated.
Similarly, the plural is applied to immediate experiences which
have become habitual, as in this summary of the doctor's
routine:

> He ate omelets on farmhouse tables, poked his arm into damp
> beds, felt the warm spurts of blood-letting in his face, listened
> for death-rattles, examined basins, turned over a good deal of
> dirty linen; but every evening he found a blazing fire, a laid-out
> table, comfortable chairs, and a well-dressed wife, so charming
> and sweet-smelling that it was hard to say whence the odor
> came, or whether her skin were not perfuming her chemise.

The second half of this highly Flaubertian sentence brings
us home to Emma, balances the attractions of her day against
the revulsions of Charles's, and registers the incompatibility
of their respective ways of life. A sequence of vividly physical
manifestations, ranging through the clinical toward the sensual,
unfolds itself for us just as it did for Charles. Strain is com-
pensated by relaxation; pain and suffering give place to comfort
and well-being; but, contrasted with the grim concreteness of
his own sensations and the tangible solidity of his cases, there
is something elusive and possibly deceptive in the person of
Emma, which is vaguely hinted by her ambiguous perfume.
More commonly we see the uxorious husband, from her vantage-
point, as the thick-skinned personification of plodding mediocrity: the medical man well suited to the village of Tostes,
whose competence is strained by the town of Yonville. From
his earliest entrance into the schoolroom, he falters between
the comic and the pathetic; his solitary youth and loveless first
marriage prepare him for the ungrateful role of the cuckold; on
his visit to the chateau he seems indeed to be playing the
bourgeois gentleman. His very schoolmates have found him too

unromantic, yet his love is the most devoted that Emma finds—
as Flaubert expressly states in his work-sheets, adding: "This
must be made very clear." His own devotion to his motherless
niece is doubtless reflected in Charles's tenderness toward his
daughter, Berthe. In the final retrospect—the analogue of that
weary reunion which rounds out *L'Education sentimentale*—
Charles, over a bottle of beer with his wife's lover, Rodolphe,
forgives him and blames the whole affair on "fatality."
Rodolphe, though he has blamed fatality in his farewell letter
to Emma, was scarcely a fatalist when he took the initiative;
while Emma has enjoyed, as long as it lasted, the poetic
illusion of liberty. Now that it has yielded to necessity, and the
probable has become the inevitable, Charles is left to bear—
and it kills him—the unpoetic truth.

The issue is poised between his materialistic plane, which
is vulgar but real, and her ideal of refinement, which is illusory.
"Charles conjugal night: plans for his career. his child. Emma:
dreams of travel. the lover. villa on the shore. until dawn. . . ."
This bare notation was expanded by Flaubert into two of his
most luminous pages—pages which reveal not only the nocturnal
reveries of the doctor and his wife, her Italianate fancies and
his Norman calculations, but the conflict within Flaubert's
dual personality between lyricism and criticism—or, to use
his synonym for the latter, "anatomy." To anatomize Emma's
imagination is succinctly to recapitulate the romantic movement itself, moving from the primitive idyll of *Paul et Virginie*
through the polychromatic mysticism of Chateaubriand's *Génie
du Christianisme* toward the vicarious passions of George Sand
and Balzac. Emma's sentimental education, accompanied by the
excitations of music and perfumed by the incense of religiosity,
is traced back to the convent where she has been schooled.
From the drab milieu she has known as a farmer's daughter,
her extracurricular reading conjures up the allurements of
escape: steeds and guitars, balconies and fountains, medieval
and Oriental vistas. Dreaming between the lines, she loses her
identity in the heroines of the novels she peruses, the mistresses
to whom verses are inscribed, the models in the fashion
magazines. The ball at the Château de Vaubyessard lends a
touch of reality to her fictitious world, which Flaubert likened—

in a discarded metaphor—to "a drop of wine in a glass of water." When she discovers a kindred soul in the young law-clerk Léon, the only person in the community who seems comparably sensitive to boredom and yearning and the arts, their friendship is "a continual traffic in books and romances." And when a neighboring landowner, the sportsman-philanderer Rodolphe, assists her to fulfill her sexual desires, fantasy and actuality seem to merge in the realization: "I have a lover!"

But adultery ends by reasserting "the platitudes of mar-riage," and neither condition teaches Emma the meaning of "the words that looked so fine in books: 'felicity,' 'passion,' and 'intoxication.'" Here, more explicit than in *Don Quixote* itself, language is of the essence; the basic misunderstanding, since it is verbal, is regulated by the flow and ebb of Flaubert's prose; and his rhetoric is constantly expanding into purple passages which are trenchantly deflated by his irony. The en-suing style, he feared, might read like "Balzac chateaubrianisé." Yet if that compound means eloquent banality rather than banal eloquence, it is not too inept a summation of what Flaubert attempted and achieved; and those literary auspices are not inappropriate for the incongruity between Emma's high-flown sentiments and Charles's pedestrian bumblings. If we ever forgot that the book was about an ill-matched pair, we should be reminded by the way that sentences double back upon themselves and episodes are paired off against one another. The two turning-points of the first part, the fourth and eighth chapters, frame a significant contrast between the peasantry and the aristocracy. The garish colors of the rustic wedding, the raw haircuts of the farmers, the lengthened com-munion-dresses of the girls, the boisterous jokes and substantial viands in the manner of Brueghel, are pointedly offset by the grand entertainment at the chateau, where the stately dancers display "the complexion of wealth, that fair complexion which is enhanced by the pallor of porcelain, the shimmer of satin, the veneer of fine furniture." In the second part a similar pair-ing occurs, which even more fatally brings out the variance be-tween Charles and Emma: the operation versus the opera. On the one hand his surgical incompetence, the gangrenescent cripple, and the amputated foot are portents of Emma's relapse. On the other the romantic libretto from Scott, *Lucia di Lammermoor,* the swaggering tenor Lagardy as Edgar, and the coruscating spectacle would corrupt purer souls than hers; we may recall Natasha in *War and Peace.* Overwhelmed by "Edgar Lagardy," Emma becomes, in effect, Lucia Bovary.

The two antithetical strains are juxtaposed in the central chapters of the book, where the agricultural exhibition takes place in the public square while Rodolphe flirts with Emma in the privacy of the deserted neo-Greek town hall. His amorous pleas are counterpointed by the bureaucratic platitudes of the political orators outside; a prize for the highest quality of manure is awarded at the delicate moment when he grasps her hand; the bifurcation is so thoroughgoing that the National Guard and the fire brigade refuse to march together; and the series of anticlimaxes culminates when nightfall brings a fizzle of dampened fireworks. Now Flaubert built up this scene by writing out continuous speeches for both sets of characters, which he thereupon broke down and rearranged within the larger framework of the situation. By such means he caught that interplay of cross-purposes which is increasingly stressed through the third and last part, above all in the cathedral and at the deathbed. He told Louise Colet that the method of *Madame Bovary* would be biographical rather than dramatic, yet biography seems to branch out into drama at all the crucial stages of Emma's career; and these, in turn, furnish the novel with its six or eight major scenes—several of which are overtly theatrical or, at any rate, ceremonial. Their relation to the rest of the book, and to his ambivalent purpose, may be gathered from his further remark that "dialogue should be written in the style of comedy, narrative in the style of epic." Mock-epic would probably be a more accurate classification of Flaubert's tone, as differentiated from the various inflections he reproduces, and softened by lyrical interludes when he is Emma. The many contrasting strands of discourse are so closely interwoven that the texture is uniformly rich, although it varies from one chapter to the next. Each of them advances the narrative a single step, scores a new point and captures another mood, much as a well-turned short story does in the hands of Flaubert's innumerable emulators.

The chapter, as Flaubert utilizes it, is in itself a distinctive literary genre. Its opening is ordinarily a straightforward designation of time or place. Its conclusion habitually imposes some striking effect: a pertinent image, an epigrammatic twist, a rhetorical question, a poignant afterthought. "She had loved him after all." The succession of episodes, like the articulation of a rosary, shapes the continuity of the work. The three-part structure allows the novelist, with a classicism seldom encountered in novels, to give his conception a beginning, a middle, and an end: to study first the conditions of Emma's marriage, then her Platonic romance and her carnal affair, and finally the train of consequences that leads to her death. Different leading men play opposite her, so to speak, in these three successive parts: Charles in the first, Rodolphe in the second, Léon in the third. The setting broadens with her aspirations, starting from the narrowest horizon, Tostes, proceeding to the main locale, Yonville, and ultimately reaching the provincial capital, Rouen. Not that she wished to stop there. "She wanted simultaneously to die and to live in Paris," Flaubert apprises us in a characteristic zeugma, and he seems to have toyed with the notion of granting her that double-barreled wish. But he wisely decided to confine her to the province, reserving his study of the metropolis for the fortunes of Frédéric Moreau. The chronology of *Madame Bovary*, which spans the decade from 1837 to 1847, roughly corresponds with the period of *L'Education sentimentale*, stopping just short of the mid-century crisis. Each of its subdivisions, conforming to a rough but Dantesque symmetry, covers slightly more than three years. The crucial season would seem to be the autumn of 1843, when Rodolphe fails to elope with Emma and she is plunged into brain fever. Up to that stage, with manic fervor, her illusions mount; after that, with steady disillusionment, she sinks toward her last depression. The dating coincides, more or less, with Flaubert's failure to pass his examinations, and with the neurotic crisis of his personal career.

Between the autumn of 1851 and the spring of 1856 his concentrated labor was the writing of *Madame Bovary*. For those who hold—with André Gide—that the gestation of art is more interesting than the finished product, no record could be more fascinating than Flaubert's correspondence during those four years and a half. The parallel lives of the author and the heroine, daily, weekly, monthly, yearly, charge the novel with their emotional tension. Imaginative effort was reinforced by documentation when Flaubert sought the proper shading for Emma's hallucinations by immersing himself in *Keepsakes* and other feminine periodicals. By plying his brother with queries about surgery and toxicology, he filled in the peculiar symptoms his outline required: "Agony precise medical details 'on the morning of the twenty-third she had vomiting spells again. . . .'" He familiarized himself with the children of his brain by drawing a map of Yonville and keeping files on its citizens. He controlled his plot—or should we say he calculated his probabilities?—by carefully drafting and firmly reworking scenarios. The embryonic material for his novel comprised some 3600 pages of manuscript. The demiurgic function of reducing that mass to its present form might be compared to the cutting of a film; and, rather than speak of Flaubert's "composition" in the pictorial sense, we might refer, in kinetic terms, to montage. To watch him arranging his artful juxtapositions, or highlighting one detail and discarding another, is a lesson in artistic economy. To trace his revision of a single passage, sometimes through as many as twelve versions, is the hopeful stylist's *gradus ad Parnassum*. It is therefore a boon to students of literature that Flaubert's drafts and variants have been gathered and printed. But to reincorporate them into a composite text of *Madame Bovary*, interpolating what he excised, reamplifying what he condensed, and thereby undoing much of what he so purposefully did—as has been done in the so-called *Nouvelle version*—is a doubtful service to his intentions. Flaubert might have preferred Bowdlerization.

He did protest against expurgations when the novel was serially published in the *Revue de Paris*; but Du Camp and his editors had not expurgated enough to appease the prudery of the imperial police; and Flaubert, together with the publisher and the printer, was prosecuted for outraging civic and religious morality. The outrage, so the prosecution alleged, was worse than pornography; it was blasphemy. Flaubert's offense was less a concern with sex than an attempt to link sex with

religion. It mattered little that the linkage had been effected on
the naïve level of Emma's confused motivation, or that his
analysis could be corroborated, by such sympathetic clerics as
Bishop Dupanloup, from their first-hand remembrance of
country confessionals. The ruse of citing passages out of context figured heavily in the trial, and the government staked
much of its case on the passage where Emma receives extreme
unction. It was a precarious example, since by definition that
sacrament hovers ambiguously between the worlds of sense and
spirit: shift the emphasis, as Joyce does in *Finnegans Wake*,
and it becomes an apology for the flesh. Flaubert's defense, by
warily refusing to admit the ambiguity, was able to claim the
support of orthodox sanctions, along with the precedent of such
diverse French writers as Bossuet and Sainte-Beuve. It argued
that *Madame Bovary* as a whole, far from tempting its readers
to sensualism, offered them an edifying object-lesson. Considerable stress was laid *ad hominem* on the bourgeois respectability
of the Flaubert family. Won by such arguments, the judge
acquitted Flaubert and his accomplices, with a parting dis-
quisition on taste and a fatherly warning against "a realism
which would be the negation of the beautiful and the good."
Six months later, when *Les Fleurs du mal* was condemned,
Flaubert must have wondered whether he or Baudelaire was
the victim of judicial error. Meanwhile, in April 1857, when
Madame Bovary came out as a book, its intrinsic ironies were
enhanced by a preliminary dedication to Flaubert's lawyer and
an appended transcript of the court proceedings.

Great books have their proverbial fates, among which
banning and burning may not be the hardest, since these involve downright conflicts of principle. It may be harder for
the serious artist, be he Flaubert or Joyce, to emerge from the
cloud of censorship into the glare of scandalous success. The
public reception of Flaubert's first book, at all events, hardened
those equivocal attitudes which had been poured into it. To
avoid the accusation of immorality, he was pushed into the
embarrassing position of a moralist. If the novel was not
pornographic, it must be didactic—or had he stopped beating
his wife? Taine spins an amusing anecdote of an English project
to translate and circulate *Madame Bovary* as a Methodist tract,

subtitled *The Consequences of Misbehavior*. The respectable Lamartine, cited on Flaubert's behalf, declared that Emma's sins were too severely expiated. Why need Flaubert have been so much less merciful than Jesus was toward the woman taken in adultery? Partly because he was not exemplifying justice, partly because he may have been punishing himself, but mainly because her infractions of the seventh commandment were the incidental and ineffectual expression of an all-pervasive state of mind: Bovarism. Her nemesis, as Albert Thibaudet shrewdly perceived, is not a love affair but a business matter: her debt to the usurious merchant, Lheureux. When the bailiffs move in to attach the property, their inventory becomes a kind of autopsy. The household disintegrates before our eyes, as its component items are ticked off, and we think of the auction in *L'Education sentimentale*. This empty outcome, by the Flaubertian rule of opposites, is a sequel to the agricultural exhibition, where rural prosperity smugly dispenses its awards. And the lonely figure of Charles, left to brood among unpaid bills and faded love-letters, has been foreshadowed by Père Rouault after Emma's wedding, "as sad as an unfurnished house."

The vacuum her absence creates for her father and husband echoes the hollowness of her own misapplied affections. Rodolphe's gallantry, after meeting her desires halfway, proves to be no more than a cynical technique of seduction. Léon's sentimentalism is quite sincere, until she seduces him, and then it vanishes like growing pains. "Every notary bears within him the ruins of a poet." Consequently, amid the most prosaic circumstances, there will still be some spark of poetry, and in Yonville-l'Abbaye it is Emma Bovary. It is not, alas, the Princesse de Clèves; nor could that model of all the compunctions have flourished there; for her delicacy presupposes reciprocal comportment on the part of others. Emma's dreams are destined, at the touch of reality, to wither into lies. Is that a critique of her or of reality? If she suffers for her mistakes, shall we infer that those who prosper are being rewarded for their merits? If we cannot, we can hardly assume—with the novel's courtroom apologists—that it preaches a self-evident moral. If it were a play, our reactions would be clearer; we are more accustomed to facing her plight in the theater; we disapprove of

Hedda Gabler's intrigues and pity the wistful Katherina in Ostrovsky's *Storm*. Though she possesses the qualities of both those heroines, Emma is essentially a novelistic creation, set forth in all her internal complexities. Entrammelled by them, we cannot pretend to judge her, any more than we can judge ourselves. But, guided by Flaubert, perhaps we can understand her: *Madame Bovary, c'est nous*. [We are Madame Bovary.] With her we look down from the town hall upon the exposition, a sordid rustic backdrop for Rodolphe's welcome advances. Again, at her rendezvous with Léon, the lovers occupy the foreground; but this time it is the massive cathedral of Rouen that looks down upon them; and its sculptured warriors and stained-glass saints, too hastily passed by, are the mute upholders of higher standards than those which Emma and Léon are engaged in flouting. "Leave by the north portico, at any rate," the verger shouts after them, baffled by their indifference to Gothic antiquities, "and see the Resurrection, the Last Judgment, Paradise, King David, and the Condemned in Hellfire!"

The heavy judgment that Flaubert suspends, and which we too withhold, is implicit in this hurried exclamation. It affects the lovers as little as the extinct abbey affects Yonville, in whose name alone it survives. Yet oblique reference accomplishes what overt preaching would not, and those neglected works of art bear an ethical purport. The category of *moraliste*, which is so much more comprehensive with the French than with us, given its condensation of morals and manners, still applied to Flaubert *malgré lui* [in spite of himself]. Whereas he seemed immoral to those who confused him with his characters, and seems amoral to those who take at face value an aloofness which is his mask for strong emotions, he protested too much when he claimed to be impersonal. If he deserves Maupassant's adjective "impassive," it is because all passion has crystallized beneath the lucent surfaces of his prose. He is not above making sententious and aphoristic pronouncements upon the behavior of his characters: "A request for money is the most chilling and blighting of all the winds that blow against love." Nor does he shrink from stigmatizing Emma's acts as phases of "corruption" and even "prostitution." More positively he betrays his sympathy, when it seems most needed, by the adjective *pauvre*. The crippled groom is a "poor devil," and so is the Blindman; the luckless Charles is "poor boy," and the gestures of Emma's agony are made by "her poor hands." The word regains its economic overtones, and Flaubert's tone is uniquely humanitarian, when he pauses before the "poor garments" of Catherine Leroux. The hands of this aged peasant woman, in definitive contrast to Emma, are deformed with toil. On the platform "before those expansive bourgeois," personifying "half a century of servitude," her mute and ascetic presence strikes the single note of genuine dignity amid the pomposities and hypocrisies of the agricultural exhibition. Flaubert deliberately classifies her with the attendant livestock, for whose impassivity he reserves his compassion. His irony intervenes to measure her reward, twenty-five francs for a lifetime of service, against two pigs which have just gained prizes of sixty francs apiece. An earlier and crueller twist, which Flaubert finally left out, pictures her deaf apprehension lest the judges accuse her of stealing the twenty-five francs.

Here is Flaubert's response to those who criticize *Madame Bovary* for its apparent lack of positive values. The human qualities he really admired, the stoic virtues of patience, devotion, work, are not less admirable when they go unrewarded. His careful portrait of Catherine Leroux—together with many landscapes, small and subdued, of his fog-tinted Normandy— belongs with the canvases then being painted by Courbet at Ornans and Millet at Barbizon. Peasant faces, though never conspicuous, are always in the background; they watch Emma through the broken window-panes of the chateau. Animals, too, are sentient characters: her mysterious greyhound, Djali, is almost a demonic familiar, which has its opposite number in the goat Djala, the mascot of *Notre-Dame de Paris*. The people that Flaubert treats sympathetically are life's victims like the clubfooted Hippolyte, those whom Hugo would name *Les Misérables* and Dostoevsky *The Insulted and the Injured*. Surely the kindest person in the story is the druggist's errand-boy, Justin, whose dumb affection is the unwitting instrument of Emma's death, and whose illicit reading-matter is her ironic epitaph: a book entitled *Conjugal Love*. The meek do not in-

herit Flaubert's earth; the good, by definition, are the ones that
suffer; and the unhappy ending, for poor little innocent Berthe,
is grim child-labor in a textile factory. The most downtrodden
creature of all, the dog-like Blindman, is linked by a grotesque
affinity with Emma herself. Envisaging him as a "monster," a
memento mori, an incarnation of fleshly frailty, Flaubert had
originally planned to make him armless and legless rather than
visionless; and he pointedly accentuated Emma's disillusion by
the swish of the driver's whip that knocks the helpless beggar
off the coach. This is coincident with the critical stroke that
once laid Flaubert prostrate on a muddy Norman road. His
Blindman dogs his heroine's missteps to her very deathbed, with
a terrible mimicry which is not unworthy of King Lear's fool;
and there his unseasonable song, a lyric from Restif de la
Bretonne about young girls' dreams of love, finds its long
awaited echo of relevance. Emma's eyes open to a recogni-
tion scene "like a person waking from a dream," like Don
Quixote when death restores his aberrant sense of reality.

The counterpoint set up in the cathedral attains its fullest
resolution—far from the rented room at the Hôtel-de-Boulogne
—Emma's bedchamber. There priestly rites alleviate clinical
symptoms; the unction allays the poison; and, taking formal
leave of her five senses one by one, Flaubert breaks off his prolonged sequence of associations between sacred and profane
love. Insofar as orchestration is based on arrangement rather
than statement, Flaubert's can best be appreciated by comparing this episode with a remotely analogous one from the
Old Curiosity Shop, the famous sermon on the reiterated text:
"Dear, gentle, patient, noble Nell was dead." Flaubert, who
evokes what Dickens invokes and elaborates what the English-
man simplifies, dismisses his heroine more abruptly and absolutely: "She no longer existed." Thereafter Emma's death-watch
unites "in the same human weakness" Father Bournisien, with
his holy water, and M. Homais, with his bottle of chlorine.
Since religion is served by the priest as inadequately as science
is by the pharmacist, it is not surprising that neither force has
operated benignly on Emma's existence, or that the antagonists
—as Bournisien predicts—"may end by understanding one
another." Homais, the eternal quacksalver, is a would-be writer

as well as a pseudoscientist, who practises the up-to-date art of journalism and is most adept at self-advertisement. Because his shop is the source of Emma's arsenic, he is an unconscious accomplice in her suicide; and he instigates the ill-advised surgery that poisons Hippolyte's leg and blackens Charles's reputation. When his own prescription, the antiphlogistic pomade, fails to cure the Blindman's scrofula, it is typical of him to add insult to injury, persecuting his patient while continuing to pose as the benefactor of mankind. M. Homais is definitively shown up by the retarded arrival of Dr. Larivière, just as the introduction of Catherine Leroux is a standing rebuke to Emma's course of conduct. Hereupon, Flaubert, inspired by memories of his father, dedicates a strongly affirmative paragraph to the understanding physician, who pursues the compassionate calling of medicine as religiously as a medieval saint. But the doctor is no god-in-the-machine, and it is too late for an antidote. With a tear he discerns the prognosis at once and with a farewell pun he diagnoses the complaint of Homais. His difficulty is not *le sang* but *le sens*—neither anemia nor hypertension, nor indeed that lack of sense from which poor Emma suffered, but insensibility, the defect of her quality.

What is worse, the disease is contagious. With the rare exception of the stranger Larivière, and the dubious hope of agreement between the cleric and the anticlerical, nobody in Yonville seems to understand anybody else. And though collective misunderstanding is comic, failure to be understood is a personal tragedy. Though Emma, misunderstood by her husband and lovers and neighbors, misunderstands them and herself as well, at least she harbors a feeling of something missed; whereas the distinguishing mark of Homais is the bland assurance that he never misses anything. His Voltairean incantations, his hymns to progress, his faith in railroads and rubber, his fads and statistics, his optimism—a hundred years later—may seem as far-fetched as Emma's delusions of grandeur. His clichés, embedded like fossils in his newspaper articles, Flaubert was momentarily tempted to say, "would enable some future Cuvier of the moral sciences to reconstruct clearly all the ineptitude of the nineteenth-century middle class, if that race were not indestructible." Of that hardy breed M. Homais survives as our prime specimen. Neither a creation nor a discovery, he represents the fine flower of the species that pervaded the *Comédie humaine,* the ripe perfection of the philosophy whose accredited spokesman was M. Prudhomme. This was enthusiastically attested when Prudhomme's creator and actor, Henry Monnier, sought permission to dramatize and enact Homais. The latter is more successful in attaining their common ambition, the decoration of the Legion of Honor; while his predecessor, M. Prudhomme, must content himself, when the curtain falls, with "a decorated son-in-law." The curtain-line of their spiritual relative, that famous father-in-law, M. Poirier, is his resolve to be "peer of France in 'forty-eight," an aspiration which has meanwhile been thwarted by the revolution of that date. But the unabashed Homais goes from strength to strength; the Empire will shower its accolades upon him and his brethren; and the dazzling glimpse of him in his hydroelectric undervest is a virtual apotheosis.

When he equipped his personage with a motto, "Il faut marcher avec son siècle!" [One must keep in step with the century!], Flaubert may have remembered his newly decorated friend, Maxime Du Camp, whose *Chants modernes* were prefaced by a Whitmanesque declaration: "Tout marche, tout grandit, tout s'augmente autour de nous. . . ." [Everything is advancing, growing, increasing about us.] Those reverberations stridently blended with the journalistic watchword of Saint-Marc Girardin, "Il faut marcher, marcher toujours. . . ." [We must go forward, always forward.] Any endeavor which aims to keep in step with one's century, as Flaubert realized better than most of his contemporaries, is bound to be outdistanced in the long run. He took the province for his ground because it was an available microcosm, because it exaggerated the ordinary, because its dearth of color sharpened its outlines; but he did not assume that provinciality was confined to the hinterland or, for that matter, to any territory. M. Homais is historically, rather than geographically, provincial. The habit of equating one's age with the apogee of civilization, one's town with the hub of the universe, one's horizons with the limits of human awareness, is paradoxically widespread: it is just what Russian novelists were attacking as *poshlost,* or self-satisfied mediocrity.

It is what stands between Emma Bovary and the all-too-easily-satisfied citizens of Yonville. Her capacity for dissatisfaction, had she been a man and a genius, might have led to Rimbaldian adventures or Baudelairean visions: "Anywhere out of the world." As things stand, her retribution is a triumph for the community, a vindication of the bourgeoisie. Flaubert, who does not always conceal his tenderness toward those who suffer, not infrequently reveals his bitterness toward those whose kingdom is of this world. We cannot sympathize with the prosperous Homais as we could with Balzac's bankrupt César Birotteau; and, unlike his prototypes on the comic stage, Flaubert's druggist is not just a harmless busybody, a well-meaning figure of fun; he is the formidable embodiment of a deeply satirical perception which was adumbrated in Le Garçon and eventuates in *Bouvard et Pécuchet*. His Bovarism would be more illusive than Emma's if the modern epoch did not conspire to support his bumptious ideology and to repay his flatteries with its honors. His *boutonnière*, like the one conferred on Tolstoy's Russian guardsman, symbolizes more than Napoleon intended—and less. For the symbol is an empty ornament, the badge of society's approval is meaningless, when it goes unsupported by reality.

What, then, is real? Not the mean guerdon awarded to Catherine Leroux, but the lifelong service that earned it so many times over. And what is realism? Not the pathology of Emma's case, but the diagnostic insight of Larivière. Charles Bovary, for all his shortcomings, remains the great doctor's disciple, and retains the peasant virtues of his own patients; he is led astray by other motives than his own, by sentimentalism through Emma and pretentiousness through Homais. As the thrice-injured party, conjugally betrayed, professionally humiliated, financially ruined, Dr. Bovary is the neglected protagonist. If Emma is a victim of the situation, he is her victim, and her revenge against the situation is to undermine his way of life. The depths of his ignominy can be gauged by the idealized achievements of Dr. Benassis in Balzac's *Médecin de campagne*. Flaubert's ideal, though it is more dishonored than observed, fortifies him against those negative values which triumph in his book, and rises to an unwonted pitch of affirmation with the character-sketch of Dr. Larivière: his disinterested skill, his paternal majesty, his kindness to the poor, his scorn for all decorations, his ability to see through falsehood. His most revealing epithet is *hospitalier*, since it connotes not only hospitality but Flaubert's birthplace, his father's hospital at Rouen, and also the stained-glass figure of Saint Julian the Hospitaller, whom the verger of the cathedral pointed out in an earlier draft, and who would later be Flaubert's knightly hero. The hospital and the cathedral: such, in retrospect, are the substance and the form of *Madame Bovary*. The attitude that embraces the distance between them, that comprehends both the painful actualities and the grandiose aspirations, and that can therefore make each paragraph comment dynamically upon itself, is Flaubertian irony. Irony dominates life, so Flaubert asserted by precept and example. So it does, particularly for those who are occupied with art as well as life, and unflinchingly face the problems of their interrelationship. Hence the irony of ironies: a novel which is at once cautionary and exemplary, a warning against other novels and a model for other novelists, the classic demonstration of what literature gives and what literature takes.

9 · Madame Bovary

INTRODUCTION

Close analyses of the text of Madame Bovary have produced many fruitful results. The present selection is an attempt to go beyond the general statement that Flaubert counsels objectivity and impassivity of presentation; it indicates instead in detail how he carries this out and what its effect is upon the reader. Like all such investigations of a single passage, it does risk being less than entirely typical; and it is not by any means easy to find another section of only a few lines which so fully embodies Flaubert's method. But the various elements here brought out for clear inspection do recur separately throughout the novel, and the reader will enjoy seeking them out for himself.

[In the lines preceding the present selection, Auerbach notes that "In Flaubert realism becomes impartial, impersonal, and objective." He then refers to an earlier study of his, which he will here abridge. It concerned a paragraph from Part I, Chapter 9, of *Madame Bovary*, which he then quotes.]

Mais c'était surtout aux heures des repas qu'elle n'en pouvait plus, dans cette petite salle au rez-de-chaussée, avec le poêle qui fumait, la porte qui criait, les murs qui suintaient, les pavés humides; toute l'amertume de l'existence lui semblait servie sur son assiette, et, à la fumée du bouilli, il montait du

Reprinted from *Mimesis* by E. Auerbach, translated by W. R. Trask, by permission of Princeton University Press. Copyright © 1953, by Princeton University Press. First published in Berne, Switzerland, 1946, by A. Francke Ltd. Co.

fond de son âme comme d'autres bouffées d'affadissement.
Charles était long à manger; elle grignotait quelque noisettes,
ou bien, appuyée du coude, s'amusait, avec la pointe de son
couteau, à faire des raies sur la toile cirée.

[But it was above all at mealtimes that she could bear it no
longer, in that little room on the ground floor, with the smok-
ing stove, the creaking door, the oozing walls, the damp floor
tiles; all the bitterness of life seemed to be served to her on
her plate, and, with the steam from the boiled beef, there
rose from the depths of her soul other exhalations as it were of
disgust. Charles was a slow eater; she would nibble a few
hazelnuts, or else, leaning on her elbow, would amuse herself
making marks on the oilcloth with the point of her table
knife.]

The paragraph forms the climax of a presentation whose
subject is Emma Bovary's dissatisfaction with her life in Tostes.
She has long hoped for a sudden event which would give a new
turn to it—to her life without elegance, adventure, and love,
in the depths of the provinces, beside a mediocre and boring
husband; she has even made preparations for such an event,
has lavished care on herself and her house, as if to earn that
turn of fate, to be worthy of it; when it does not come, she is
seized with unrest and despair. All this Flaubert describes in
several pictures which portray Emma's world as it now appears
to her; its cheerlessness, unvaryingness, grayness, staleness, air-
lessness, and inescapability now first become clearly apparent
to her when she has no more hope of fleeing from it. Our
paragraph is the climax of the portrayal of her despair. After
it we are told how she lets everything in the house go, neglects
herself, and begins to fall ill, so that her husband decides to
leave Tostes, thinking that the climate does not agree with her.

The paragraph itself presents a picture—man and wife
together at mealtime. But the picture is not presented in and
for itself; it is subordinated to the dominant subject, Emma's
despair. Hence it is not put before the reader directly: here
the two sit at table—there the reader stands watching them.
Instead, the reader first sees Emma, who has been much in
evidence in the preceding pages, and he sees the picture first
through her; directly, he sees only Emma's inner state; he sees
what goes on at the meal indirectly, from within her state, in

the light of her perception. The first words of the paragraph, *Mais c'était surtout aux heures des repas qu'elle n'en pouvait plus* . . . state the theme, and all that follows is but a development of it. Not only are the phrases dependent upon *dans* and *avec*, which define the physical scene, a commentary on *elle n'en pouvait plus* in their piling up of the individual elements of discomfort, but the following clause too, which tells of the distaste aroused in her by the food, accords with the principal purpose both in sense and rhythm. When we read further, *Charles était long à manger*, this, though grammatically a new sentence and rhythmically a new movement, is still only a resumption, a variation, of the principal theme; not until we come to the contrast between his leisurely eating and her disgust and to the nervous gestures of her despair, which are described immediately afterward, does the sentence acquire its true significance. The husband, unconcernedly eating, becomes ludicrous and almost ghastly; when Emma looks at him and sees him sitting there eating, he becomes the actual cause of the *elle n'en pouvait plus*; because everything else that arouses her desperation—the gloomy room, the commonplace food, the lack of a tablecloth, the hopelessness of it all—appears to her, and through her to the reader also, as something that is connected with him, that emanates from him, and that would be entirely different if he were different from what he is.

The situation, then, is not presented simply as a picture, but we are first given Emma and then the situation through her. It is not, however, a matter—as it is in many first-person novels and other later works of a similar type—of a simple representation of the content of Emma's consciousness, of *what* she feels *as* she feels it. Though the light which illuminates the picture proceeds from her, she is yet herself part of the picture, she is situated within it. . . . Here it is not Emma who speaks, but the writer. *Le poêle qui fumait, la porte que criait, les murs qui suintaient, les pavés humides*—all this, of course, Emma sees and feels, but she would not be able to sum it all up in this way. *Toute l'amertume de l'existence lui semblait servie sur son assiette*—she doubtless has such a feeling; but if she wanted to express it, it would not come out like that; she has neither the intelligence nor the cold candor of self-accounting necessary

for such a formulation. To be sure, there is nothing of Flaubert's life in these words, but only Emma's; Flaubert does
nothing but bestow the power of mature expression upon the
material which she affords, in its complete subjectivity. If
Emma could do this herself, she would no longer be what she
is, she would have outgrown herself and thereby saved herself.
So she does not simply see, but is herself seen as one seeing,
and is thus judged, simply through a plain description of her
subjective life, out of her own feelings. Reading in a later passage (Part 2, Chapter 12); *jamais Charles ne lui paraissait aussi
désagréable, avoir les doigts aussi carrés, l'esprit aussi lourd, les
façons si communes* . . . [never had Charles seemed to her so
disagreeable, his fingers so stubby, his mind so heavy, his
manners so common], the reader perhaps thinks for a moment
that this strange series is an emotional piling up of the causes
that time and again bring Emma's aversion to her husband
to the boiling point, and that she herself is, as it were, inwardly
speaking these words; that this, then is an example of *erlebte
Rede*. But this would be a mistake. We have here, to be sure,
a number of paradigmatic causes of Emma's aversion, but they
are put together deliberately by the writer, not emotionally by
Emma. For Emma feels much more, and much more confusedly; she sees other things than these—in his body, his
manners, his dress; memories mix in, meanwhile she perhaps
hears him speak, perhaps feels his hand, his breath, sees him
walk about, good-hearted, limited, unappetizing, and unaware;
she has countless confused impressions. The only thing that is
clearly defined is the result of all this, her aversion to him,
which she must hide. Flaubert transfers the clearness to the
impressions; he selects three, apparently quite at random, but
which are paradigmatically taken from Bovary's physique, his
mentality, and his behavior; and he arranges them as if they
were three shocks which Emma felt one after the other. This
is not at all a naturalistic representation of consciousness. Natural shocks occur quite differently. The ordering hand of the
writer is present here, deliberately summing up the confusion
of the psychological situation in the direction toward which it
tends of itself—the direction of "aversion to Charles Bovary."
This ordering of the psychological situation does not, to be

sure, derive its standards from without, but from the material of the situation itself. It is the type of ordering which must be employed if the situation itself is to be translated into language without admixture.

In a comparison of this type of presentation with those of Stendhal and Balzac, it is to be observed by way of introduction that here too the two distinguishing characteristics of modern realism are to be found; here too real everyday occurrences in a low social stratum, the provincial petty bourgeoisie, are taken very seriously (we shall discuss the particular character of this seriousness later); here too everyday occurrences are accurately and profoundly set in a definite period of contemporary history (the period of the bourgeois monarchy)—less obviously than in Stendhal or Balzac, but unmistakably. In these two basic characteristics the three writers are at one, in contradistinction to all earlier realism; but Flaubert's attitude toward his subject is entirely different. In Stendhal and Balzac we frequently and indeed almost constantly hear what the writer thinks of his characters and events; sometimes Balzac accompanies his narrative with a running commentary—emotional or ironic or ethical or historical or economic. We also very frequently hear what the characters themselves think and feel, and often in such a manner that, in the passage concerned, the writer identifies himself with the character. Both these things are almost wholly absent from Flaubert's work. His opinion of his characters and events remains unspoken; and when the characters express themselves it is never in such a manner that the writer identifies himself with their opinion, or seeks to make the reader identify himself with it. We hear the writer speak; but he expresses no opinion and makes no comment. His role is limited to selecting the events and translating them into language; and this is done in the conviction that every event, if one is able to express it purely and completely, interprets itself and the persons involved in it far better and more completely than any opinion or judgment appended to it could do. Upon this conviction—that is, upon a profound faith in the truth of language responsibly, candidly, and carefully employed—Flaubert's artistic practice rests.

This is a very old, classic French tradition. There is already something of it in Boileau's line concerning the power of the rightly used word (on Malherbe: *D'un mot mis en sa place enseigna le pouvoir* [Taught the power of a word put in the right place]); there are similar statements in La Bruyère. Vauvenargues said: *Il n'y aurait point d'erreurs qui ne périssent d'elles-mêmes, exprimées clairement.* [There would be no errors which would not die of themselves if they were phrased clearly.] Flaubert's faith in language goes even further than Vauvenargues': he believes that the truth of the phenomenal world is also revealed in linguistic expression. Flaubert is a man who works extremely consciously and possesses a critical comprehension of art to a degree uncommon even in France; hence there occur in his letters, particularly of the years 1852–1854 during which he was writing *Madame Bovary* (*Troisième Série* in the *Nouvelle édition augmentée* of the *Correspondance*, 1927), many highly informative statements on the subject of his aim in art. They lead to a theory—mystical in the last analysis, but in practice, like all true mysticism, based upon reason, experience, and discipline—of a self-forgetful absorption in the subject of reality which transforms them (*par une chimie merveilleuse* [by a marvelous chemistry]) and permits them to develop to mature expression. In this fashion subjects completely fill the writer; he forgets himself, his heart no longer serves him save to feel the hearts of others, and when, by fanatical patience, this condition is achieved, the perfect expression, which at once entirely comprehends the momentary subject and impartially judges it, comes of itself; subjects are seen as God sees them, in their true essence. With all this there goes a view of the mixture of styles which proceeds from the same mystical-realistic insight: there are no high and low subjects; the universe is a work of art produced without any taking of sides, the realistic artist must imitate the procedures of Creation, and every subject in its essence contains, before God's eyes, both the serious and the comic, both dignity and vulgarity; if it is right and surely reproduced, the level of style which is proper to it will be rightly and surely found; there is no need either for a general theory of levels, in which subjects are arranged according to their dignity, or for any analyses by the writer commenting upon the subject, after its presentation with a view to better comprehension and more accurate classification; all this must result from the presentation of the subject itself. It is illuminating to note the contrast between such a view and the grandiloquent and ostentatious parading of the writer's own feelings, and of the standards derived from them, of the type inaugurated by Rousseau and continued after him; a comparative interpretation of Flaubert's *Notre coeur ne doit être bon qu'à sentir celui des autres* [Our heart should be used only to feel that of others], and Rousseau's statement at the beginning of the *Confessions, Je sens mon coeur, et je connais les hommes* [I can feel my own heart, and I know men], could effectually represent the change in attitude which had taken place. But it also becomes clear from Flaubert's letters how laboriously and with what tensity of application he had attained to his convictions. Great subjects, and the free, irresponsible rule of the creative imagination, still have a great attraction for him; from this point of view he sees Shakespeare, Cervantes, and even Hugo wholly through the eyes of a romanticist, and he sometimes curses his own narrow petty-bourgeois subject which constrains him to tiresome stylistic meticulousness (*dire à la fois simplement and proprement des choses vulgaires*) [to say vulgar things both simply and properly]; this sometimes goes so far that he says things which contradict his basic views: . . . *et ce qu'il y a de désolant, c'est de penser que, même réussi dans la perfection, cela* [Madame Bovary] *ne peut être que passable et ne sera jamais beau, à cause du fond même* [and what is so very sad is to realize that, even if I succeed perfectly, it (*Madame Bovary*) can at best be only passable and will never be beautiful, because of the basic subject matter]. Withal, like so many important nineteenth-century artists, he hates his period; he sees its problems and the coming crises with great clarity; he sees the inner anarchy, the *manque de base théologique* [lack of a theological base], the beginning menace of the mob, the lazy eclectic Historism, the domination of phrases, but he sees no solution and no issue; his fanatical mysticism of art is almost like a substitute religion, to which he clings convulsively, and his candor very often becomes sullen, petty, choleric, and neurotic. But this sometimes perturbs his impartiality and that love of his subjects which is comparable to the Creator's love.

The paragraph which we have analyzed, however, is untouched by such deficiencies and weaknesses in his nature; it permits us to observe the working of his artistic purpose in its purity.

The scene shows man and wife at table, the most everyday situation imaginable. Before Flaubert, it would have been conceivable as literature only as part of a comic tale, an idyll, or a satire. Here it is a picture of discomfort, and not a momentary and passing one, but a chronic discomfort, which completely rules an entire life, Emma Bovary's. To be sure, various things come later, among them love episodes; but no one could see the scene at table as part of the exposition for a love episode, just as no one would call *Madame Bovary* a love story in general. The novel is the representation of an entire human existence which has no issue; and our passage is a part of it, which, however, contains the whole. Nothing particular happens in the scene, nothing particular has happened just before it. It is a random moment from the regularly recurring hours at which the husband and wife eat together. They are not quarreling, there is no sort of tangible conflict. Emma is in complete despair, but her despair is not occasioned by any definite catastrophe; there is nothing purely concrete which she has lost or for which she has wished. Certainly she has many wishes, but they are entirely vague—elegance, love, a varied life; there must always have been such unconcrete despair, but no one ever thought of taking it seriously in literary works before; such formless tragedy, if it may be called tragedy, which is set in motion by the general situation itself, was first made conceivable as literature by romanticism; probably Flaubert was the first to have represented it in people of slight intellectual culture and fairly low social station; certainly he is the first who directly captures the chronic character of this psychological situation. Nothing happens, but that nothing has become a heavy, oppressive, threatening something. How he accomplishes this we have already seen; he organizes into compact and unequivocal discourse the confused impressions of discomfort which arise in Emma at sight of the room, the meal, her husband. Elsewhere too he seldom narrates events which carry the action quickly forward; in a series of pure pictures—pictures transforming the nothingness of listless and uniform days into an

oppressive condition of repugnance, boredom, false hopes, para-
lyzing disappointments, and piteous fears—a gray and random
human destiny moves toward its end.

The interpretation of the situation is contained in its description. The two are sitting at table together; the husband divines
nothing of his wife's inner state; they have so little communion
that things never even come to a quarrel, an argument, an open
conflict. Each of them is so immersed in his own world—she in
despair and vague wish-dreams, he in his stupid philistine self-
complacency—that they are both entirely alone; they have nothing in common, and yet they have nothing of their own, for
the sake of which it would be worthwhile to be lonely. For,
privately, each of them has a silly, false world, which cannot
be reconciled with the reality of his situation, and so they both
miss the possibilities life offers them. What is true of these two,
applies to almost all the other characters in the novel; each of
the many mediocre people who act in it has his own world of
mediocre and silly stupidity, a world of illusions, habits, instincts, and slogans; each is alone, none can understand another, or help another to insight, there is no common world of
men, because it could only come into existence if many should
find their way to their own proper reality, the reality which is
given to the individual—which then would be also the true
common reality. Though men come together for business and
pleasure, their coming together has no note of united activity;
it becomes one-sided, ridiculous, painful, and it is charged with
misunderstanding, vanity, futility, falsehood, and stupid hatred.
But what the world would really be, the world of the "intelligent," Flaubert never tells us; in his book the world consists of
pure stupidity, which completely misses true reality, so that the
latter should properly not be discoverable in it at all; yet it is
there; it is in the writer's language, which unmasks the stupidity
by pure statement; language, then, has criteria for stupidity
and thus also has a part in that reality of the "intelligent" which
otherwise never appears in the book.

Emma Bovary, too, the principal personage of the novel, is
completely submerged in that false reality, in *la bêtise humaine*,
as is the "hero" of Flaubert's other realistic novel, Frédéric
Moreau in the *Education sentimentale*. How does Flaubert's

manner of representing such personages fit into the traditional categories "tragic" and "comic"? Certainly Emma's existence is apprehended to its depths, certainly the earlier intermediate categories, such as the "sentimental" or the "satiric" or the "didactic," are inapplicable, and very often the reader is moved by her fate in a way that appears very like tragic pity. But a real tragic heroine she is not. The way in which language here lays bare the silliness, immaturity and disorder of her life, the very wretchedness of that life, in which she remains immersed (*toute l'amertume de l'existence lui semblait servie sur son assiette*), excludes the idea of true tragedy, and the author and the reader can never feel as at one with her as must be the case with the tragic hero; she is always being tried, judged, and, together with the entire world in which she is caught, condemned. But neither is she comic; surely not; for that, she is understood far too deeply from within her fateful entanglement—though Flaubert never practices any "psychological understanding" but simply lets the state of the facts speak for itself. He has found an attitude toward the reality of contemporary life which is entirely different from earlier attitudes and stylistic levels, including—and especially—Balzac's and Stendhal's. It could be called, quite simply, "objective seriousness." This sounds strange as a designation of the style of a literary work. Objective seriousness, which seeks to penetrate to the depths of the passions and entanglements of a human life, but without itself becoming moved, or at least without betraying that it is moved—this is an attitude which one expects from a priest, a teacher, or a psychologist rather than from an artist. But priest, teacher, and psychologist wish to accomplish something direct and practical—which is far from Flaubert's mind. He wishes, by his attitude—*pas de cris, pas de convulsion, rien que la fixité d'un regard pensif* [no cries, no convulsion, nothing but the fixity of a thoughtful look]—to force language to render the truth concerning the subjects of his observation: "style itself and in its own right being an absolute manner of viewing things" (*Correspondance*, 2, 346). Yet this leads in the end to a didactic purpose: criticism of the contemporary world; and we must not hesitate to say so, much as Flaubert may insist that he is an artist and nothing but an artist. The more one studies

Flaubert, the clearer it becomes how much insight into the problematic nature and the hollowness of nineteenth-century bourgeois culture is contained in his realistic works; and many important passages from his letters confirm this. The demonification of everyday social intercourse which is to be found in Balzac is certainly entirely lacking in Flaubert; life no longer surges and foams, it flows viscously and sluggishly. The essence of the happenings of ordinary contemporary life seemed to Flaubert to consist not in tempestuous actions and passions, not in demonic men and forces, but in the prolonged chronic state whose surface movement is mere empty bustle, while underneath it there is another movement, almost imperceptible but universal and unceasing, so that the political, economic, and social subsoil appears comparatively stable and at the same time intolerably charged with tension. Events seem to him hardly to change; but in the concretion of duration, which Flaubert is able to suggest both in the individual occurrence (as in our example) and in his total picture of the times, there appears something like a concealed threat: the period is charged with its stupid issuelessness as with an explosive.

Through his level of style, a systematic and objective seriousness, from which things themselves speak and, according to their value, classify themselves before the reader as tragic or comic, or in most cases quite unobtrusively as both, Flaubert overcame the romantic vehemence and uncertainty in the treatment of contemporary subjects; there is clearly something of the earlier positivism in his idea of art, although he sometimes speaks very derogatorily of Comte. On the basis of this objectivity, further developments became possible. . . . However, few of his successors conceived the task of representing contemporary reality with the same clarity and responsibility as he; though among them there were certainly freer, more spontaneous, and more richly endowed minds than his.

The serious treatment of everyday reality, the rise of more extensive and socially inferior human groups to the position of subject matter for problematic-existential representation, on the one hand; on the other, the embedding of random persons and events in the general course of contemporary history, the fluid historical background—these, we believe, are the foundations of modern realism, and it is natural that the broad and elastic form of the novel should increasingly impose itself for a rendering comprising so many elements. If our view is correct, throughout the nineteenth century France played the most important part in the rise and development of modern realism. In England, though the development was basically the same as in France, it came about more quietly and more gradually, without the sharp break between 1780 and 1830; it began much earlier and carried on traditional forms and viewpoints much longer, until far into the victorian period. Fielding's art (*Tom Jones* appeared in 1749) already shows a far more energetic contemporary realism of life in all its departments than do the French novels of the same period; even the fluidity of the contemporary historical background is not entirely lacking; but the whole is conceived more moralistically and sheers away from any problematic and existential seriousness; on the other hand, even in Dickens, whose work began to appear in the thirties of the nineteenth century, there is, despite the strong social feeling and suggestive density of his milieux, almost no trace of the fluidity of the political and historical background. Meanwhile Thackeray, who places the events of *Vanity Fair* (1847–1848) most concretely in contemporary history (the years before and after Waterloo), on the whole preserves the moralistic, half-satirical, half-sentimental viewpoint very much as it was handed down by the eighteenth century.

10 · Madame Bovary

INTRODUCTION

Several of the preceding selections have sought to define the excellence of Flaubert's novel or to ascertain its limits; they stem from the line of approach first used by Baudelaire. But the fundamentally hostile attitude of a Sainte-Beuve (or later of a Henry James) has not disappeared from criticism with the passing of time. Rather, the gradual enshrining of Madame Bovary as a classic has continued to elicit commentary intended to explain the real distaste which some readers feel for the characters of the novel, its tone, and the apparent attitude of its author.

The following selection shows the reactions of a contemporary English critic and popular commentator on the BBC's famous Third Program, as he seeks to elucidate his own distaste. He shares a widespread tendency among certain critics to do what their opponents are apt to call reading into a work of literature something which is not demonstrably there. The practice is too common to be dismissed with a shrug by those who do not like it, and the results deserve a fair hearing from any reader of Madame Bovary. The reader will here find identified a number of symbols, many of which, beyond a doubt, he will not have found for himself. He will find it challenging to make his own decisions as to whether in fact they are really there in the book and, if so, in what sense.

Occasionally the translations adopted by Turnell seem questionable; but I have felt it wiser to leave them, as they suggest what he believes he sees in the French passages.

Madame Bovary is a study of the Romantic outlook. Its principal theme is the Romantic longing for a happiness which the world of common experience can never satisfy, the disillusionment which springs from the clash between the inner dream and an empty, hostile universe. Emma's misfortunes are caused by her inability to adapt herself to the world of everyday life. Her hunt for a Romantic passion leads to adultery which undermines her character, involves her in a life of subterfuge and deceit, and in the dubious financial transactions which ultimately drive her to suicide.

Flaubert's intentions in writing the book were exemplary. His early work—particularly the first version of *La Tentation de Saint Antoine*—had been marred by the excesses and extravagances which are commonly associated with nineteenth-century Romanticism. His friends Louis Bouilhet and Maxime Du Camp had convinced him that he needed discipline. They persuaded him that this could be achieved by abandoning legend and writing a novel based on fact and using the society which he knew as a setting. Their advice was eminently sound. The strength of *Madame Bovary* lies largely in the fact that it is not merely a study of the Romantic outlook, but of the Romantic outlook in a realistic setting which effectively prevented it from degenerating into another extravaganza in the manner of *René* or from being no more than a superior version of *Novembre*. The setting was not only a discipline; it made the book into a novel. For Emma's disillusionment does not spring merely from her desire for an impossible happiness. It springs from the conflict between impulses and emotions which are often sound and the pervading middle-class *bêtise* which corrodes them.

The Romantic malady has become a permanent part of our consciousness. Emma has her counterparts to-day among the millions who crowd hungrily to the cinema to escape from a drab existence by battening on the impossible loves and the luxury palaces of American films. Now day-dreaming is not the monopoly or the vice of any one class. Emma appeals to those "stock responses" from which not even the most sensitive readers are completely free. This leads them to assume that she is a symbol of universal validity without considering the value of the emotions which she symbolizes, and it explains their somewhat exaggerated estimate of the novel.

Madame Bovary is a remarkable book because of the subtlety with which Flaubert explored his theme, but it is not the flawless masterpiece for which it is usually taken. Its weaknesses lie partly in its execution and partly in the novelist's attitude towards his principal character. When Stendhal used the story of Berthet as his starting-point in *Le Rouge et le noir*, it became an *opportunity* for the display of his magnificent gifts and he created something which far transcended his original. Although the story of the Delamare family provided Flaubert with a discipline, it was also a *temptation*. We may suspect that he attempted a dispassionate analysis of the Romantic malady in the unconscious hope of curing himself of its ravages, but he was not really successful. It became an excuse, as we shall see, for exploiting all sorts of private manias.

Flaubert's relation to the Romantic Movement was a curious and an interesting one. Its impress is apparent on almost every page he wrote. But though it accounts for some of his most serious weaknesses, it also enabled him to make some of his most important discoveries. The French classic novel was the product of a small homogeneous society which possessed a common language. Its precision enabled the novelist to make a profound study of human nature, but he worked in a field which was necessarily restricted. He was confined in the main to the great primary emotions, to a settled round of feelings. The break-up of this society in the eighteenth century transformed the scene. Man became a problem to be explored and there were no longer any limits to the exploration, no longer any clear-cut outlines. The change did not come overnight. The process was a gradual one. Constant and Stendhal made discoveries about human nature, but they combined them with an eighteenth-century discipline. The "outsider" may be unpredictable, but we are aware of the rational being underneath. He never becomes a welter of conflicting impulses or a mere succession of moods. We do not have this feeling with their contemporaries. For the break-up of society led in the end to the break-up of man. The Romantic Movement did far more than release emotions which had been repressed by eighteenth-century decorum. It blurred the division between man and nature, dream and reality, creating a new kind of awareness which could not be expressed in classic French prose. Its writers had moments of insight, but their work reveals a progressive movement away from the psychological realism of the seventeenth and eighteenth centuries, and it tends to dissolve into a flood of unrelated words and images. Flaubert attempted, with varying success, to create a style which was capable of exact analysis and which would at the same time make use of the colour and suggestiveness discovered by the Romantics.

There is a striking passage in Part I, Chapter 7, which throws some light on Flaubert's originality:

> *Elle songeait quelquefois que c'étaient là pourtant les plus beaux jours de sa vie, la lune de miel, comme on disait. Pour en goûter la douceur, il eût fallu, sans doute, s'en aller vers ces pays à noms sonores où les lendemains de mariage ont de plus suaves paresses! Dans des chaises de poste, sous des stores de soie bleue, on monte au pas des routes escarpées, écoutant la chanson du postillon qui se répète dans la montagne avec les clochettes des chèvres et le bruit sourd de la cascade. Quand le soleil se couche, on respire au bord des golfes le parfum des citronniers; puis, le soir, sur la terrasse des villas, seuls et les doigts confondus, on regarde les étoiles en faisant des projets. Il lui semblait que certains lieux sur la terre devaient produire du bonheur, comme une plante particulière au sol et qui pousse mal toute autre part. Que ne pouvait-elle s'accouder sur le balcon des chalets suisses ou enfermer sa tristesse dans un cottage écossais, avec un mari vêtu d'un habit de velours noir à longues basques, et qui porte des bottes molles, un chapeau pointu et des manchettes!*

[She thought, at times, that these days of what people called the honeymoon, were the most beautiful that she had ever known. To savour their sweetness to the full, she should, of course, have travelled to those lands with sounding names where newly wedded bliss is spent in exquisite languor. Seated in a post-chaise behind curtains of blue silk, she should have climbed, at a foot's pace, precipitous mountain roads, listening to the postillion's song echoing from the rocks to the accompaniment of goats' bells and the muted sound of falling water. She should have breathed at sunset, on the shores of sea bays in the South, the scent of lemon trees, and at night, alone with her husband on a villa terrace, have stood hand in hand, watching the stars and planning for the future. It seemed to her that happiness must flourish better in some special places than elsewhere, as some plants grow best in certain kinds of soil. Why was it not her fate to lean upon the balcony of a Swiss chalet or hide her melancholy in some Highland cottage, with a husband dressed in a black, long-skirted velvet coat, soft leather boots, a pointed hat, and ruffles at his wrist?]

At a first reading one might pardonably suppose that this is no more than an unusually well-written description of a Romantic day-dream, but in reality it is far more than that. It is not only one of the central passages in *Madame Bovary*, it is also a landmark in the development of the European novel. The feelings are not in the nature of the undertaking very profound or very original, but in analysing the content of the Romantic *rêverie* Flaubert comes closer, perhaps, than any of his predecessors to the intimate workings of consciousness and his method clearly points the way to the inner monologue.

The passage, so far from being a straightforward description, is a deliberate piece of stylization which anticipates the method that was later used with conspicuous success by the Symbolists. For Flaubert translates feelings into *visual* images, enabling him to control expression by building each image into the final picture—in this case an imaginary voyage—and to register the transitions from one set of feelings to another with greater fidelity than had been possible before. The result seems to me to be a complete success and the passage an artistic whole. It is not, strictly speaking, a description at all, but the dramatic presentation of a "mental event." There is complete identity between image and feeling. Every image is a particle of Emma's sensibility and a strand in the final pattern. The "lune de miel" is the symbol of a vague feeling of happiness associated with Emma's childhood, but its function is complex. It is the first of a series of images—landscapes, sounds, perfumes—which lead naturally from one to the other, and it also marks the point at which Emma's contact with the actual world ends and the *rêverie* begins. Her feeling of happiness is the material out of which she constructs an adventure in an imaginary world which has the sharpness and heightened reality of an hallucination. The *noms sonores*, the *douceur* and the *suaves paresses* build up a general impression of softness and languor, a lazy voluptuous happiness. As they echo and answer one another, so too do the sounds—the song which reverberates in the mountains is answered by the tinkle of the goats' bells, mingles with the muffled sound of the cascade and finally dies away in the silence of a summer night. When we come to "Il lui semblait que certains lieux . . ." we notice a change in the tone of the passage. The note of exaltation symbolized by "lune de miel," with which it opens, changes to a wistfulness as she contemplates a *bonheur* which already belongs to the past, and this is followed by a sudden sinking as the *bonheur* is transformed into *tristesse*. The image which dominates the first part of the passage and gives the whole its particular flavour is the image of the blue silk blinds with their smooth vivid tactile suggestions. Flaubert had a particular fondness for blue and we may suspect that here it was unconsciously suggested by statues of the Madonna which he had seen in churches. The blinds are drawn and are supposed to conceal strange depths of passion at play within the coach. So we have the impression of a blue mist radiating over the whole scene and enveloping it. The most striking thing about the passage, however, is the absence of the Romantic lover. The drawn blinds do not conceal an exotic passion, but an empty coach or a coach in which there is only a lonely woman. We catch a glimpse of "les doigts confondus," but they are anonymous fingers—fingers without hands. There is, too, the "mari vêtu d'un habit de velours noir," and we see the black velvet jacket with its long tails very clearly. We also see the "chapeau pointu," but we never see the features of the man inside because there is no one there, only a tailor's dummy rigged out in extravagant garments.

The passage leaves us with a sense of absence and this is the crux of the book. The account of the *physical* absence of the lover here is completed by the account of his *psychological* absence in another place:

> *Elle se promettait continuellement, pour son prochain voyage, une félicité profonde, puis elle s'avouait ne rien sentir d'extraordinaire. Cette déception s'effaçait vite sous un espoir nouveau, et Emma revenait à lui plus enflammée, plus avide.*

Elle se déshabillait brutalement, arrachant le lacet mince de son corset, qui sifflait autour de ses hanches comme une couleuvre qui glisse. Elle allait sur la pointe de ses pieds nus regarder encore une fois si la porte était fermée, puis elle faisait d'un seul geste tomber ensemble tous ses vêtements;— et pâle, sans parler, sérieuse, elle s'abattait contre sa poitrine, avec un long frisson.

[On the eve of each of their meetings she told herself that *this* time their happiness would be unclouded, only to confess, after the event, that she felt no emotions out of the ordinary. Such recurrent disappointments were always swept away by a renewed surge of hope, and when she next saw him, she was more on fire, more exigent, than ever. She flung off her clothes with a sort of brutal violence, tearing at her thin stay-lace so that it hissed about her hips like a slithering snake. She tip-toed across the room on her bare feet to make sure that the door was really locked, and then, with a single gesture, let her things fall to the floor. Pale, speechless, solemn, she threw herself into his arms with a prolonged shudder.]

The first sentence describes with great insight the central experience of Flaubert's work. The sensation of "falling out of love" is not, perhaps, an unusual one, but Flaubert invests it with immense significance. He is the great master of negation. Some of the most impressive pages in his books describe the sudden collapse of all feeling, the void which suddenly opens at the supreme moments of life and the realization that not simply one's emotional life, but one's whole world has fallen into ruin. There is no crash, no disaster—it is this that makes it so horrifying—life simply comes to an end. When you look into it, you find that there is nothing there.

What I have called physical and psychological absence is combined in the *long frisson*. Emma's tragedy is twofold. It lies in her inability to adapt herself to the normal world and in her failure to construct a durable inner life which would compensate for its drabness. The *long frisson* reflects the tendency of the human mind to escape from the disenchantment of awakening and from the pressure of thought by deliberately submerging itself in primitive animal contacts, as Emma does here. It is a mental blackout, a voluptuous swoon in which the intelligence is completely suspended. The placing of the closing words and the punctuation—"et pâle, sans parler, sérieuse, elle s'abattait . . ."—convey the sensation of someone losing consciousness, falling into nothingness. The words are interesting for another reason. They mark the limit of Flaubert's power of analysis. His preoccupation with negative states almost certainly reflects his own inability to penetrate deeply into the content of experience. This makes the contrast between "elle s'avouait ne rien sentir d'extraordinaire" and "elle se déshabillait brutalement" of particular interest. For here the novelist intervenes in the life of his creature. It is his own starved sensibility, his own incapacity for deep feeling that he portrays in Emma. The violent actions which follow are an attempt to whip up the feelings that he is convinced he ought to experience, to obtain a vicarious satisfaction of feelings which life had refused him.

"Je me suis toujours défendu de rien mettre de moi dans mes oeuvres" [I have always sought not to put anything of myself into my works], Flaubert had said in a letter to Louise Colet, "et pourtant j'en ai mis beaucoup" [and yet I did put in a great deal].[1] Although these words were written ten years before the publication of *Madame Bovary*, they suggest that he was already conscious of a divided purpose which later disturbed the unity of the book. *Madame Bovary* purports to be a study of the Romantic outlook, but it is only partly that and partly an expression of the novelist's personal attitude which could not always be conveyed through the symbols that he chose and was sometimes in flagrant conflict with them. "Madame Bovary, c'est moi," he said on another occasion. She was, but she was also the narrator as well as the heroine of *Novembre*. The similarity of outlook between the autobiographical story written when he was twenty-one and *Madame Bovary* is striking, and it brings home forcibly how little Flaubert developed.

"In sum," wrote M. André Maurois, "Mme de La Fayette had studied love as a metaphysician, Rousseau as a moralist, Stendhal as a lover, Flaubert as a disbeliever and an iconoclast."[2] This comment draws attention to interesting possibilities. There was nothing new in Flaubert's preoccupation with sexual passion, but his approach differs sensibly from that of his predecessors. The great dramatists and novelists of the

1 *Correspondance*, I, 254.
2 *Sept visages de l'amour* (Paris, 1946), p. 219.

past had concentrated on it because it is one of the profoundest of human instincts and enabled them to make some of the most searching studies of human nature that we possess. In Flaubert it had the reverse effect, narrowing instead of widening the scope of his work. He was aware of its importance, but he was only interested in its destructive effect on personality, and he selected it because it was the most vulnerable point for his carefully planned attack on human nature. For when we look into the structure of *Madame Bovary*, we find that so far from being a detached study of sexual mania and in spite of its superficial moral orthodoxy, it is an onslaught on the whole basis of human feeling and on all spiritual and moral values.

The first fifty pages, where he keeps his personal preoccupations severely under control, are amongst the best that Flaubert ever wrote. The main characters are introduced and their significance sketched. The narrative moves swiftly and economically forward. There is no padding and none of those disastrous descriptions of external reality which contribute so much to the ruin of *L'Education sentimentale*.

The book opens with the arrival of the absurd Charles Bovary as a new boy at his school. It is a delightful piece of comedy, but Flaubert's intention was serious. The description of his peculiar hat is a characteristic example of his symbolism which enables him to prepare the setting for Emma:

> *C'était une de ces coiffures d'ordre composite, où l'on retrouve les éléments du bonnet à poil, du chapska, du chapeau rond, de la casquette de loutre et du bonnet de coton, une de ces pauvres choses, enfin, dont la laideur muette a des profondeurs d'expression comme le visage d'un imbécile. Ovoïde et renflée de baleines, elle commençait par trois boudins circulaires; puis s'alternaient, séparés par une bande rouge, des losanges de velours et de poils de lapin; venait ensuite une façon de sac qui se terminait par un polygone cartonné, couvert d'une broderie en soutache compliquée, et d'où pendait, au bout d'un long cordon trop mince, un petit croisillon de fils d'or, en manière de gland. Elle était neuve; la visière brillait.*

> [It was a nondescript sort of object, combining a number of different features—part woollen comforter, part military headdress, part pillbox, part fur bonnet, part cotton nightcap; one of those shoddy affairs which, like the face of an idiot,

seems to express a certain secretive significance. Its general shape was that of an egg, and the upper part, stiffened with whalebone, rose from a base consisting of three bulging, circular, sausage-like protuberances. Above these was a pattern of alternating lozenges of rabbit-fur and velvet separated from one another by strips of some scarlet material. Higher still was a species of sack ending in a polygon of cardboard covered with a complicated design in braid, and finished off with a long, and excessively thin, cord from which depended a small cross of gold thread in place of a tassel. The whole contraption was brand new, and had a bright, shining peak.]

I felt inclined to assume at first that no special significance should be attached to the five different kinds of military and civilian headdress mentioned in the first sentence, but I think that this view was mistaken. The busby [3] and the lancer cap are almost certainly an allusion to Charles's father. For we learn, a page or two later, that he had been a professional soldier, had had to leave the army on account of some discreditable transaction, had married the daughter of a prosperous hosier and taken to heavy drinking. The catalogue, which begins with a busby and ends with a nightcap, is clearly arranged in descending order and points to the moral and material decline of father and son. The ironical *composite* is one of the operative words. Charles's hat may contain "elements" of several different kinds of hat, but it does not belong completely to any recognizable category. It is a stupid, shapeless muddle like the wearer and the society in which he lives. The downward movement leads naturally to

une de ces pauvres choses . . . dont la laideur muette a des profondeurs d'expression comme le visage d'un imbécile.

The poor, silly, good-natured Charles becomes the incarnation of *la bêtise*, and Flaubert emphasizes the depth of his stupidity. The second sentence develops not merely the idea of shapelessness, but its nature and extent. The downward movement is succeeded by an unwinding movement whose importance will shortly become apparent. The grotesque, egg-shaped hat, with its tiers of ridiculous ornaments, suggests a society con-

3 Mr. Hopkins translates *bonnet à poil* as "woollen comforter," but it seems to me to mean "busby."

structed in layers where each layer exemplifies its particular kind of stupidity. Nor should we overlook the point of the "trois boudins circulaires." For the novel is in a sense a widening "circle." Flaubert is concerned to explore stupidity at one level —the middle-class level. The cord with the cross on the end is probably intended to suggest a clown's hat and looks forward to Charles's failure as a doctor. He thus becomes one of a "circle" which includes Bournisien and Homais. In this circle he stands, as they do, for professional incompetence. When later on, his incompetence leads to the amputation of Hippolyte's leg, the unfortunate man becomes a projection of Bovary's stupidity, and the thud of his wooden leg on the paving drives home remorselessly the idea of professional failure.

I have spoken of the unwinding movement of the second sentence. The story which "unfolds" in the novel appears to be no more than a development of something which is implicit in the image of Charles's hat. The wearer, you feel, is bound to come to grief. The stolid, unimaginative Charles is not merely a bad doctor; he stands for the ordinary man, for humdrum everyday reality, and the first phase closes with his disastrous alliance with the unbalanced over-imaginative Emma.

The rift between them begins shortly after their marriage. They are invited to stay with the Comte de Vaubyessard for the family ball. Emma finds herself for a moment in an aristocratic world, a world of luxury and romance which suddenly seems to offer everything for which she has unconsciously been longing:

> Leurs habits, mieux faits, semblaient d'un drap plus souple, et leurs cheveux, ramenés en boucles vers les tempes, lustrés par des pommades plus fines. Ils avaient le teint de la richesse, ce teint blanc que rehaussent la pâleur des porcelaines, les moires du satin, le vernis des beaux meubles, et qu'entretient dans sa santé un régime discret de nourritures exquises. Leur cou tournait à l'aise sur des cravates basses; leurs favoris longs tombaient sur des cols rabattus; il s'essuyaient les lèvres à des mouchoirs brodés d'un large chiffre, d'où sortait une odeur suave. Ceux qui commençaient à vieillir avaient l'air jeune, tandis que quelque chose de mûr s'étendait sur le visage des jeunes. Dans leurs regards indifférents flottait la quiétude des passions journellement assouvies; et, à travers leurs manières douces, perçait cette brutalité particulière que communique

*la domination de choses à demi faciles, dans lesquelles la force
s'exerce et où la vanité s'amuse, le maniement des chevaux
de race et la société des femmes perdues.*

[Their evening coats, better cut than those of their fellow
guests, seemed to be made of a more elastic cloth; their hair,
which they wore in clustered curls over their temples, and
lustrous with pomade, of a silkier texture. They had the colouring which comes of wealth, that pallor which is enhanced by
the white sheen of china, the iridescence of watered satin, the
polish of fine furniture, and is maintained by a diet of exquisite
food never indulged in to excess. Their necks moved freely
above low cravats, their long whiskers fell over turned-down
collars, and they wiped their lips with embroidered handker-
chiefs marked with large monograms and diffusing a sweet
perfume. Those on the threshold of middle age looked young,
while the more youthful of their company had an air of
maturity. Their indifferent glances told of passions dulled by
daily satisfaction, and through their polished manners showed
that peculiar aggressiveness which comes of easy conquests,
the handling of thoroughbred horses and the society of loose
women.]

I think we must admit that Flaubert achieves something
here which his predecessors had not attempted, something of
which classical French prose for all its merits was perhaps incapable. In a few lines, with a few deft touches, he *evokes* the
life of a highly civilized society; the description of the cut of a
coat, the turn of a head, is sufficient to reveal the essential gifts
of the ruling class which had made France great. The final
sentence, with its restrained irony, indicates both the strength
and the weakness of this society. It would be difficult to improve
on his description of its patrician dignity and pride: "Dans
leurs regards indifférents flottait la quiétude des passions jour-
nellement assouvies; et, à travers leurs manières douces, perçait
cette brutalité particulière. . . ." Nor would it be easy to improve upon the way in which Flaubert hints at the weaknesses
which had led to the ruin of the French nobility when he speaks
of "la domination de choses à demi faciles . . . le maniement
des chevaux de race et la société des femmes perdues." This sort
of language—this combination of evocation and critical appraisal—is one of Flaubert's most effective and important inno-
vations.

The damage done by Emma's experience to the Bovarys' married life is irreparable:

> *Son voyage à la Vaubyessard avait fait un trou dans sa vie, à la manière de ces grandes crevasses qu'un orage, en une seule nuit, creuse quelquefois dans les montagnes.*

[Her journey to la Vaubyessard had opened a yawning fissure in her life, a fissure that was like one of those great crevasses which a storm will sometimes make on a mountain-side in the course of one short night.]

It is a characteristic sentence. The fact of the rift is stated with Flaubert's customary forthrightness in the first clause; the commonplace image which follows shows how he tried to force his sensibility, giving us a feeling of a vain and unrewarding hunt for the *mot juste* which always eludes him.

The third phase opens with the Bovarys' removal to Yonville-l'Abbaye and Emma's first encounter with Léon. The confused and excited feelings released by her visit to la Vaubyessard seek an outlet. She hovers on the verge of adultery and is only saved by Léon's departure for Paris. In her perplexity her mind turns to religion and Flaubert takes the opportunity of making a critique of religion:

> *Un soir que la fenêtre était ouverte, et que, assise au bord, elle venait de regarder Lestiboudois, le bedeau, qui taillait le buis, elle entendit tout à coup sonner l'Angelus.*
>
> *On était au commencement d'avril, quand les primevères sont écloses; un vent tiède se roule sur les plates-bandes labourées, et les jardins, comme des femmes, semblent faire leur toilette pour les fêtes de l'été. . . . La vapeur du soir passait entre les peupliers sans feuilles, estompant leurs contours d'une teinte violette, plus pâle et plus transparente qu'une gaze subtile arrêtée sur leurs branchages. Au loin, des bestiaux marchaient, on n'entendait ni leurs pas ni leurs mugissements; et la cloche, sonnant toujours, continuait dans les airs sa lamentation pacifique.*
>
> *A ce tintement répété, la pensée de la jeune femme s'égarait dans ses vieux souvenirs de jeunesse et de pension. Elle se rappela les grands chandeliers, qui dépassaient sur l'autel les vases pleins de fleurs et le tabernacle à colonnettes. Elle aurait voulu, comme autrefois, être encore confondue dans la longue ligne des voiles blancs, que marquaient de noir çà et là les capuchons raides des bonnes soeurs inclinées sur leur prie-Dieu;*

*le dimanche à la messe, quand elle relevait sa tête, elle
apercevait le doux visage de la Vierge, parmi les tourbillons
bleuâtres de l'encens qui montait. Alors un attendrissement la
saisit; elle se sentit molle et tout abandonnée . . . ce fut sans
en avoir conscience qu'elle s'achemina vers l'église, disposée à
n'importe quelle dévotion, pourvu qu'elle y absorbât son âme
et que l'existence entière y disparût.*

[One evening when she was sitting by the open window
watching Lestiboudois, the sexton, trimming the box-hedge,
she suddenly heard the sound of the Angelus bell.
It was the beginning of April, when the primroses are in
bloom. A warm wind was blowing over the dug flower-beds,
and the gardens, like women, seemed to be furbishing their
finery for the gaieties of summer. . . . The mist of evening
was drifting between the leafless poplars, blurring their outline
with a violet haze, paler and more transparent than a fine gauze
hung upon their branches. Cattle were moving in the distance,
but her ear could catch neither the noise of their hooves nor
the sound of their lowing. The bell, continuously ringing,
struck upon the air with its note of peaceful lamentation.
The repeated tolling took the young woman's mind back
to the memories of childhood and of her school. She remembered the branched candlesticks which used to stand upon the
altar, overtopping the flower-filled vases and the tabernacle
with its little columns. She would have liked, as then, to be an
unnoticed unit in the long line of white veils in which, here
and there, the stiff coifs of the good sisters kneeling at their
desks, showed as accents of black. At Mass, on Sundays,
whenever she raised her head, she could see the sweet face of
the Virgin in a blue cloud of eddying incense. At such
moments she had been conscious of deep emotion, had felt
alone and immaterial. . . . It was almost without knowing
what she was doing, that she set out towards the church,
ready to enter into any act of devotion provided only that her
feelings might be wholly absorbed, and the outer world forgotten.]

It is an admirable example of Flaubert's art at its finest.
The insistent ringing of the church bell through a process of
sensuous suggestion, which bears a striking resemblance to
Proust's *mémoire involontaire*, sets the mechanism of memory
in motion. The dying away of the sounds from the external
world marks the beginning of the *rêverie*, so that the final stroke
of the bell merges into the remembered sound of the bell at the
convent. The images dovetail perfectly into one another. "Les

jardins, comme des femmes, semblent faire leur toilette pour les fêtes de l'été," suggests the flowers on the altar and the white veils of the schoolgirls on feast days. The "vapeur du soir . . . d'une teinte violette" floats into the "tourbillons bleuâtres de l'encens." There is no direct comment, but Flaubert by employing the same method that he used in the account of the ball at la Vaubyessard shows that Emma's religion is of the same quality as her dreams of Romantic love. It is largely emotional, a desire to return to her childhood and be one of a row of little girls in white veils, or to plunge into "n'importe quelle dévotion" provided that like the *long frisson* it brings oblivion, "que l'existence entière y disparût."

On her way to the church she meets the Abbé Bournisien to whom she turns for help, but he completely fails to understand her. The intention of this memorable scene is to show the inability of the Church to provide a solution. It reminds us to some extent of the Russian films with their hideous, bloated bourgeois; but while one is reading it, it is effective enough. This criticism disposes of religion and Emma is now ripe for a fall.

The fourth phase is the liaison with Rodophe. The outstanding scene, which from a technical point of view has had an immense influence, is the visit of Emma and Rodolphe to the Comices Agricoles. Flaubert was very proud of it, as he had every right to be, and compared it to a symphony. Thibaudet shrewdly suggested that it was arranged in three tiers like a mediaeval mystery. The animals and peasants were at the bottom, the platform with the distinguished visitor and the local notabilities in the middle, and the lovers at the window above. He went on to point out that the animal noises, the speeches from the platform and the conversation between the lovers were all varieties of *la bêtise* which blended in the symphony.[4] The *conseiller de préfecture*'s speech certainly alternates with the dialogue between the lovers; the platitudes about religion, duty, progress and patriotism and Rodolphe's platitudes about enduring passion and the new morality answer one another mockingly, cancel one another out, leaving the reader with the impression that love and duty are mere shams, that

---

4 *Gustave Flaubert*, p. 117.

nothing has value. The effect is intensified when the speech is followed by the distribution of prizes to deserving farmers:

Et il saisit sa main; elle ne la retira pas.
"Ensemble de bonnes cultures!" cria le président.
—"Tantot, par exemple, quand je suis venu chez vous. . . ."
"A M. Bizet, de Quincampoix."
—"Savais-je que je vous accompagnerais?"
"Soixante et dix francs!"
—"Cent fois même j'ai voulu partir, et je vous ai suivie, je suis resté."
"Fumiers."
"Comme je resterais ce soir, demain, les autres jours, toute ma vie!"
"A M. Caron, d'Argueil, une médaille d'or!"
—"Car jamais je n'ai trouvé dans la société de personne un charme aussi complet."
"A M. Bain, de Givry-Saint-Martin!"
—"Aussi, moi, j'emporterai votre souvenir."
"Pour un bélier de mérinos. . . ."
—"Mais vous m'oublierez, j'aurai passé comme une ombre."
"A M. Belot, de Notre-Dame. . . .
—"Oh! non, n'est-ce pas, je serai quelque chose dans votre pensée, dans votre vie?"
"Race porcine, prix ex aequo: à MM. Lehérissé et Cullembourg; soixante francs!"

[He pounced upon her hand. She did not withdraw it.
"We must work together for the good of farming," cried the President.
"Recently, for instance, when I came to your house. . . ."
". . . To Monsieur Bizet of Quincampoix. . . ."
"Did I know that we should be together in this place?"
". . . Seventy francs!"
"A hundred times I even strove to break from you, but ever followed, ever stayed. . . ."
". . . Manures. . . ."
"As I should so dearly love to stay this evening, to-morrow, all the days of my life!"
". . . To Monsieur Caron of Argueil, a gold medal. . . ."
"For never have I found a charm so powerful in the companionship of anybody. . . ."
". . . To Monsieur Bain of Givry-Saint-Martin. . . ."
"This memory of you will be with me always. . . ."
". . . For a merino ram. . . ."
"But you will forget me: I shall be for you as a shadow that has passed. . . ."

". . . To Monsieur Belot of Notre-Dame. . . ."
"But no! Tell me I shall count for something in your
thoughts and in your life!"
"Pig class—a prize of sixty francs, divided between
Monsieur Lehérissé and Monsieur Cullembourg. . . ."]

The opening announcement is an ironic comment on
Emma and Rodolphe, standing furtively hand in hand. For we
know that at bottom they are anything but "bonnes cultures."
When Rodolphe cries: "Savais-je que je vous accompagnerais?"
the mocking voice, which chimes in with "Soixante et dix
francs," becomes the voice of the courtesan announcing the
price of her favours or of the hard-boiled man of the world
making an offer for those favours. When Rodolphe whispers
that he stayed because he could not tear himself away, the
strident voice answers jeeringly: "Fumiers." The promise to
remain "this evening, to-morrow, all the days of my life" is
greeted derisively by: "Une médaille d'or!" "J'emporterai votre
souvenir" is answered by "Un bélier de mérinos." In the final
announcement the irony grows savage. "I shall count for something in your thoughts and in your life, shan't I?" asks
Rodolphe. The voice retorts, brutally: "Race porcine *ex aequo*—
Pigs, the pair of you." [5]

I think it will be agreed that this scene is a decidedly impressive performance, an ironical commentary not merely on
Emma's assumed modesty and Rodolphe's vows of eternal fidelity, but on the whole basis of love. It ends by transforming the
pair into a couple of pigs rolling over each other on the dung-
heap. For the words which give it its particular tone are *fumiers*
and *race porcine*. They sum up Rodolphe's views on love and
there seems little doubt that Flaubert himself shared them, or
that he used this slick, shallow adventurer as part of his general
plan for bringing it into discredit. Later in the book we read
of him:

5 The account of the Comices Agricoles is more than an attack on
sexual passion. The ceremony, which closes with the presentation of a
silver medal worth twenty-five francs to Catherine-Nicaise-Elisabeth Leroux
for fifty-four years' service on the same farm, is also an attack on the whole
life of the French agricultural community. For Flaubert shows no appreciation of agricultural life. It is reduced to the same boring monotony as everything else.

*Ce qu'il ne comprenait pas, c'était tout ce trouble dans une
chose aussi simple que l'amour.*
*Il jugea toute pudeur incommode. Il la traita sans façon. Il
en fit quelque chose de souple et de corrompu.*

[He could not see why she should make such a fuss about
anything so simple as love.
He had no use for modesty, and rode over it roughshod. He
turned her into something supple and corrupt.]

When he comes to write his *lettre de rupture,* Emma already means so little to him that he has to turn up some of her
old letters to him to provide inspiration. He comes across a
mass of letters from different women:

*En effet, ces femmes, accourant à la fois dans sa pensée,
s'y gênaient les unes les autres et s'y rapetissaient, comme sous
un même niveau d'amour qui les égalisait. . . .*
"Quel tas de blaques! . . ."
*Ce qui résumait son opinion; car les plaisirs, comme des
écoliers dans la cour d'un collège, avaient tellement piétiné
sur son coeur, que rien de vert n'y poussait, et ce qui passait
par là, plus étourdi que les enfants, n'y laissait pas même,
comme eux, son nom gravé sur la muraille.*

[All these women, crowding together in his thoughts,
got in one another's way. They seemed to shrink in size, to
assume an identity when reduced to the same level of
love. . . .
"Just a lot of nonsense!"
The phrase did, in fact, sum up what he felt, for the succession of his pleasures, like boys in a school playground, had so
trodden his heart underfoot that now not a single shoot of
green could show above the ground, and what passed over
it, more scatterbrained than children, did not, as they might
have done, leave even a name scribbled on the wall.]

The final phase of the novel opens with Léon's return and
Emma's liaison with him. The prelude is their meeting in
Rouen Cathedral which is followed by the celebrated drive in
the cab with its drawn blinds. It is interesting to recall that
when the novel was originally published in serial form in the
Revue de Paris this was one of the first scenes which the editors
insisted on cutting. It may seem strange that the people who
had apparently passed the ride with Rodolphe and the seduction
in the forest should have felt any scruples over the second

scene. I think we must assume that they sensed obscurely what to-day is plain. It is possible to argue that the symbolism is sometimes a little obvious, but on the whole it is an impressive display of literary craftsmanship with the pompous, boring guide pursuing the distracted lovers round the cathedral, the cab travelling at breakneck speed, the wretched perspiring *cocher* and the furious voice bellowing at him from inside the cab every time he slows down.

The cathedral and the cab both possess a moral significance, but there is a contrast between them. When Léon compares the cathedral mentally to "un boudoir gigantesque [qui] se disposait autour d'elle," the significance is clearly sexual and anticipates the highly Freudian moral support before she gives in. The drive "sans parti pris ni direction, au hasard" stands for a loss of moral direction which can only have one end:

> Une fois, au milieu du jour, en pleine campagne, au moment où le soleil dardait le plus fort contre les vieilles lanternes argentées, une main nue passa sous les petits rideaux de toile jaune et jeta des déchirures de papier qui se dispersèrent au vent et s'abattirent plus loin, comme des papillons blancs, sur un champ de trèfle rouge tout en fleurs.

> [Once, about midday, out in the open country, with the sun striking full on the plated lamps, a bare hand emerged from behind the little curtains of yellow canvas, and scattered some scraps of paper which eddied in the wind and settled afar off, like so many white butterflies, on a field of red flowering clover.]

I suspect that there is an ironic contrast between this drive and Emma's youthful daydream of the romantic honeymoon drive in the "pays à noms sonores." The fragments of paper belong to the *lettre de rupture* which she had intended to hand to Léon in the cathedral; but, whether consciously or unconsciously, they also suggest clothes. For the "naked" hand stretching out of the closed cab is a signal that "marriage vows" have once more been "torn up," that "virtue has succumbed." [6] The "butterflies" stand for the transitoriness of the relationship with Léon. The "red" clover is a symbol of adultery (contrasted with

6 There may be a reference to the opening of the shutters of the farmhouse at the beginning of the book which was old Rouault's "signal" to Bovary that his daughter accepted the proposal of marriage.

the "white" pieces of paper) as the "blue" blinds of the carriage
in the imaginary honeymoon were a symbol—a traditional symbol—of innocence. In a comment on the liaison with Rodolphe the novelist
remarks:

> *Alors elle se rappela les héroïnes des livres qu'elle avait lus,
> et la légion lyrique de ces femmes adultères se mit à chanter
> dans sa mémoire avec des voix de soeurs qui la charmaient.*

[Then she called to mind the heroines of the books that she
had read; the lyrical legion of those adulterous ladies sang in
her memory as sisters, enthralling her with the charm of their
voices.]

We are told of the affair with Léon:

> *Emma retrouvait dans l'adultère toutes les platitudes du
> mariage.*

[Emma found in adultery nothing but the old commonplaces of marriage.]

They are characteristic of the book. The sudden expansion
signified by *lyrique* collapses inevitably from within into *plati-
tude; mariage* and *adultère* cancel out. Marriage or adultery, it
is always the same story of frustration and disappointment.

There is another passage which sums up not only Emma's
experience, but the author's intention:

> *Les premiers mois de son mariage, ses promenades à cheval
> dans la forêt, le vicomte qui valsait, et Lagardy chantant, tout
> repassa devant ses yeux. . . . Et Léon lui parut soudain dans
> le même éloignement que les autres.*
> *"Je l'aime pourtant!" se disait-elle.*
> *N'importe! elle n'était pas heureuse, ne l'avait jamais été.*
> *D'où venait donc cette insuffisance de la vie, cette pourriture
> instantanée des choses où elle s'appuyait?*

[She saw in imagination the early months of her marriage,
her days of riding through the woods; she saw the Vicomte
waltzing and Lagardy singing . . . and suddenly, she saw
Léon too, diminished in the same perspective of time.
"But I do love him!" she said to herself.
But what good did that do? She was not happy; she never
had been happy. Why had her life been such a failure? Why
did everything on which she leaned crumble immediately to
dust?]

Fumiers, race porcine, pourriture and *corruption* reflect the novelist's own personal outlook, a mood which envelopes everything, undermining, dissolving feeling into nothingness. We read, for example, of Charles after Emma's death:

> *Il mettait du cosmétique à ses moustaches, il souscrivit comme elle des billets à ordre. Elle le corrompait par delà le tombeau.*

[He put pomade on his moustache, and followed her example in the matter of signing bearer bills. Her power to corrupt him was still active from beyond the grave.]

The last fifty pages possess the same qualities as the first fifty. They are the traditional excellences of the finest European novels. In these pages, too, Flaubert displays all his technical mastery. Emma becomes a trapped animal trying desperately to escape from her enemies. All through the novel we are conscious of the dialogue which goes on ceaselessly—sometimes in an undertone, sometimes openly—between Bournisien and Homais, between the Ecclesiastic and the Progressive, between the religious and the secularist *bêtise*. In the final pages the other characters also become symbolic figures, and we see them crowding in on Emma with hostile faces. Lheureux is the Usurer demanding, insistently, his pound of flesh; the beggar, with his hideous deformity and his ghastly song, is Death, or, possibly, as Thibaudet suggests, the Devil to whom she throws her last five-franc piece. Rodolphe and Léon are both variations of the Faithless Lover. The sense of her enemies closing in on Emma in a constantly narrowing circle gives the final chapters their dramatic force. The clandestine journeys to Rouen to see Léon when she is supposed to be having music lessons are replaced by a different sort of journey. Emma rushes to and fro between Rouen and Yonville in a frantic attempt to borrow money to keep her creditors at bay and avoid being sold up. She fails. Her main outlet has been blocked and she is confined to Yonville. She moves hither and thither at Yonville, seeks refuge with the old nurse where, by an ominous association of ideas, the sound of the spinning-wheel recalls the sound of Binet's lathe on the day she nearly committed suicide after Rodolphe's defection. She is on the point of selling herself to the local solicitor, pays a visit to the tax-gatherer. As so often happens in Flaubert, these scenes remind us of a film in which we watch the action from different angles and different heights. We go with her into Rodolphe's château and into the solicitor's breakfast-room, but we watch her visit to Binet from above and through the eyes of spiteful neighbours:

"*Viendrait-elle lui commander quelque chose?*" *dit Mme Tuvache.*

"*Mais il ne vend rien!*" *objecta sa voisine.*

Le percepteur avait l'air d'écouter, tout en écarquillant les yeux, comme s'il ne comprenait pas. Elle continuait d'une manière tendre, suppliante. Elle se rapprocha; son sein haletait, ils ne parlaient plus.

"*Est-ce qu'elle lui fait des avances?*" *dit Mme Tuvache.*

Binet était rouge jusqu'aux oreilles. Elle lui prit les mains.

"*Ah! c'est trop fort!*"

Et sans doute qu'elle lui proposait une abomination, car le percepteur . . . tout à coup, comme à la vue d'un serpent, se recula bien loin en criant:

"*Madame! y pensez-vous?*"

"*On devrait fouetter ces femmes-là!*" *dit Mme Tuvache.*

"*Où est-elle donc?*" *reprit Mme Caron.*

Car elle avait disparu durant ces mots. . . .

["Is she going to give him an order?" said Madame Tuvache.

"But his things aren't for sale!" objected her neighbour.

The Collector seemed to be listening. He was blinking his eyes as though finding it difficult to grasp what was being said. Madame Bovary talked on in a gentle, supplicating manner. She went close to him, her breast rising and falling. Neither was saying anything now.

"D'you think she's making advances to him?" said Madame Tuvache.

Binet had flushed crimson to the tips of his ears. Emma took his hands.

"That really is too much!"

She must be making some abominable suggestion, because the Collector . . . suddenly recoiled as though he had seen a snake, exclaiming:

"Madame, what can you be thinking of?"

"Women like that ought to be whipped!" said Madame Tuvache.

"Where has she gone now?" asked Madame Caron.

For during this brief exchange, Emma had disappeared. . . .]

We hear the old women's comments, but we do not hear the conversation between Emma and Binet. We simply suspect that she is trying to persuade him to lend her the tax-payers' money as she had tried to persuade Léon to "borrow" money for her from the office where he worked. Suddenly, the horrified "Madame! y pensez-vous?" reaches us. Then she disappears, to reappear in the main street. We go with her into Lheureux's shop, into Homais' store where she takes the arsenic, and into the room where she dies horribly to the sound of the beggar's song:

> Souvent la chaleur d'un beau jour
> Fait rêver fillette à l'amour. . . .

There is another important change in these closing pages. The novelist manages to forget himself and keep his eye on his principal figure. The morbid satisfaction with which he has recorded her misfortunes gives way to a pity which adds another dimension to the book. The scene in which she tries to obtain money from Rodolphe shows Flaubert at his best:

> Mais, lorsqu'on est si pauvre, on ne met pas d'argent à la crosse de son fusil! On n'achète pas une pendule avec des incrustations d'écailles!" continuait-elle en montrant l'horloge de Boulle; "ni des sifflets de vermeil pour ses fouets"—elle les touchait!—"ni des breloques pour sa montre! . . . Eh! quand ce ne serait que cela," s'écria-t-elle en prenant sur la cheminée ses boutons de manchettes, "que la moindre de ces niaiseries! on en peut faire de l'argent! . . . Oh! je n'en veux pas! garde-les."
>
> Et elle lança bien loin les deux boutons, dont la chaîne d'or se rompit en cognant contre la muraille.
>
> "Mais, moi, je t'aurais tout donné, j'aurais tout vendu, j'aurais travaillé de mes mains, j'aurais mendié sur les routes, pour un sourire, pour un regard, pour t'entendre dire: 'Merci.' "

["But a poor man like you doesn't lavish silver on the butt of a gun, or buy a clock inlaid with tortoiseshell"—she went on, pointing to a buhl timepiece—"or silver-gilt whistles for riding-crops"—she touched them as she spoke—"or trinkets for watch-chains. . . . Why, the smallest of these knick-knacks could be turned into money. . . . Not that I want them . . . you can keep the lot for all I care!"

She threw the links from her so violently that the gold chain broke against the wall.

"I would have given you everything, would have sold all I had. I would have worked with my hands, would have begged on the roads, just for a smile, a look, just to hear you say 'thank you.' "]

This is a different Emma from the unbalanced romantic who is studied throughout the greater part of the book. Her voice, freed from the confusing undertones of her creator, has a different accent. There is no blur here. The simple, direct words contrast strangely with her muddled dreams. They come straight from the heart and appeal to something far deeper in us.

We cannot help noticing that Flaubert displayed a marked reluctance to give due weight to what was valid and genuine in Emma. She was not, as Henry James alleged, a woman who was "naturally depraved." She possessed a number of solid virtues which were deliberately played down by the novelist. It was after all to her credit that she possessed too much sensibility to fit comfortably into the appalling provincial society of Yonville-l'Abbaye and it was her misfortune that she was not big enough to find a way out of the dilemma. We cannot withhold our approval from her attempts to improve her mind or from the pride that she took in her personal appearance and in the running of her house. The truth is that Flaubert sacrificed far too much to his *thèse*. These virtues express his instinctive appreciation of what was sane and well-balanced in the French middle classes. In sacrificing them to a doctrinaire pessimism, which was held intellectually instead of arising from his contemplation of his material, he destroyed the findings of his own sensibility and involved himself in a confusion of values. We may conclude, too, that it was this nihilism, this sense that nothing—neither religion, morals, nor love—has value rather than a few lurid scenes which really upset French *mères de famille* in the year 1857 and led to Flaubert's prosecution for indecency.

The critic is faced with another problem. While *Madame Bovary* is admittedly only partly successful on account of conflicting attitudes, it still has to be decided what value should be attached to Flaubert's pessimism, whether it was a mature conception of life or an immature cynicism which is masquerading as mature vision.

Thibaudet was in no doubt about the answer:

> The world described in *Madame Bovary* he said is a world
> which is falling apart. . . . But in every society when some-
> thing is destroyed, another thing takes its place. When the
> Bovarys' fortune collapses, Lheureux's rises. . . . The novel
> has two sides—the defeat of Emma and the triumph of
> Homais.[7]

The book does, indeed, end with a remarkable stroke of
irony. "Homais," we are told

> *Homais inclina vers le pouvoir. Il rendit secrètement à M. le
> préfet de grands services dans les élections. Il se vendit, enfin,
> il se prostitua. . . .*
> *Depuis la mort de Bovary, trois médecins se sont succédé à
> Yonville sans pouvoir y réussir, tant M. Homais les a tout de
> suite battus en brèche. Il fait une clientèle d'enfer; l'autorité
> le ménage et l'opinion publique le protège.*
> *Il vient de recevoir la croix d'honneur.*

[In pursuit of his ambition, he consented to bow the knee
to Authority. Unknown to anybody, he rendered the Prefect
great service at election time. In short, he sold, he prostituted
himself. . . .
Since Bovary died, there have been three doctors in Yonville.
None of them, however, has made a success of the practice,
so violently hostile has Homais shown himself to all of them.
He himself is doing extremely well. The authorities handle him
with kid gloves, and he is protected by public opinion.
He recently received a decoration.]

There is no doubt that Thibaudet correctly described
Flaubert's intentions. And if sheer technical power were sufficient, we should have to agree that *Madame Bovary* was one
of the greatest of novels. Yet somehow we remain unconvinced
by the irony as we are unconvinced by the pessimism. For
Flaubert's figures will not bear the weight of the symbolism that
he tried to attach to them. We cannot fail to notice that he
was continually tipping the scales, trying to give these sordid
provincials an importance which they were far from possessing.
What he exhibits with superb accomplishment is in fact an
immature cynicism masquerading as mature vision.

7 *Op. cit.*, pp. 120, 122.

John C. Lapp

11 · Art and Hallucination in Flaubert

INTRODUCTION

In recent years much interest has attached to matters of how an artist creates, in the particular sense of how his basic make-up and, frequently, his physiology lead him to certain perceptions not normally available to average people. In Flaubert's case, it has been pointed out, for instance, that his hearing was unusually acute, that his visual memory was extraordinary, and that his nerves were almost incredibly on edge. All of these represent capacities for experience beyond the normal and allowed Flaubert certain sensitivities which led to elements in the novel that are of major importance for the reader. Thanks to Flaubert's heightened sensitivity the reader learns to become aware for himself of experiences he would otherwise have passed by without noticing. Further, Flaubert not infrequently lent his own reactions to his characters, in particular to Emma Bovary herself.

The analysis of these abnormal physiological states or capacities in Flaubert has been carried out for some time both in France and the United States. Perhaps the most significant study in English is the following one, which examines some of the relationships between Flaubert's "nervous ailment" and his creativity, and between it and the temperaments with which he endowed his characters. When the article was published, it had not yet been established what this ailment was. Recent work in France and, independently, in this country has established the fairly definitive diagnosis that it was temporal lobe epilepsy. Further investigations in Flaubert's private papers also make clear that, in fact, the disorder never completely subsided; there were major recurrences in 1860 and during most of the last decade of Flaubert's life until his death in 1880. As the present article suggests, one of the principal works in which Flaubert utilizes his own abnormal nervous experience is Madame Bovary; but it recurs in most of his works thereafter.

Once again the reader will return to reconsider a number of passages which he has examined earlier in the course of this collection; and once again he will discover the extraordinary riches of these paragraphs, which may be approached from so many different vantage points. I have added to the original article translations of these French passages. A comparison with the translations of the same passages given earlier (and prepared by other translators) will show that I have not always felt satisfied with them. But this is only to say that no two translators ever quite agree.

On a cold evening in January 1844, Gustave Flaubert was driving with his brother along a country road near Pont-l'Évêque. Suddenly, as a farmer's cart loomed up out of the dark, he dropped the reins and slumped unconscious to the floor. For several hours afterwards he lay as if dead, and when he awoke, weak and sweating, he told of strange visions: a thousand images and the bursting of dazzling lights, "like a fireworks display." This was the first of a series of attacks, resembling in several details the lesser form of epilepsy known as *petit mal*, that were to recur with some frequency for about ten years, while he was completing the first *Education sentimentale, La. Tentation de Saint Antoine,* and *Madame Bovary.*

Although it is well known that Flaubert suffered from these convulsive seizures, no complete or detailed attempt has been made, as far as I know, to demonstrate the extent to which he exploited them and the phenomena which characterized them. René Dumesnil has declared, without elaboration, that "Flaubert utilise très nettement sa maladie nerveuse, par un

Reprinted from *French Studies*, X (1956), 322–34 (Oxford: Basil Blackwell). By permission.

phénomène d'auto-observation, et il se sert de cette observation pour créer des images." [1] [Flaubert does, clearly, use his nervous ailment by means of self-observation, and he makes use of this observation to create images.] D. L. Demorest, in the course of his work on Flaubert's imagery, refers frequently to the hallucinations and their importance, but the scope of his study precluded a detailed examination of their use.[2] It has occurred to me, although I am aware that this is dangerous ground for the literary critic,[3] that it might be of value to try to determine with some exactness just how the hallucinatory experiences affected Flaubert's art. Fortunately for our purpose, he carefully described the sensations accompanying them in several letters, in particular those he wrote to Taine when the latter was gathering data concerning the artistic imagination for *De l'intelligence*. The fact that these significant letters have only recently been published undoubtedly goes far to explain why such a study has not been undertaken before.[4]

If I had been asked, before reading these letters, which of Flaubert's works would best lend itself to a study of this kind, I would have been tempted to answer *Madame Bovary*. First of all, for its richness of imagery; it is, as Thibaudet has said, "parmi ses romans, le seul qui fournisse une moisson d'images" [5] [among his novels, the only one which furnishes a rich harvest of images]. And secondly, I feel that what Lionel Trilling has remarked of the neurotic artist in general is applicable to Flaubert and *Madame Bovary*: "the more a writer takes pains with his work and the further he removes it from the

1 René Dumesnil, *Gustave Flaubert, l'homme et l'oeuvre*, Paris, Desclée et Brouwer, 1947, pp. 450–52. There is a masterful discussion of Flaubert's illness, which Dumesnil does not believe was epilepsy, in the Appendix. I should like here to thank Professor L. E. Cole of the Department of Psychology, Oberlin College, for valuable advice in connection with this paper.
   2 D. L. Demorest, *L'Expression figurée et symbolique dans l'oeuvre de Gustave Flaubert*, Paris, Presses Universitaires, 1931, p. 472.
   3 A chief danger is, of course, that we should equate genius with neurosis or degeneracy, and, as Kenneth Burke has put it (*The Philosophy of Literary Form*, Baton Rouge, 1941, pp. 17–18), we must remind ourselves that "the true locus of assertion is not in the disease, but in the structural powers by which the poet encompasses it."
   4 G. Flaubert, *Correspondance. Supplément*, II, 90–96.
   5 A. Thibaudet, *Gustave Flaubert*, Paris, 1930, p. 210.

personal and the subjective, the more—and not the less—he is expressing his unconscious." [6]

This feeling was confirmed when I first read the letter to Taine in which Flaubert most vividly recalls his hallucinations. After first describing, without knowing it, what modern psychiatrists would call his "aura"—"il y a toujours terreur, on sent que votre personnalité vous échappe, on croit qu'on va mourir" [there is always a feeling of terror, you feel as though your personality were slipping from you, you think you are about to die]—he writes:

> Puis, tout à coup, comme la foudre, envahissement ou plutôt irruption instantanée de la mémoire, car l'hallucination proprement dite n'est pas autre chose—pour moi, du moins. C'est une maladie de la mémoire, un relâchement de ce qu'elle recèle. On sent les images s'échapper de vous comme des flots de sang. Il vous semble que tout ce qu'on a dans la tête éclate comme les mille pièces d'un feu d'artifice, et on n'a pas le temps de regarder ces images internes qui défilent avec furie.—En d'autres circonstances, ça commence par une seule image qui grandit, se développe et finit par couvrir la réalité objective, comme par exemple une étincelle qui voltige et devient un grand feu flambant. Dans ce dernier cas, on peut très bien penser à autre chose, en même temps; et cela se confond presque avec ce qu'on appelle "les papillons noirs," c'est-à-dire ces rondelles de satin que certaines personnes voient flotter dans l'air, quand le ciel est grisâtre et qu'elles ont la vue fatiguée.

[Then suddenly, like lightning, there is an invasion or rather an instantaneous irruption *of the memory*, for a true hallucination is exactly that—for me, at least. It is an illness of the memory, a loosing of what it contains. You feel the images escaping from you like spurts of blood. It seems as though everything you had in your head were bursting like the thousands of bits of a fireworks display, and you don't have time to look at all these internal images which pass madly by. —In other cases, it begins with a single image which grows larger, fills out, and ends by covering objective reality completely, for instance a spark which flutters about and then becomes a great flaming fire. In this latter case, you can perfectly well think of other things *at the same time;* and it is almost like what is called having spots before your eyes (in French:

---

6 "À Note on Art and Neurosis," *Partisan Review,* XII (1945), 45.

black butterflies), those little, round, satin spots that some
people see floating in the air, when the sky is leaden and their
eyes are tired.]

The reader will have seen at once how very similar to this is
Emma's fearful experience just before her fatal visit to Homais's
capharnaüm with its waiting jar of arsenic:

> *Tout ce qu'il avait dans sa tête de réminiscences, d'idées,*
> *s'échappait à fois, d'un seul bond, comme les mille pièces d'un*
> *feu d'artifice. Elle vit son père, le cabinet de Lheureux, leur*
> *chambre là-bas, un autre paysage. La folie la prenait, elle eut*
> *peur, et parvint à se ressaisir, d'une manière confuse, il est*
> *vrai; car elle ne se rappelait point la cause de son horrible état,*
> *c'est-à-dire la question d'argent. Elle ne souffrait que de son*
> *amour, et sentait son âme l'abandonner par ce souvenir, comme*
> *les blessés, en agonisant, sentent l'existence qui s'en va par*
> *leur plaie qui saigne.*
> *La nuit tombait, des corneilles volaient.*
> *Il lui sembla tout à coup que des globules couleur de feu*
> *éclataient dans l'air comme des balles fulminantes en s'aplatis-*
> *sant, et tournaient, tournaient, pour aller se fondre sur la neige,*
> *entre les branches des arbres. Au milieu de chacun d'eux, la*
> *figure de Rodolphe apparaissait. Ils se multiplièrent, et ils se*
> *rapprochaient, la pénétraient; tout disparut. Elle reconnut les*
> *lumières des maisons, qui rayonnaient de loin dans le brouil-*
> *lard.*[7]

[All the memories and ideas that she had in her head were
let loose in a single flood, like the thousands of bits of a fireworks display. She saw her father, Lheureux's office, the bed-
room back there, a different landscape. Madness was coming
over her. She became frightened, and managed to get hold
of herself, but only confusedly, in fact; for she had no memory
of the cause of her horrible condition, that is, the question of
money. She suffered only from her love, and felt her soul
abandoning her through this recollection, as badly wounded
people on their death bed feel life itself slipping out through
their bleeding wound.
Night was falling, crows were flying about.
Suddenly it seemed to her that fiery globules were bursting

---

7 P. 432. Demorest has noted that the "globules couleur de feu" are
"une reminiscence des crises de Flaubert et des hallucinations qui les ac-
compagnent," op. cit., p. 458, n. 47. J. P. Richard, *Littérature et Sensation,*
Paris, Éd. du Seuil, 1954, p. 146, mentions briefly Flaubert's letter to Taine
in this connection.

in the air and flattening out like exploding bullets; they whirled and revolved until they dropped and melted on the snow amongst the branches of the trees. In the middle of each appeared Rodolphe's face. They multiplied and, drawing nearer, penetrated within her; then everything disappeared. She recognized the lights of the houses which shone from afar through the fog.]

The one striking image in this passage that is not found in the letters to Taine (although he speaks there of his "personality escaping," and compares the rapidity of the images to the flow of blood) Flaubert had already used in writing of his seizures to Louise Colet (December 27th, 1852); "J'ai souvent senti nettement mon âme qui m'échappait, comme on sent le sang qui coule par l'ouverture d'une saignée." [8] [I have often clearly felt my soul escaping from me, as you feel your blood escaping through the incision during a blood-letting.]

Another character, earlier in the novel, has an hallucination, but of a non-violent type, the kind Taine called "benevolent." In the last of the four questions he addressed to Flaubert, he wrote:

> Vous connaissez sans doute les images intenses, mais tranquilles, et les hallucinations bienfaisantes qui précèdent le sommeil. Quand on s'endort après dîner ou en tisonnant, elles sont très faciles à remarquer, il reste encore assez de conscience. L'intuition ou l'image artistique et poétique du romancier, telle que vous la connaissez, en diffère-t-elle beaucoup pour l'intensité? Ou bien la différence est-elle simplement que ces images ou hallucinations situées sur le seuil du sommeil, sont désordonnées et non volontaires?

> [Of course you know the intense but quiet images and the benevolent hallucinations which precede sleep. When you drift off to sleep after dinner or before your fire, they are very easy to observe because you are still sufficiently conscious. Is intuition or the artistic and poetic image of the novelist, as you know it, much different in intensity? Or is the difference simply that these images or hallucinations which come on the edge of consciousness are disorganized and involuntary?]

Here is Charles Bovary on his way to Les Bertaux farm in the grey light of early morning:

8 *Correspondance*, III, 77.

La pluie ne tombait plus; le jour commençait à venir, et, sur les branches des pommiers sans feuilles, des oiseaux se tenaient immobiles, hérissant leurs petites plumes au vent froid du matin. La plate campagne s'étalait à perte de vue, et les bouquets d'arbres autour des fermes faisaient, à intervalles éloignés, des taches d'un violet noir sur cette grande surface grise, qui se perdait à l'horizon dans le ton morne du ciel. Charles, de temps à autre, ouvrait les yeux; puis, son esprit se fatiguant et le sommeil revenant de soi-même, bientôt il entrait dans une sorte d'assoupissement où, ses sensations récentes se confondant avec des souvenirs, lui-même se percevait double, à la fois étudiant et marié, couché dans son lit comme tout à l'heure, traversant une salle d'opérés comme autrefois. L'odeur chaude des cataplasmes se mêlait dans sa tête à la verte odeur de la rosée; il entendait rouler sur leur tringle les anneaux de fer des lits et sa femme dormir (pp. 16–17).

[The rain had stopped; daylight was beginning, and on the leafless apple trees motionless birds were fluffing out their little feathers in the cold morning air. The flat landscape stretched away as far as the eye could see, and the clumps of trees around the farms at distant intervals made splotches of black velvet on the great, grey surface, which disappeared in the distance into the mournful tone of the sky. From time to time Charles would open his eyes, but then his mind would tire and sleep would return unbidden; soon he would be overcome with drowsiness and he would see himself double, both student and married man, lying abed as shortly before or traversing a roomful of patients who had been operated on, as he used to do. The warm odor of the dressings would mingle in his head with the green scent of the dew; he would hear the chain-metal springs of the beds creak and at the same time hear his wife asleep.]

The dozing Charles's "benevolent" hallucination does not, of course, include fiery visions. But what features do these experiences of Charles and Emma have in common? In both, what strikes one immediately is a characteristic simultaneity evident first of all in the use of background. It is against a dim screen of dawn or twilight sky that in Emma's case, fiery visions explode, or in Charles's, birds with ruffled feathers perch on deeply etched bare branches. Without relating them to the seizures, Faguet aptly called Flaubert's landscapes "des hallucinations précises," possessing "ce relief, cette saillie forte des angles et des contours, que les objets rêvés prennent brusquement, alors, sur le rideau noir du sommeil." [9] ["precise hallucinations," possessing "that high relief and three-dimensional quality and angles and contours which objects in dreams take on then suddenly against the black curtain of sleep."] This sharpness of contour depends on the use of background, and Flaubert's characteristic use of the tiny detail against a dull surface has manifold effects, since it occurs in the most disparate passages. If he wants to suggest the calmness and immobility of a summer afternoon he sketches the thin legs of insects on lily pads; if he would show ironically how far the indolent nobility have retrogressed from their glorious ancestors, he describes not the paintings in the busy billiard-room at La Vaubyessard, but only the fine cracks in the canvases.

The landscape itself exists simultaneously with and independently of the inner visions, which are themselves simultaneous. Charles sees himself as two selves, *at the same time* a student and a married man. The pictures from Emma's past burst *all at once* upon her consciousness like a thousand fireworks going off. And in both passages the subject retains a sensorial anchor to the real world; as Flaubert told Taine: "Dans l'hallucination pure et simple on peut très bien voir une image fausse d'un oeil, et les objets vrais de l'autre," and again: "on peut très bien penser à autre chose, *en même temps*." [In hallucinations pure and simple you can perfectly well see an unreal image with one eye and real objects with the other, and again: you can perfectly well think of other things, *at the same time*.]

Besides this characteristic simultaneity, this co-existence of the real and the visionary worlds in which mental visions are superimposed upon reality, we may list as typical of the hallucinations: (1) Visual, aural, or olfactory memories, lacking chronological order, and (2) Unreal visual phenomena, especially lights having a whirling or hovering movement.

We may now consider how *Madame Bovary* reflects these characteristics. The hallucinations involve questions of time; not only do they have simultaneity, they consist, in Flaubert's own words, of a "sickness of the memory"—a brutal invasion

---

9 E. Faguet, *Gustave Flaubert*, Paris, Hachette, 1899, p. 163.

of the past. The time scheme of the novel itself seems to reflect certain of these temporal characteristics. For one thing, there is a recurring pattern of simultaneity, and it is this pattern more than any other single factor that effectively prevents the novel from having any real forward movement. A famous example of Flaubert's simultaneous technique, in which the see-saw from one level of action to another dissolves the narrative sequence, is the "symphony" of the *comices agricoles,* which has already been discussed by Joseph Frank in his pioneer article on spatial form.[10] But despite Frank's conclusion that "with this one exception, the novel maintains a clear-cut narrative line," the technique reaches far beyond the single instance he cites. Besides Binet's lathe, famous as a symbol of monotony, but even more an ironic accompaniment to the crises in Emma's life, we have the many occasions on which Flaubert juxtaposes sounds and actions, like the clinking of cutlery from Homais's dining-room as Emma is finding and devouring the arsenic. The technique may even be extended to dialogue, as in the long scene when Emma first meets Léon at the inn, and two conversations (Charles and Homais, Léon and Emma) go on at the same time. In general, Flaubert thus evokes the inevitable presence of indifferent society, so that Emma's actions, which taken singly might seem dynamic and forward-moving, are muffled by the contrasting habitual actions of the Binets and the Homais.[11]

If the novel's vertical rather than horizontal time-scheme can be related to the simultaneity of the hallucinations, the action itself can be described in terms of Emma's futile struggle against the "sickness of the memory," ending in a final triumph

10 J. Frank, "Spatial Form in Modern Literature," in *Criticism: The Foundations of Modern Literary Judgment,* eds. M. Schorer, J. Miles, and G. McKenzie (New York, Harcourt Brace, 1948), pp. 379–92.

11 He achieves a similar ironic counterpointing by using the present tense in his description of Yonville in Part II. The town as described is not contemporaneous with the heroine, but with the author; its permanence overwhelms her subsequent actions: "Depuis les événements que l'on va raconter, rien, en effet n'a changé à Yonville" [Since the events which are about to be told took place, nothing as a matter of fact has changed in Yonville], etc. (p. 100). He establishes the pastness of all the actions to follow; the future towards which Emma looks with such anticipation is really a past, the progression Tostes-Yonville is robbed of its dynamism.

of past over present. At carefully selected moments, beginning
with the ball at La Vaubyessard, external stimuli confront her
with images out of her past. The very first instance reminds one
unmistakably of the hallucinations, with its suggestion of an
inability to distinguish past and present:

> *Alors le souvenir des Bertaux lui arriva. Elle revit la
> ferme, la mare bourbeuse, son père en blouse sous les pom-
> miers, et elle se revit elle-même, comme autrefois, écrémant
> avec son doigt les terrines de lait dans la laiterie (p. 72).*

> [Then the memory of the farm, Les Bertaux, came back to
> her. She could see the farm, the muddy pond, her father in
> shirt-sleeves under the appletrees and she could see herself
> once again, as she used to be, using a finger to skim the cream
> off the jars of milk in the creamery.]

It is true that a moment later the splendour of the ball blots
out these memories, and the present, overshadowing the past,
implies future triumphs:

> . . . *aux fulgurations de l'heure présente, sa vie passée, si
> nette jusqu'alors, s'évanouissait tout entière, et elle doutait
> presque de l'avoir vécue (p. 72),*

> [. . . before the flaming illuminations of the present moment,
> her past life, which had been so clear, disappeared entirely,
> and she almost felt as though she had never lived it,]

but this supremacy is short-lived. As the novel continues,
Emma's look is increasingly backward. Neatly balancing and
seemingly intended to recall the earlier passage are the homely
images of the farm that crowd in upon her consciousness as
she reads a letter from her father long after her marriage and
first unhappy love-affair:

> . . . *elle crut presque apercevoir son père se courbant vers
> l'âtre pour saisir les pincettes. Comme il y avait longtemps
> qu'elle n'était plus auprès de lui, sur l'escabeau, dans la
> cheminée, quand elle faisait brûler le bout d'un bâton à la
> grande flamme des joncs marins qui pétillaient! . . . Elle se
> rappela des soirs d'été tout pleins de soleil. Les poulains hen-
> nissaient quand on passait, et galopaient, galopaient. . . . Il y
> avait sous sa fenêtre une ruche à miel, et quelquefois les
> abeilles, tournoyant dans la lumière, frappaient contre les
> carreaux comme des balles d'or rebondissantes. Quel bonheur
> dans ce temps-là! quel espoir! quelle abondance d'illusions!
> Il n'en restait plus maintenant! (p. 239)*

[. . . she almost thought she could see her father leaning toward the hearth to grasp the fire tongs. How long it was since she had been with him, seated on the stool by the fireplace, and burning the tip of a branch in the great flames of reeds which were crackling and sparkling! . . . She remembered summer evenings which were so sunny. The foals would whinny as you went by and then would gallop about. . . . Under her window there was a honey-bee hive, and sometimes as the bees buzzed about in the sunlight, they would strike against the windowpanes like bouncing, golden balls. How much happiness she had then! what hopes for the future! what an abundance of illusions! There were none left any longer!]

If we contrast two other passages, similarly balanced one against the other, we shall see how Flaubert depicts the gradual disintegration of her personality through different degrees of obtrusiveness of the past. Just before her visit to the village priest Bournisien, she hears the Angelus and at once she is lost in memories of convent life. Certain verbs (*elle se rappela, elle aurait voulu*) show that she still retains control, that her summoning up of the convent scenes is at least partially willed, but in the last lines there is already a hint that the anchor is dragging:

> A *ce tintement répété, la pensée de la jeune femme s'égarait dans ses vieux souvenirs de jeunesse et de pension. Elle se rappela les grands chandeliers, qui dépassaient sur l'autel les vases pleins de fleurs et le tabernacle à colonnettes. Elle aurait voulu, comme autrefois, être confondue dans la longue ligne des voiles blancs, que marquaient de noir çà et là les capuchons raides des bonnes soeurs inclinées sur leur prie-Dieu; le dimanche à la messe, quand elle relevait la tête, elle apercevait le doux visage de la Vierge, parmi les tourbillons bleuâtres de l'encens qui montait. Alors un attendrissement la saisit; elle se sentit molle et tout abandonnée, comme un duvet d'oiseau qui tournoie dans la tempête; et ce fut sans en avoir conscience qu'elle s'achemina vers l'église, disposée à n'importe quelle dévotion, pourvu qu'elle y absorbât son âme et que l'existence entière y disparût (pp. 153-54).*

[This repeated tinkling of the bell made the young woman's mind wander back through old memories of her youth and her days in the boarding school. She recalled the great candlesticks, which rose above the flower vases and the columned tabernacle on the altar. She would have liked to be lost once

again in the long line of white veils, set off now and again by
the stiff black hoods of the sisters kneeling at their prayer
stools. On Sundays at mass, when she used to raise her head,
she could see the gentle face of the Virgin amidst the bluish
clouds of rising incense. Then a tender feeling came over her;
she felt herself melting and abandoned like a bit of down
tossed in a storm; and no doubt she did not realize what she
was doing as she took the path to the church, disposed in her
heart for any devotions providing only that she might lose
herself in them and that her entire existence would disappear
into them.]

Much later, as the liaison with Léon is drawing to a close,
when she sits down for a moment beside the convent of her
youth, she slips quite effortlessly into a swirl of memory images:

> Quel calme dans ce temps-là! Comme elle enviait les inef-
> fables sentiments d'amour qu'elle tâchait, d'après des livres,
> de se figurer!
> Les premiers mois de son mariage, ses promenades à cheval
> dans la forêt, le vicomte qui valsait, et Lagardy chantant, tout
> repassa devant ses yeux. . . . [sic] Et Léon lui parut soudain
> dans le même éloignement que les autres (p. 392).

[How calm things were then! How she envied the ineffable
feelings of love which she used to try to imagine from her
reading!
The first months of her marriage, her horseback rides in the
forest, the Viscount waltzing, and Lagardy singing, all passed
before her eyes again. . . . (sic) And Léon suddenly appeared
before her, as distant as the others.]

After all her possessions have been seized, and she has taken
refuge with the nurse, Mme Rolet, she must actually ride the
wave of images to reach the immediate past:

> Un jour, avec Léon. . . . Oh! comme c'était loin . . . le
> soleil brillait sur la rivière et les clématites embaumaient. . . .
> Alors, emportée dans ses souvenirs comme dans un torrent qui
> bouillonne, elle arriva bientôt à se rappeler la journée de la
> veille (p. 424).

[One day with Léon. . . . Oh! how far off it seemed . . .
the sun was shining on the river and the clematis perfumed
the air. . . . Then carried along in her memories as in a
swirling, bubbling torrent, she soon succeeded in recalling the
moment of the day before.]

In these instances the automatic influx of memories appears as a sign of Emma's disintegration, as a preparation for her death, and they produce a dream-like, supra-temporal quality. But Flaubert imparts a hallucinatory tinge to Emma's triumphs as well as her defeats. These triumphs are, of course, sexual, and it is significant that Flaubert frequently described his sensations during an attack in sexual terms. In this connection there is the very explicit and revealing comparison in a letter to Taine between his aura and the sexual act, as well as a similar, though more veiled statement to Louise Colet; [12] and a phrase he wrote to her, describing, not his feelings during a hallucination, but his contentment after a rendezvous with her—"*J'avais dans mon âme des océans de crême*" [I had oceans of cream in my soul]—should also be borne in mind when we consider the following passage, quoted by G. Poulet as an example of "*une durée qui s'étale*" [13] [a duration which is stretching out], one which seems to occur independently of the flow of time:

> *Les ombres du soir descendaient; le soleil horizontal, passant entre less branches, lui éblouissait les yeux. Çà et là, tout autour d'elle, dans les feuilles ou par terre, des taches lumineuses tremblaient, comme si des colibris, en volant, eussent éparpillé leurs plumes. Le silence était partout; quelque chose de doux semblait sortir des arbres; elle sentait son coeur, dont les battements recommençaient, et le sang circuler dans sa chair comme un fleuve de lait (pp. 222–23).*

[The evening shadows were descending; the horizontal rays of the sun, passing through the branches, blinded her. Here and there all about her, on the leaves or the ground, luminous spots vibrated, as if hummingbirds had scattered their plumage as they flew about. Silence was everywhere; something soft seemed to distill from the trees; she could feel her heart, as it began to beat again and her blood started to circulate through her body like a river of milk.]

There is scarcely need to point out the elements typical of the hallucination: the dark background, the hovering spots of light. The odd final simile becomes clarified in the context of the

12 *Correspondance, Supplément*, II, 94, and *Correspondance*, III, 77.
13 G. Poulet, *Etudes sur le temps humain*, Edinburgh, 1949, p. 321.

phrase to Louise Colet and Flaubert's frequent comparison of his sensations to the blood flowing from a wound.

Emma's first awareness of sexual power had been accompanied by a hallucinatory experience; as she sat with Rodolphe in an upper room of the Town Hall she caught sight of L'Hirondelle, the stage coach that had borne Léon away to Paris:

> *Elle crut le voir en face, à sa fenêtre; puis tout se confondit, des nuages passèrent; il lui sembla qu'elle tournait encore dans la valse, sous le feu des lustres, au bras du vicomte, et que Léon n'était pas loin, qu'il allait venir (p. 204).*

[She thought she saw him across from her at his window; then everything became confused, clouds passed before her eyes; she seemed to be still whirling about in the waltz under the bright lights of the candelabra on the Viscount's arm; Léon seemed to be somewhere near; he was going to come to her.]

At the same moment, Rodolphe's pomade, of an odour similar to the Viscount's, excites in her vague sexual desires:

> *La douceur de cette sensation pénétrait ainsi ses désirs d'autrefois, et, comme des grains de sable sous un coup de vent, ils tourbillonnaient dans la bouffée subtile du parfum qui se répandait sur son âme (ibid.).*

[The gentleness of this sensation penetrated into her former desires and, like grains of sand before a gust of wind, they whirled about in the subtle breath of the perfume which spread over her soul.]

In the first of these quotations we note the deliberate confusion of real and visionary in the phrase "tout se confondit, des nuages passèrent" [everything became confused, clouds passed before her eyes], and of course once again the verbs of whirling.

The imprint of the hallucinations is frequently found where the author is not immediately concerned with unusual affective states in his characters. What may seem purely expositional passages, such as the chapter describing Emma's identification with the Romantic heroines of history and fiction suddenly falls into the pattern when we read that these women "se détachaient comme des comètes sur l'immensité ténébreuse de l'histoire" [stood out like comets for her against the dark immensity of history]. Leo Spitzer may have spoken truer than he knew when he called this simile "an impressionistic, almost schizoid picture of world history." [14] In the same chapter swans on a lake in one of Emma's illustrated books "se détachent en écorchures blanches, sur un fond d'acier gris" (p. 52) [stood out like white wounds against a background of steel grey]. Of his whirling lights Flaubert told Taine, we remember, that they may occasionally be confused with what people call *les papillons noirs*—"ces rondelles de satin que certaines personnes voient flotter dans l'air, quand le ciel est grisâtre et qu'elles ont la vue fatiguée" [spots before your eyes—those little, round, satin spots that some people see floating in the air, when the sky is leaden and their eyes are tired]. From this derives one of the most startling images in the novel, startling not merely for its evocation of the physical scene, but because it conveys Emma's mood of detachment, her hypnotized upward gaze as she watches, against the background of the fire-back, the floating ashes of her discarded wedding-bouquet:

> *Elle le regarda brûler. Les petites baies de carton éclataient, les fils d'archal se tordaient, le galon se fondait; et les corolles de papier, racornies, se balançant le long de la plaque comme des papillons noirs, enfin s'envolèrent par la cheminée (p. 94).*

> [She watched it burn. The little cardboard berries burst, the brass wires twisted, the braid melted; and the shrivelled paper petals fluttered against the fire-back like black butterflies and finally flew up the chimney.]

Of significantly similar texture and movement are the passages describing the scattered pieces of Emma's note, falling upon a field of red clover "comme des papillons blancs" [like white butterflies], and the cloud of flies whirling in the bright air of afternoon just in front of Emma and Léon as they walk along the river.

The reader will have noticed in the passages already quoted that the turning movement is frequently expressed by verbs like *tourbillonner*, which evoke related images of wind and water. Very early in the novel Emma feels "un insaisissable malaise qui change d'aspect comme les nuées, qui tourbillonne comme le vent" [an ill-defined discomfort, which changes its character like the clouds, which twists and turns like the wind]. The incense upon the convent altar rises in bluish whorls, and in the same passage she feels lax and abandoned "comme un duvet d'oiseau qui tournoie dans la tempête" (p. 154) [like a bit of down tossed in a storm]. Past desires whirl through her mind "comme des grains de sable dans une tempête" (p. 204) [like grains of sand in a storm]; when she is on the verge of leaping from the attic window, "Le bleu du ciel l'envahissait, l'air circulait dans sa tête creuse" (p. 285) [The blue of the sky was invading her, the air was circulating through her empty head]; she is carried off by her memories "comme dans un torrent qui bouillonne" (p. 424) [as in a swirling, bubbling torrent]. Or again the swirling movement combines with Baudelairean metaphors in which the heart or the soul is an empty building or an abyss: the blind beggar's cry, "lui descendait au fond de l'âme comme un tourbillon dans un abîme" (p. 369) [descended to the bottom of her heart like a whirlwind in a chasm].

In describing his hallucinations, Flaubert linked the whirling motion to sensations like Emma's sinking feeling ("Le sol sous ses pieds était plus mou qu'une onde" [The ground gave beneath her feet more gently than water would]): "C'était dans ma pauvre cervelle un tourbillon d'idées et d'images où il me semblait que ma conscience, que mon *moi* sombrait comme un vaisseau sous la tempête" [15] [There was a whirlwind of ideas and images in my poor brain which made it seem as though my consciousness, my *self*, was sinking like a ship in a tempest]. In such moments she is possessed of an abnormally acute sense of hearing: she hears the pulsing of her own arteries, and Rodolphe's letter crumpling in her hand crackles like sheet metal (pp. 284, 432). Perhaps in the latter case, recalling the auditory phenomenon that accompanied his seizures (the sound of cart wheels), he hit on this method of conveying his char-

15 *Correspondance*, IV, 180. G. Poulet calls the circle image "l'image essentielle par laquelle s'exprime les rapports du monde et de l'être dans l'imagination flaubertienne" [the essential image through which the relationships of the world and of being are expressed in the Flaubertian imagination]—"La Pensée circulaire de Flaubert," NNRF, 1er juillet 1955, p. 34.

acter's tension. And to intensify the characteristic sensation of
the blood flowing through his veins by making it audible (in
an interesting reminiscence of Poe) [16] would have been a relatively simple step.

In a less specific way, the strangeness of certain metaphorical passages becomes explicable in the light of our knowledge of the hallucinations. The two-page description of Emma's
melancholy following Léon's departure for Paris reveals many
typical ingredients. In the beginning, "tout lui parut enveloppé
par une atmosphère noire qui flottait confusément sur l'ex-
térieur des choses" (p. 171) [everything seemed to her to be
enveloped in a black vapor which floated confusedly on the
exterior of things], and her sorrow is compared to the winter
wind howling in abandoned castles. She recalls La Vaubyessard
"quand les quadrilles tourbillonnaient dans sa tête" [when the
quadrilles twisted and turned in her head], and her visions of
Léon, though still controlled and orderly visual and auditive
associations, have the quality of hallucination. There follows
(pp. 172–73) that strange metaphor, extending through two
long paragraphs, in which Emma's love is a traveller's fire on
the Russian steppe, the metaphor Thibaudet despairingly called
"la plus longue peut-être et la plus laborieuse de toute la langue
française" [17] [perhaps the longest and the most laborious of the
whole French language]. Yet this fantastic structure becomes at
least understandable when we recall the content of Flaubert's
visions. Its very involutions remind us of the chaotic images he
described; here, as in the hallucinations, a flame glows against
a large expanse; ennui is spatialized. The search for the dry
wood of memories past and present ("les réminiscences les plus
lointaines comme les plus immédiates occasions" [p. 172] [the
most distant recollections as well as the most recent occasions])
to feed the fire of love prefigures the "sickness of memory," and
the fading of her emotion, like the aftermath of the visions of
whirling lights, is a shivering darkness and cold.

16 Cf. *Correspondance*, IV, 169: "Tout ce qu'il y a dans Sainte
Thérèse, dans Hoffmann et dans Edgar Poë, je l'ai senti, je l'ai *vu*, les
hallucinés me sont fort compréhensibles." [Everything in Saint Theresa, in
Hoffmann, and in Edgar Poe I have felt and *seen*; I can easily understand
people who have hallucinations.]
17 *Op. cit.*, p. 211.

At this juncture I should like to say that, although I have restricted the scope of this essay, I do not mean that any discussion of the particular images considered here should henceforth be confined to the context of the hallucinations, although I think a case can be made for calling Flaubert's style "hallucinatory" rather than "apoplectic," as Kenneth Burke has proposed.[18] It is quite likely, for example, that the "river of milk" image discussed above could be related to various images involving rivers or streams. And as I have tried to suggest by linking the "simultaneity" of the hallucinations with the novel's time-scheme, their impact undoubtedly goes far beyond the close verbal relationship between Flaubert's description of his visions and his metaphorical language in the novel. It would not, I believe, be far-fetched to see in the structure itself, consisting as it does of a series of crescendi and decrescendi—big moments followed by let-downs—a reflection of Flaubert's successive periods of relative good health, sudden attacks and *détentes*.[19]

It should also be emphasized that the question of realism is not pertinent here. Had Flaubert been creating a character who suffered from some sort of nervous malady of which hallucinations would be symptoms, he could have been presumed to have been aiming at scientific realism in the manner of Zola. But Emma's hallucinations are not intended to suggest physical ills; of her final traumatic experience Flaubert says, simply: "elle ne souffrait que de son amour" [she was suffering only from her love]. Thus, apart from the multiple instances where his own visions coloured his descriptive language, even the abnormal visions of his character remain in the realm of metaphor: they are remarkably effective metaphorical representations of states of mind.[20]

18 *Op. cit.*, p. 17.

19 Significantly Flaubert calls Emma's feelings after Léon goes to Paris "cette douleur, enfin, que vous apportent l'interruption de tout mouvement accoutumé, la cessation brusque d'une vibration prolongée" (p. 171) [that distress, finally, which comes to you through the interruption of any customary movement, the sudden ceasing of a prolonged vibration].

20 There are, to be sure, dangers in this method. Emma's final hallucination is prepared for by the many hallucinatory moments we have noted, by her frequent alternations between calm and distress, suggestive of the *aura*. But Flaubert lends certain of his symptoms to Farmer Rouault

Perhaps the most obvious reason why, of all Flaubert's works, *Madame Bovary* reflects the hallucinations most prominently[21] was that of all the characters this "grand féminin" created, Emma was closest to his own nature; "Madame Bovary, c'est moi" was no *boutade*. The Correspondence suggests another reason. We are frequently told that the writing of *Madame Bovary* had cathartic properties for its author; it was to purge him of Romanticism, and so forth. But it may well have had a therapeutic value of another sort. Despite periods of despondency, Flaubert never lost confidence in his own power of reason. In the series of letters we have discussed, he told Taine that he had frequently rid himself of his seizures "by force of will." Elsewhere he actually asserted that he was responsible for his own recovery. While it is impossible to tell accurately what the span of the illness was, he seems to have stopped having attacks some time between 1852 and 1857.[22] In the letter dated May 18th, 1857, he confided to Mlle Leroyer de Chantepie how he had brought about his own cure:

> *Vous me demandez comment je me suis guéri des hallucinations nerveuses que je subissais autrefois? Par deux moyens:*

---

as well. Nothing whatever has led us to suspect that this "gros petit homme de cinquante ans" [fat little man of fifty] would twice fall down in a faint, first at the news of Emma's poisoning, and then at the sight of the funeral cloth, or that en route to her bedside he should suddenly see a vision of her lying dead in the middle of the road (p. 461)!

21 Perhaps because *La Tentation de Saint Antoine* is so overtly *about* hallucinations the Saint's visions are elaborate structures having little in common with Flaubert's. A final image in the work does recall Emma's vision of Rodolphe's face in the fiery globes: "dans le disque même du soleil rayonne la face de Jésus-Christ" (p. 296). Cf. J. Seznec, *Nouvelles Études sur la Tentation de Saint Antoine*, London, Warburg Inst., 1949, p. 89, for a discussion of this vision. In the first *Education sentimentale* there occurs a hallucinatory passage when the hero, wandering by moonlight, meets a strange dog whose eyes dart fire, then grow and take on human form (Paris, Conard, 1910), pp. 251–52. Curiously the fire-darting eyes are not only present in *La Tentation*, but in *Madame Bovary*: "Il s'échappa des prunelles d'Hilarion comme deux flèches rouges" (p. 232) and "Elle fixait sur Charles la pointe ardente de ses prunelles comme deux flèches de feu prêtes à partir" (p. 255).

22 Probably in 1854. He wrote to Mlle Leroyer de Chantepie, March 30th, 1857: ". . . à vingt et un ans, j'ai manqué mourir d'une maladie nerveuse . . . Cette maladie m'a duré dix ans" [. . . at twenty-one I almost died of a nervous ailment . . . This ailment lasted ten years], *Correspondance*, IV, 169.

1° *en les étudiant scientifiquement, c'est-à-dire en tâchant
de m'en rendre compte, et 2° par la force de la volonté. J'ai
souvent senti la folie me venir. C'était dans ma pauvre cervelle
un tourbillon d'idées et d'images où il me semblait que ma
conscience, que mon moi sombrait comme un vaisseau sous
la tempête. Mais je me cramponnais à ma raison. Elle dominait
tout, quoique assiégée et battue. En d'autres fois, je tâchais, par
l'imagination, de me donner facticement ces horribles souf-
frances. J'ai joué avec la démence et le fantastique comme
Mithridate avec les poisons. Un grand orgueil me soutenait et
j'ai vaincu le mal à force de l'étreindre corps à corps.*[23]

[You ask me how I got over the nervous hallucinations which
I used to have? In two ways: 1) by studying them scientifically,
that is by trying to understand them, and 2) by *will power*. I
often felt madness coming on. There was a whirlwind of ideas
and images in my poor brain which made it seem as though
my consciousness, my *self*, was sinking like a ship in a tempest.
But I held fast to my reason. Even battered and besieged it
dominated everything. On other occasions I tried inducing
these horrible sufferings artificially by a deliberate act of
imagining. I played with madness and the fantastic as
Mithridates did with poisons. A great deal of pride kept me
going and I conquered the ailment by wrestling with it.]

Might we not be permitted to interpret this "scientific study,"
this triumphant "coming to grips" with his malady as the
artist's successful attempt to transform his experience, to
exorcise its spell by endowing the world of his novel with
its sensations and visions? Without this struggle, of course,
the hallucinations would have little importance. They were an
occasion, an impersonal factor like the condensations of moisture
on the horizon which produce sunsets. As William James once
said, to the majority these illuminated bits of cloud will suggest
supper-time, to a few, heroes' deaths. That Flaubert happened
to combine artistic genius and a nervous malady is far from
unusual; that he strove, with a large measure of success, to
sublimate his abnormal experiences in his novel's characterization, structure and imagery, offers yet another reason why he is
unique among novelists.

23 *Ibid.*, p. 180.

B. F. Bart

12 · Madame Bovary *after a Century*

INTRODUCTION

*With what I hope will be judged pardonable bias, I have
left to myself the last word in this collection. The following
selection is, with only a few changes, an address to the Modern
Language Association on the occasion of the Centenary of
Madame Bovary. Neither so harsh as Turnell nor so unreservedly laudatory as Baudelaire, I have sought to embrace in
one perspective the various points of view from which readers
have envisaged the novel. It may then perhaps serve as a conclusion to these essays.*

Flaubert's masterpiece is alive a century after its publication because it is the successful embodiment of a new esthetic.
This esthetic has long proved confusing and still today needs
redefinition. Critics who have studied it have tended to call
it realism and have tried to see Flaubert as some sort of
amalgam, compound, or mixture of romanticism and this new
element, but this traditional approach has very serious defects.
In the first place, Flaubert always rejected the claim that he
was a realist; he had no use for the school [VII, 359 and 377].[1]
In the second place, it seems very difficult to define "realism"
satisfactorily in connection with Flaubert: either one makes it
impossible to include those of his works which are like

Reprinted from *The French Review*, XXXI (1958), 203–10. By
permission.
   1 All bracketed volume and page indications refer to Flaubert's *Correspondance*.

Salammbô within the definition, or one has a series of statements which are not meaningful when applied to realists other than Flaubert, for instance to William Dean Howells, who would never have written books akin to *Salammbô*. Under the circumstances, it would be wise to try for a new understanding of Flaubert's esthetic based on what he had to say about it himself while writing *Madame Bovary* and leaving aside the word "realism," which does no more than confuse the issue.

Certain of Flaubert's observations to Baudelaire form a ready starting point. He wrote to the poet: "You have found a way to rejuvenate romanticism," and "You have found a way to be a classicist while still remaining the transcendent romantic we admire" [IV, 205 and 408]. It is significant that, while Flaubert does speak of romanticism, he makes no mention at all of realism and instead names classicism as the other pole in this esthetic. And his phrasing makes it clear that he, too, believed in rejuvenating romanticism by a return to the long classical tradition. This is, in fact, his new esthetic.

To understand Flaubert's statement, one must determine what he meant by romanticism and above all by classicism: both are slippery terms. To Flaubert romanticism (at least in this context) was emotionalism unbridled by Art. A classical approach, on the other hand, was precisely that discipline which limits emotion and thereby makes Art possible, for Art has among its characteristics chasteness, precision, and ultimately serenity [II, 398, 451; III, 264, 340; IV, 164]. Flaubert would say that the writer with unbridled emotions is romantic and wrong. He prefers the author who first dominates these emotions and only then seeks the proper form to express them. Such a man is classical and right. "You must write with your head. If your heart warms it, all the better, but don't say so" [III, 50; see also IV, 5]. In point of fact, he felt that Art, to be Art at all, had to separate itself from this emotionalism. To rejuvenate romanticism, then, was in part to stop mistaking the feeling for the poem. It was, for instance, to abjure the errors of a Musset, whom Flaubert condemned for his failure to separate poetry from the sensations. It is the function of Art to complete these (and not, incidentally, to reproduce them, as the realists thought) [II, 446–47 and 460].

This classical aspect of Flaubert's esthetic has been under-rated. It is what leads to mastering what he called the transcendent romanticism of Baudelaire, so as to transmute it into Art. Flaubert always felt that Beauty was calm; it was itself serene and it evoked serenity. Baudelaire's sonnet, *La Beauté*, aroused his intense admiration. Here Beauty states in part:

> *Je trône dans l'azur comme un sphinx incompris;*
> *J'unis un coeur de neige à la blancheur des cygnes,*
> *Je hais le mouvement qui déplace les lignes,*
> *Et jamais je ne pleure et jamais je ne ris.*

> [I reign in the sky like a mysterious sphinx;
> I join a heart of snow to the whiteness of swans,
> I hate movement which upsets the lines,
> And I never weep nor laugh.]

The highest goal of Art, Flaubert once asserted, was to set one to dreaming; the best works are serene of aspect and in-comprehensible; and, he added, "something strangely gentle and sweet hovers over it all," "it is calm! so calm!" [III, 322, 323; see also III, 340].

Flaubert's classicism is calm, it is true, but it is not the pale ink of French nineteenth-century neo-classicism, nor is it the French seventeenth century, except incidentally. Flaubert liked La Fontaine, Boileau, Molière; but "the gentle Racine" only bemused him [II, 120, 297, 426; III, 138]. When he uses words like "classic," he really means Greece and Rome and the long tradition that fully derives from them: a true progeny, going always beyond the parents. Taking his cue from the ancient literatures—and from the romantic concept of the grotesque—Flaubert sought an all-inclusive literature. Thus he objected that Leconte de Lisle, for all his "classicism," was not a true "classicist" and therefore not a good artist, since the Parnassian poet was rejecting the modern world. Flaubert held that the ideal world of the artist, ancient or modern, is fertile only if the artist includes everything in it. Art is a work of love, not of exclusion [IV, 15; see also III, 215, 281]. Hence, to the classical tradition, Flaubert insisted on adding a modern feeling. The artist must not return to antiquity; he must rather take its procedures. One should be as artistic as the Greeks, but in other ways, because the scope of humanity had broadened since Homer's day and "the belly of Sancho Panza strains the girdle of Venus" [III, 137, 157, 281].

Various aspects of this doctrine have formed the commonplaces of critical observations on Flaubert: they all take their place within this rejuvenation of romantic emotionalism attained by controlling it so as to transmute it into a serene classical vision which would be Art. His effort to achieve comprehensiveness and universality led to a primary emphasis on impersonality and impartiality; the serenity necessitated impassivity. The absolute awareness that Beauty was the only goal of the artist led to the unremitting search for perfect form, the striving for the artistically right word, the agonies of the struggle over style. All are parts in a total process, which has meaning only when all of the parts are understood together, for the whole is an entity itself, and not just the sum of its parts.

Flaubert did not think of himself as an innovator or a revolutionary; rather he considered that he was a traditionalist. He is indeed one of the masters who moved the great line of western literature a step forward by a real return to the problem of Form. He was a classicist in the sense that he was in the Tradition, and he knew it. He was deeply irritated by those who set up little schools of the Beautiful—romantic, realistic, or classical for that matter: there was for him only one Beautiful, with varying aspects [III, 336].

Classicism was an integral part of his life and of his book *Madame Bovary*. He wanted the novel to have "a haughty, classical air" [III, 180]. Yet his was essentially a doctrine of innutrition. Born a romantic and never losing his passionate responses, he longed also to nurture himself, as Ronsard had, on the classics and to take to himself what excellences they had. One must be, he wrote, more classical than the classicists and infuriate the romantics by surpassing their intentions. He was sure it could be done, that one could be, like Baudelaire, a classicist while remaining a transcendent romantic [III, 249].

What then becomes of the familiar image of Flaubert, *chef d'école* of the French realists? It is true that he frequently asserted the absolute need for the artist to see things as they are, to penetrate into an object before writing of it. He did say, "When you can see your model clearly, you always write well . . ." [III, 269; see also III, 138]. He also wrote, "I will have produced written reality, which is rare" [III, 268]. But this does not mean that Flaubert is, after all, a realist: it is more complicated than that.

To call Flaubert a realist (as opposed to noting realistic elements in his work) is to confuse the issue seriously. It was not, he felt, a good method to look at something and then go write about it; its essence had to be digested first. He was aware that people thought him "fascinated with reality"; in fact, he hated it, he said [III, 263 and IV, 134]. This misinterpretation of his works bothered him throughout his lifetime and still troubles the critic today. Twenty-five years after writing the *Bovary*, Flaubert was still struggling to make himself understood, insisting that though he had always been incredibly scrupulous about reading all relevant documents and books, amassing all possible information and travelling wherever necessary, still he regarded all of this as secondary and inferior. So-called material reality should, he stated, never be more than a pattern used to mount higher [VIII, 374]. "Written reality," his phrase of a moment ago, is not the same thing as "reality." Art completes reality; it does not reproduce it. And this doctrine is not and cannot be called realism.

Flaubert is not a realist, nor is he a romantic; nor, for that matter, is he a naturalist or a symbolist. He sought rather to include all of these partial views of life and of Art in a larger synthesis, the Beautiful. He was preoccupied with the basic problem of the great writers of all ages, life itself: what meaning it has, what its parts really are, and (lastly) how they may be portrayed so as to display life's meaning.

Flaubert's efforts to learn what life was made up of in Normandy have been studied many times and need no lengthy rehearsal here. This is where he made his first impact. This is his documentation and the fabulous sheaves of notes. More important this is his scientism, and the prescient observation that Art would become scientific and science artistic in the future, a comment which the Freudian novel and the attitudes of an Einstein have borne out. Art was to gain in this process:

gain in accuracy and truth by laying aside personal susceptibilities and affections, gain in precision by adopting a rigorous method [II, 395–96; IV, 164].

The ways Flaubert adopted to portray what he saw are perhaps his most enduring contribution. This aspect—the style —was to him the great and overriding problem of the book. He felt sure enough of his basic plan (upon which everything depended, as he well knew) so that style instead, even though a secondary issue, was the main difficulty [II, 316, 362; III, 21, 140, 248, etc.]. Truly great geniuses, he sadly confessed, often wrote badly and could readily afford it; the lesser people, like himself, were of worth only if the style were perfect. Hence he sought "style, form, indefinable Beauty, *resulting from the concept itself* and which is the splendor of the True, as Plato used to say" [IV, 165]. The *concept* of *Madame Bovary* was, unfortunately, wholly alien to Flaubert, which made the book very hard for him to write and something of a *tour de force*. He achieved it only by constantly reminding himself that there was a style for every subject and that he must find this style [II, 346, 432; III, 3, 156, 201]. This was a further aspect of Baudelaire's work which delighted him: "The originality of the style derives directly from the concept. The sentence is filled to the brim with the idea; it is almost overflowing" [IV, 205].

Problems of form—or rather, brilliant resolutions of them— have become dominant as one surveys the influence of the novel. Taking his place beside Stendhal, the earlier master of irony, there now stands Flaubert, too, evolving new dimensions and forms for the ironic view of life. Anticipating Proustian sensitivities, Flaubert, too, knew much of the passage of time and the fleeting memory: to display this required bold new forms. And towering above other mid-century French advocates of pessimism, Flaubert showed how one might work up into a novel a philosophy of despair. The use of symbols, the handling of dialogue, simile, and metaphor, problems of tempo, the place of ethics, these and innumerable other formal questions he met and resolved. But, as most of these are familiar, it is perhaps well to move beyond them, leaving to another time and place the investigation of their import after a century. In sum, style was Flaubert's chief concern; he saw clarity of concept as the true

source of good form, and he rejuvenated romanticism by returning behind its looseness to the great tradition of western literature.

The question of Flaubert's view of life, the meaning he
attached to it and, hence, to his book, remains to be examined.
Flaubert himself directs attention to it when he says, "Everything depends on the concept" [II, 339]. What was it that he
had to say? What meanings did he discover and then display
with such excellence? If a work is to reach the summits and
take its place on the shelf, the very small shelf, of truly world
literature, its form and its content, the what as well as the
how, must both be superlative and must both fuse wholly into
a totality which will speak cogently to later ages. *Madame
Bovary* is good enough so that one may, without absurdity, ask
whether it belongs on this select shelf.

Each reader must answer for himself, and my purpose must
be quite as much to provide a framework for the answers of
others as it is to give my own reply. Flaubert's book had a point,
and he knew it: "this novel has a perfectly clear meaning. . . ."
He went on, however, to say that it was a matter of perfect
indifference to him and that style alone mattered [IV, 136].
But can it properly be a matter of indifference to the rest of
us, his readers, who are not writers and for whom style is
therefore less important? For my own part, I must answer "No,"
and must further urge that Flaubert himself in his better
moments knew his assertion was an exaggeration.

If, then, we ask what the message of the book is, I think
we must answer that it is one of distilled hatred and disgust,
for romanticism, for the bourgeois, for provincial life, for
orthodox religion: for nearly everything portrayed. Some parts
of the book, some paragraphs or even short episodes show
Flaubert as serene as he felt the masters had been, reaching
beyond the exasperation and disillusionment which are the
price of wisdom, to that calm which he knew was necessary to
Art. It is these moments which produced the great pages, the
scene by moonlight as Emma and Rodolphe plan their trip,
the Catherine Leroux episode, Doctor Larivière's visit, the
death of Charles, and a host of others.

Flaubert can, upon occasion, rise to the real heights of

the great western tradition. Few books can ever do so, and it
is great praise to say that some pages of his book do. But its
essential message and its normal level are perhaps less than that:
they certainly are for me, and it may be that in the pages which
remain, I can suggest why.

It is Flaubert's reiterated contention in his letters that life
is hateful, farcical, grotesque; that it consists of ignominy and
stupidity. It is so hideous that the only way to stand it is to
avoid it and to look upon the human race as "a vast assembly of
monsters and rascals." He enjoys seeing humanity and all it
respects "crushed, humiliated, dishonored, spat upon" [II, 321,
325, 472; III, 63, 420; IV, 33, 182]. Like Baudelaire, Flaubert sees
the evil in life; but unlike the poet, he does not see anything
else. His is a limited view.

This is the burden of *Madame Bovary* as well. Flaubert
felt that there was no escape for Emma and his effort was to
prove this "irony of fate" by closing off, one after another, every
means of salvation. "Fate" is the key word of Flaubert's own
philosophy, and it is used recurrently through the book at
critical moments, finally and most cogently by Charles in his
conversation with Rodolphe after Emma's death: "Fate is to
blame." Emma is necessarily destroyed, and the world is necessarily given over to the Homais and the Lheureux of our society.
Their success is even less palatable than her failure.

Any reasonable or sensitive man will reject life if this
is its true and ultimate import. Flaubert asked repeatedly what
meaning could possibly be attributed to this grotesque and horrible spectacle either of tears, unhappiness, and misery, or else
of stupidity, infamy, cowardice, and dishonor. For his fellow
man, he could feel at most a serene hatred or what he termed
"so inactive a pity that it amounts to the same thing." No
wonder, then, that he had to conclude that life was tolerable
only providing one refused to live it: "through all the *hideous-
ness* of existence, we must always contemplate the great blue
vault of poetry. . . ." By living in Art, he once said, it seemed
to him, in his conscience, that he was accomplishing his duty,
that he was obeying a higher fate, that he was doing the Good,
that he was in the Right [II, 396; III, 107, 108–109, 144, 251,
350].

We cannot all be artists, so what Flaubert knew of how to give dignity and meaning to life was of no value to his fellow man and he never proffered these views on Art in works he published himself. I am aware that life may be viewed as having no more significance than Flaubert attaches to it; I am aware of the pervasiveness nowadays of the doctrine of irony, which Flaubert upheld truculently. But I do believe that, upon examination, the really great books of the western tradition counsel the understanding of life and urge terms in which it may be accepted. They go beyond the bitter taste of irony to some form of love. The *Iliad* shows sure knowledge of how vicious man may be to man, but before it closes it shows the mastery of the vice it portrays, and it ends in serenity and acceptance. And this pattern, it seems to me, has been followed by all the later books which I should wish to place on my own private shelf of truly world literature. But if I would place *Madame Bovary* on the shelf below, now a century later, it would still be done affectionately and with deep respect for the man who could write in one of his letters that he would probably never be able to succeed in his attempt to write the style he imagined, that it was perhaps absurd or at best merely a worthy attempt and highly original; but that in any case, he would have passed his life in a way that was noble, and often delicious [III, 142–43].